FINAL VICTORY

FINAL VICTORY

FDR's Extraordinary World War II
Presidential Campaign

STANLEY WEINTRAUB

DA CAPO PRESS
A Member of the Perseus Books Group

Designed by Linda Mark
Set in 11.5 point Plantin Light by the Perseus Books Group

Published by Da Capo Press
A Member of the Perseus Books Group
www.dacapopress.com

Library of Congress Cataloging-in-Publication Data
Weintraub, Stanley, 1929–
  Final victory : FDR's extraordinary World War II presidential campaign/
Stanley Weintraub.
    p. cm.
  Includes bibliographical references and index.
  ISBN 978-0-306-82113-4 (hardcover : alk. paper)
—ISBN 978-0-306-82112-7 (e-book) 1. Presidents—United
States—Election—1944. 2. Roosevelt, Franklin D. (Franklin Delano),
1882–1945. 3. Dewey, Thomas E. (Thomas Edmund), 1902–1971.
4. United States—Politics and government—1933–1945. I. Title.
  E812.W38 2012
  973.917092—dc23

                                                    2011047065

Da Capo Press books are available at special discounts for bulk purchases in the U.S. by corporations, institutions, and other organizations. For more information, please contact the Special Markets Department at the Perseus Books Group, 2300 Chestnut Street, Suite 200, Philadelphia, PA 19103, or call (800) 810-4145, ext. 5000, or e-mail special.markets@perseusbooks.com.

10 9 8 7 6 5 4 3 2 1

For Bob Benson,
who sailed on a troopship with me to the next war—Korea.

Contents

Daisy Stanley, on the telephone, ca. 1941:
"Mrs. Roosevelt, Mr. Stanley didn't vote for your husband,
but I did, and I'd like to vote for him again!"

The Man Who Came to Dinner,
film adaptation, 1942, from the play by
George S. Kaufman & Moss Hart

Lady at her desk turning toward
her husband, who is reading a newspaper:
"What shall I do with your Roosevelt button?
Do you want me to put it away again?"

Alan Dunn
cartoon in the *New Yorker,*
November 18, 1944

Four More Years?

P resident Roosevelt's rare wartime trips overseas were supposedly secret until he was actually seen. Troops in North
Africa were astonished to encounter him early in 1943,
when he waved his fedora from an open car near Casablanca,
where he was to confer with Winston Churchill. "Oh my God,"
FDR recalled a GI blurting out in surprise. "Just for one more
term, son," said the President.

Even earlier, talk had revived about Roosevelt's running yet
again, and it was not limited to the States. Late in 1942, when
Eleanor Roosevelt was on a goodwill visit to Britain as, in effect,
her husband's legs, she planned to visit the Virginia-born Lady
Astor, an MP. Bernard Shaw, then eighty-six, postcarded Nancy
Astor, an old friend, quipping, "Bring the First Lady to tea. . . .
When she returns home the first question they will ask her is
'Have you seen Shaw?' If she has to say No, it will cost Franklyn"—
GBS's misspelling, as he had once created a character named

Franklyn Barnabas—"at least half a dozen votes in the next election."

With the war certain to go on after the November 1944 election—much of Europe was still in Nazi hands, and the Japanese controlled a vast swath of the Pacific Rim—the President, however failing in health and long crippled by polio, had long been thinking about having to run once more to finish the job. Although enemies across both oceans had been put on the defensive, victory, in mid-1944, was on the still-distant horizon, and many Americans focused their interests on more mundane matters than the wars across the world and the imminent presidential election. The possibilities of political change were vague, but the immediate, mundane realities regard-less of party affiliation were not: It was difficult to buy tires, even retreads, for aging automobiles. To conserve rationed gasoline, speed limits were reduced to a crawling and often violated 35 miles an hour. Chewing gum and chocolate bars were nearly unobtain-able, having gone to war. As victory loomed, rationing of butter and beef, shoes and sheets, seemed a nagging inconvenience—to remind Americans that there was still an ongoing war. Despite the new affluence of war industry workers, and the once-crushing un-employment, with twelve million men in uniform, now near zero, burgeoning consumerism was at odds with rationing and restraint, and energized a robust black market in bacon and sugar, bedding and gasoline, coffee and razor blades, whiskey and cigarettes.

An ocean away from the war both east and west, Americans griped about makeshift purchasing and price controls and ex-pressed their tepid patriotism by blue (or, disconsolately, gold) stars on pennants in their windows recognizing family members in uniform, or only now in memory. Of more immediate interest than the headlines about the war in local newspapers were the inside pages about what really mattered. Superman and Lil' Abner were not even in military service, nor were Mutt & Jeff, Jiggs or Blondie's Dagwood, and millions more readers scrutinized the comic strips and the sports pages than the speeches of political candidates and abrasive editorials in the press. Hollywood flicks like *Going My Way*, *Canterville Ghost* and Abbott and Costello's *In Society* sold more tickets than *Marine Raiders* and *U-Boat Prisoner*, and even *I Love a Soldier*. Although a few major box-office stars— Clark Gable and James Stewart among them—were in active and real military service, Bing Crosby, Sonny Tufts, Pat O'Brien and Gary Cooper remained civilians, sometimes playing soldier. Ronald Reagan, an army captain in California, made movies.

The war and the presidential election meant less to many than the heated baseball season, in which the St. Louis Browns, perennial losers, won their first American League championship. It was an event as rare as a third term. Many teams were bereft of stars. Now a pilot and a sailor, Ted Williams and Bob Feller were in uniform. The Browns even played an undraftable one-armed outfielder, Pete Gray. Their World Series opponent from the rival National League—the baseball world was limited to teams otherwise east of the Mississippi—would be the St. Louis Cardinals, creating a "subway series" in a city without a subway. Professional football had a truncated league of largely older players. Sunday football had been interrupted on December 7, 1941, by loudspeaker appeals, which did not mention Pearl Harbor, urging military men and government officials to exit and return to their bases and offices. In 1943 the Pittsburgh Steelers and Philadelphia Eagles combined their shorthanded teams into the Steagles; in 1944 the perennial doormat Chicago Cardinals merged for the season with the Steelers and lost all ten games.

Radio was the newest mass information source, and war news often came on the hour with dramatic immediacy. FDR's long mastery of the medium was unparalleled, but the public preferred afternoon soap operas and evening Big Band programs, and pop music that turned toaster-sized Bakelite radios into home juke boxes that offered songs less about patriotism and the war than about a soldier's nostalgia for home and the home dweller's dream for the return of the serviceman beloved. In 1944 the most popular song was probably "I'll Be Seeing You"—a melancholy ballad not about victory to come but about the end of absence. It was that mood which campaign politics had to penetrate. Issues and slogans and bitching about scrimping and shortages competed with collective yearning for the restoration of bland everyday life.

The partisan Republican challenge was to exploit the recognizable urge in the electorate to withdraw from what domestic sacrifices there were, blaming them not on the war but upon the alleged ineffectiveness, shortcomings and paternalism of an administration in office too long. The agony of a world in turmoil was somewhere else on some other continents, seen only in the distancing of black-and-white photographs. Henry Luce's monthly for the moneyed, *Fortune,* called the war "a painful necessity." To win an election and replace a noticeably ailing Franklin Delano Roosevelt in Washington, the voting public at home—often apathetic, and often willfully uninformed—had to be made more resentful, and more aware of the President's increasing, if hidden, frailty. (Many Americans did not realize that since 1921 his legs had been immobilized by polio, and that he had made heroic efforts to campaign for office, and function as governor, and then as President, as if he were not disabled.)

Men (and now women) in military service, millions of them overseas and at hazard, had to be persuaded by the "outs" to be more eager at the ballot box to abandon the war and go home. As a *Life* editorial later put it about the President, "Whether one liked this or that policy or not, one knew that he would do what he would do. It was easier to let him worry for the whole country." For other millions who wanted change after twelve years of FDR, that wasn't enough. But were there enough voting millions to remove "that Man in the White House"?

Stanley Weintraub
Beech Hill
Newark, Delaware

One

Bungled Beginnings

President Roosevelt's face was white and contorted in agony. He lay sprawled in the aisle of his special armor-plated railway car, the *Ferdinand Magellan*. "Jimmy, I don't know if I can make it," he gasped. "I have horrible pains."

Despite security men somewhere, FDR's only companion was his eldest son, James, a Marine major on the intelligence staff of Rear Admiral Ralph O. Davis at Camp Pendleton, on the Pacific coast in California. The presidential train lay, heavily guarded, in the rail yards at San Diego. Franklin Delano Roosevelt, President of the United States longer than any other chief executive before or since, was scheduled, imminently, to review an amphibious landing exercise. The 5th Marine Division was preparing for the invasion of Japan.

Frightened by the sudden seizure, James offered to call the President's doctor, Vice Admiral Ross McIntire, the Surgeon General, who often traveled with Roosevelt. James hoped that the matter was a digestive upset rather than something worse, as the initial symptoms suggested cardiac complications.

The President resisted summoning McIntire. The pain that shook him, he struggled to claim, would pass. He had just downed his breakfast too quickly. Canceling his appearance and creating alarm, he said, struggling to get the words out, "would be very bad. But help me out of my berth, and let me stretch out flat on the deck for a while—that may help."

The President's legs were long helpless from polio. Jimmy had to assist him down. "Father lay on the floor of the railroad car," he recalled, "his eyes closed, his face drawn; his powerful torso occasionally convulsed as the waves of pain stabbed him." The younger Roosevelt watched in panic yet in silence as his father's agony began to ease. "Never in my life had I felt so alone with him—and so helpless."

As his pallor began to recede, the President opened his eyes and exhaled deeply. "Help me up now, Jimmy," he appealed. "I feel better." It was the morning of July 20, 1944.

The episode remained unspoken and unreported. Major Roosevelt got his father ready to leave. Aides arrived on schedule to lift the Commander-in-Chief under his shrunken and limp thighs out of the railway car and into an open convertible flanked by security vehicles. As if nothing had happened, FDR waved his battered hat and smiled warmly at spectators while the presidential party motored toward a high bluff to observe the invasion rehearsal on the beach at Oceanside, north of San Diego. Five thousand marines and three thousand sailors were involved, emerging from landing craft which disgorged men and equipment onshore.

To Eleanor Roosevelt, who had been with her husband but flown east from California, FDR wrote, reversing the timing and making deliberate light of it, "Yesterday a.m. Jimmy & I had a grand view of the landing operation at Camp Pendleton, and then I got the collywobbles & stayed in the train in the p.m. Better today. . . . It was grand having you come out with me."

The three pool reporters with the President's party were supposed to pretend as part of the "invisible traveling" code that they were filing from Washington. They did not know of Roosevelt's episode. Nor did Grace Tully, who as principal secretary rode along as far as San Diego. "Damn it, Grace," said Merriman Smith of United Press, "everybody at the Convention knows the Boss is on the West Coast. Thousands of people have seem him or some of the party while crossing the country. If we put 'Washington' on our stories, it won't be [for] security; it will just be a damned lie." She went to the President for advice. "It's completely ridiculous, Child," he said. "I'm saying in the [acceptance] speech that I am talking from a West Coast naval base." The stories filed carried as dateline "A West Coast Naval Base."

FDR observing amphibious landing maneuvers from his car at Oceanside, California, July 20, 1944. He had just experienced an unreported cardiac seizure aboard his presidential train.
FDR Library

When *Chicago Tribune* investigative journalist Walter Trohan saw a photo taken afterwards as FDR spoke to the nation by radio, he was shocked by the President's "emaciated face and slumping body," which the camera could not conceal. Trohan also noticed in one corner the hand and lower sleeve of a naval officer. He checked with the Navy Department. It was Dr. Howard Bruenn, a navy lieutenant colonel and heart specialist.

Although it was evident that the President was increasingly frail, and that his clothes now seemed several sizes too large, Eleanor Roosevelt had little specific knowledge of her husband's downturn until informed by their daughter, Anna Boettiger. He seldom confided to Eleanor, and they lived, but for public cordiality and token domesticity, separate lives. Aside from special occasions, when they were under the same roof she spent fifteen minutes with him while he had his breakfast, as befitted his infirmity, in bed. Mrs. Roosevelt had her own cottage at the Hyde Park estate on the Hudson and kept an apartment at 9 Washington Square in Manhattan. He had never visited it. She knew that Dr. McIntire oversaw the President's physical condition, but she had not realized until a few months earlier that the admiral had rarely taken his charge's elevated blood pressure and did little more than tinker daily with FDR's chronic bronchitis and sinus problems. It was a curiously passive doctor-patient relationship. Somehow despite it the President functioned.

Visiting earlier from Seattle, in November 1943, Mrs. Boettiger stayed on at the White House once she discovered her father's obvious decline. "Sis" became alarmed when his shirt collars seemed so large, and his clothes hung shapelessly. With FDR—briefly— nearly every day, Eleanor did not take seriously anything but his loss of weight and poor appetite, and bouts of what was described as "grippe," but Grace Tully had become nervous about FDR's nodding off while dictating to her, or while reading memoranda and mail. She had confided her worries to Anna. The dark circles under the President's eyes were more pronounced; he slumped in the wheeled kitchen chair that had enabled his mobility for twenty-three years; his hands often shook as he lighted his Camels, which should have been medically off-limits. He had long used an over-sized coffee cup at breakfast; now he employed it all the time to limit spillage.

McIntire had been an ear, nose and throat physician decades earlier, and other than pursuing his limited naval duties, dawdled medically with the Commander-in-Chief. Grossly minimizing Roosevelt's deterioration, he told the press as FDR turned sixty-two on January 30, 1944, that the President "is in better health than at any time since he came into office in 1933." Accordingly, *The New York Times* headlined on January 29, "President's Health Called Better than Ever; McIntire Hails His Ability to Bounce Back." For Admiral McIntire, FDR was "just an average patient with no operations and no interesting complaints."

Late in March 1944 the President seemed slow in recovering from what was reported as winter influenza. Most of his daily appointments remained canceled. One he kept was with Turner Catledge of *The New York Times*'s Washington Bureau. It was, Catledge recalled, "my first glimpse of him in several months. I was shocked and horrified. . . . I felt I was seeing something I shouldn't see. He had lost a great deal of weight. His shirt collar hung so loose on his neck that you could have put your hand inside it. He was sitting there with a vague, glassy-eyed expression on his face and his mouth hanging open." Catledge wondered how to exit gracefully. He had expected a lively conversation about politics: it was an election year. But Roosevelt "would start talking about something, then in midsentence he would stop and his mouth would drop open and he'd sit staring at me in silence. I knew I was looking at a terribly sick man."

Eventually Roosevelt revived, chatted to Catledge about his conferences in Iran with Winston Churchill and Josef Stalin late in 1943, and was stimulated by his own humorous spin on them.

When his appointments secretary, Major General Edwin ("Pa") Watson, kept coming to the door to hint at abbreviating the session, "Roosevelt would raise his hand (a hand so thin you could almost see through it) and tell me to stay. I had the impression of a man who very badly wanted someone to talk to. . . . It was an agonizing experience for me. Finally, a waiter brought his lunch, and . . . I was able to make my escape."

When the President's temperature peaked at 104, Anna had enough of McIntire's apparent blindness. Even Mrs. Roosevelt became more anxious. Together, Anna and Grace Tully confronted the admiral and demanded that he order a thorough checkup. Suppressing his annoyance, McIntire suggested that a week away for the President under a southern sun would do the trick. Still, Anna challenged, "Do you ever take his blood pressure?" McIntire's lame concession that he did so only when necessary raised her impatience. (Records would reveal that he had last done so four years earlier, on February 27, 1941.) Reluctantly, the admiral scheduled an examination at the Naval Hospital in Bethesda* for March 27, and agreed to discuss her father's health privately in Anna's rooms on the third floor of the White House.

During their meeting, McIntire told Anna, brushing her off, that the President's appearance was nothing serious. But Eleanor had told Anna that FDR in an unexpected burst of frustration and concern, had confessed, abruptly, "I cannot live out a normal life span. I can't even walk across the room to get my circulation going." He had not been able to "walk" without steel leg braces and assistance since 1921. Yet his therapeutic philosophy since then had been, "When you get to the end of your rope, tie a knot and hang on."

---

* FDR had already been, very briefly, to Bethesda to have a wen removed from the back of his head under local anesthetic. He told a press conference about it on February 4, soon after, but had never reported a much earlier procedure, cosmetic removal of a benign keratosis over his left eyebrow, which led to posthumous suspicions of melanoma. Yet melanoma would have had rather immediate metastatic consequences, which did not occur.

At 10:35 on the morning of March 27, 1944, Anna accompanied her father and his valet, Chief Petty Officer Arthur Prettyman, amid a phalanx of Secret Service cars, to the stately naval hospital far out on Wisconsin Avenue, dedicated by the President in 1942. "I'll wait in the car," she said as Prettyman wheeled the President toward the hospital rotunda. It was just after 11 a.m., and it would be a long wait.

Little could be kept secret in Washington. Doctors, nurses, guards and patients, waiting for FDR's arrival, broke into cheers, and he waved back as he was wheeled though. Yet, no reporters were present. The press, often tipped off, had not been alerted. All the President had been told was that his slow recovery from flu suggested that he have a fuller examination than the minimal White House clinic afforded. In a cleared medical suite waiting for him was Lieutenant Commander Howard Bruenn, M.D., a cardiologist, then thirty-nine, drawn into service from Columbia-Presbyterian Medical Center in New York. Admiral McIntire had telephoned Bruenn at nine that morning to be ready to examine the President—and to report his findings only to the admiral, by messenger to the White House. Roosevelt was to be told as little as possible. However surprised, Bruenn warned that to perform a proper examination he would need, for comparison, records of earlier findings. McIntire was uncertain that he could locate any. It was clear that the President's health had long been in the care of a medical nobody.

Prettyman wheeled FDR into an anteroom and with two male nurses helped undress him and slip his arms through a loose hospital gown. "I suspected something was terribly wrong as soon as I looked at the President," Bruenn recalled, from his notes, in the *Annals of Internal Medicine* in 1970. "His face was pallid and there was a bluish discoloration of his skin, lips, and nail beds. When the hemoglobin is fully oxygenated it is red. When it is impaired it has a bluish tint. The bluish tint indicated that the tissues were not being supplied with adequate oxygen."

As Bruenn continued his examination, the President kept up an amiable one-way conversation, the doctor only nodding, then excusing himself briefly when McIntire's inadequate medical records arrived from the White House with instructions to send them back forthwith. Scanning them and returning, Bruenn applied his stethoscope and listened to Roosevelt's heart, which he found was "worse than I feared." He also perceived rales, an abnormal rattling sound indicating fluid in both lungs. Fluoroscopy, requiring that two nurses support the president under both arms to hold him erect before a screen, then conventional X-rays and an electrocardiogram confirmed that the President was suffering from congestive ("left ventricular") cardiac failure and hypertensive heart disease.

Respectfully, Bruenn waited to leave the examination room until Roosevelt was dressed, then shook his hand. He offered no information to the President. FDR asked for none. "Thanks, Doc," he said as Arthur Prettyman wheeled him out to the car where Anna waited. A Secret Service squad from an accompanying car masked much of the exit of their boss, blurring his handicap. (Normally, Charles Fredericks of the Secret Service, Roosevelt's bodyguard and wheelchair assistant, propelled the President.)

Once the party left, Bruenn began writing up the test results for McIntire, along with his findings and recommendations. They were grim. By early evening the report was delivered, and the next morning, by order, Bruenn was at the White House. The President, he had warned, could expire at any time. If he remained untreated— and medication might be useless given such advanced stages of heart failure—FDR would not survive a year. "What do you propose that we should do with the patient?" McIntire asked.

"It's here," Bruenn said, offering his recommendations on a small sheet of paper—at least two further weeks of bed rest, digitalis to strengthen the heart and assist breathing, a light diet with potassium chloride rather than ordinary salt in a shaker; drastic reduction in smoking and alcohol intake, codeine to control coughing, sedation at night.

Mr. Roosevelt, McIntire insisted, would not submit to further restrictions on his already curtailed working regimen. With Bruenn present he discussed the situation with four other Naval Hospital physicians he had called in, including Captain John Harper, commandant at Bethesda. "The President can't take time off to go to bed," McIntire concluded. You can't simply say to him, 'Do this or do that.' This is the President of the United States!"

Bruenn mused aloud, with Churchill and Stalin in mind, "For better or worse, the war was being run by just three men, and it was not over yet." He overshot his rank and demanded that his findings be reviewed by qualified outside consultants. Backing down, McIntire and the others agreed. Meanwhile, would Bruenn serve under the admiral as physician-in-attendance? Although that meant he would be under McIntire's heavy thumb, Bruenn agreed to leave Bethesda immediately on detached service to the White House.*

Consultants brought in by McIntire on March 31 met with Bruenn and Harper at Bethesda and reviewed the President's charts and prognosis. Dr. Frank H. Lahey of the Lahey Clinic in Boston, a surgeon specializing in gastrointestinal problems, and Dr. James Paullin of Emory University in Atlanta, a specialist in endocarditis, both honorary naval consultants, were joined by Captain Robert A. Duncan, executive officer at Bethesda; Captain Charles Behrens, chief of radiology; and Dr. Paul Dickens, clinical professor of medicine at nearby George Washington University. All were sworn to secrecy. As Bruenn explained his findings, recommending a severe limitation of presidential activities, the senior physicians appeared unimpressed. The five unanimously vetoed his recommendations as excessive. Rank seemed to have its usual privileges, which here included protecting Admiral McIntire.

---

* According to Bruenn, "The original hospital chart in which all clinical progress notes as well as the results of the various laboratory tests were incorporated was kept in the safe at . . . Bethesda, Maryland. After the President's death this chart could not be found."

One physician in the group observed that because the admiral had been treating Roosevelt for years, and had observed no alarming pathology, it was impossible to imagine that FDR had suddenly deteriorated. Why, asked a second consultant utterly blind to Bruenn's findings, had McIntire asked to have a cardiologist examine a patient recovering from flu? However thwarted, Bruenn remembered, "I knew I was right, so I held my ground." Grudgingly giving way, Paullin and Lahey asked Bruenn to withhold further judgment until they could personally examine the President, which they did at the White House that afternoon, returning on two successive days.

Roosevelt never questioned the sudden influx of physicians, who conceded that Bruenn was correct and recommended that the President be informed of the gravity of his health in order to secure his cooperation. Even without that, digitalis could be administered to regulate the heart without the patient being aware of it. (More sophisticated medications now routine were then unknown.) Impulsively, McIntire rejected the advice. The harsh truth might have a serious emotional impact.

The physicians compromised on a combination of medical silence and a modicum of new treatment: low doses of digitalis, a careful diet, limitation of the Camels he smoked, a reduction in alcoholic beverages, less work and more sleep. McIntire was also directed to rush the President away into rest and sunshine. Bruenn began to pop digitalis pills into Roosevelt's mouth each morning, with the President never asking what the medication was or why Bruenn was also there daily to check blood pressure and other vital signs. (Not entirely uninformed, FDR saw a veteran in-house physical therapist, Lieutenant Commander George A. Fox, who took regular readings for which McIntire never asked. Fox had been in White House service as early as the Wilson administration.)

Although Roosevelt never asked a medical question, he understood, very likely through Fox, the gravity of his health. In the draft

of a letter he did not send to Margaret ("Daisy") Suckley, his devoted distant cousin and near-neighbor in Rhinebeck, he confided—
it was probably a month later—that Bruenn "is one of the best
heart men." The President claimed to her to be "definitely better"
although his heart "does queer things still." A descendant of the
colonial Dutch Beekmans, the wren-like Daisy, nine years younger
than FDR, described herself as "a prim spinster." Since Franklin's
polio, she had been a welcome presence at Hyde Park, and then the
White House—her emotional ties to her cousin guarded yet evident as he evolved through adversity.

Misleading the press as usual, Admiral McIntire on April 3 told
newspapermen that the President was fine, and that a medical
checkup had confirmed it. "For a man of sixty-two we had very
little to argue about, with the exception that we have had to combat the influenza plus respiratory complications that came along
afterwards." At the Naval Hospital in Bethesda, *TIME* reported
uninformatively, "They X-rayed Franklin Roosevelt's chest. It was
a mild case of bronchitis, going into its third week." At the press
conference, according to *TIME,* "The President pooh-poohed his
illness, continued to smoke from his long cigaret holder, continued
to cough softly but persistently."

The President's charts would show improvement, Bruenn
noted, as McIntire was persuaded to discontinue dosing Roosevelt
nightly with a nose spray that contained adrenaline. It had been the
reflex treatment of an old-fashioned ENT physician.

Newspapermen on the White House beat were well aware that the
Chicago convention was less than four months away. Although the
President had not announced his candidacy for a fourth term, no
one else had either. "If Roosevelt should not run," Secretary of the
Interior Harold Ickes wrote to a Chicago friend, Stacey Mosser,
"the result is likely to be a shambles." One newsman had been
asked by his office to investigate rumors that Roosevelt had been
smuggled, for unspecified surgery, into a hospital in Boston or to

the Mayo Clinic in Minnesota. When crack White House reporter Merriman Smith claimed to have identified the doctors involved, Steve Early, the President's press secretary, suggested that Smith check out his tip. He turned up nothing.

Where Roosevelt did go for "rest and sunshine" was elderly financier Bernard Baruch's secluded estate in South Carolina, just off the Atlantic coast. "Hobcaw" had an additional lure. At Aiken, 140 miles away, was the widowed Lucy Mercer Rutherfurd, who at twenty-seven had been Eleanor's former social secretary when in September 1918 Mrs. Roosevelt discovered Lucy's liaison with Franklin. Other than his being stricken with polio, the Lucy Mercer affair was the greatest personal crisis of FDR's life, and nearly ended his marriage, which became only pro forma afterward. Dismissed but unforgotten, Lucy had married a wealthy socialite stockbroker, much older and with grown sons. Winthrop, her husband, had died at eighty-two on March 18. Roosevelt, who had met her secretly and affectionately over the years, was determined to see more of her, and abetted by Anna Boettiger and Daisy Suckley, who hoped that Lucy's far-from-unwilling presence would be restorative, he did.

Only a week after Winthrop Rutherfurd's burial, with Mrs. Roosevelt away, Lucy visited at Hyde Park from her estate at Allamuchy, New Jersey. Daisy, who as an accomplice referred to Mrs. Rutherfurd as "my new cousin," was also there, ostensibly poring through Roosevelt's old papers. The President treasured his collections, which Librarian of Congress Archibald MacLeish had not long before described to FDR, anticipating the future of the papers, as the "Franklin Delano Roosevelt Memorial Library." In return the President wrote, "Dear Archie, You have been grossly deceived. I am still alive."

On April 28, as a new widow in black, with black gloves, her abundant brown hair greying, and still gracious and beautiful, Lucy quietly came for lunch at Hobcaw. For FDR her presence was bracing. It was also off the record. To Churchill on March 20,

Roosevelt had fudged about his coming convalescence in South Carolina, to be relieved, he suggested, only by deliveries of White House paperwork. "I am very angry with myself. The old attack of grippe"—he identified every ailment as grippe—"having hung on and on, leaving me with an intermittent temperature, Ross [McIntire] decided about a week ago that it is necessary for me to take a complete rest of about two or three weeks in a suitable climate which I am definitely planning to do beginning at the end of this month. I see no way out and I am furious." He said nothing about running again, but Churchill had learned dismayingly from his confidant, Lord Beaverbrook, that former ambassador to Britain, Joseph Kennedy, now hostile to Roosevelt, believed that FDR would run, and would be defeated. "The Republican candidate would be [Governor] Dewey. . . . Roosevelt's chances are declining steadily."

The President had first thought of staying at the naval station at Guantanamo Bay, Cuba, and in preparation, his Filipino navy cooks and two navy fishing experts flew there with a Secret Service agent. Cuba was reportedly unsafe, and FDR's doctors recommended against air travel. The staff relocated to Baruch's secluded twenty-three thousand acres, and the President's special train followed on April 8. Three physicians accompanied Roosevelt—McIntire, Bruenn and Robert Duncan of Bethesda—as well as FDR's physiotherapist, George Fox. (Duncan soon returned to Washington.) A dozen Secret Service agents on the train would be beefed up for security at sprawling Hobcaw by Coast Guardsmen from a patrol station at Georgetown, 8 miles away, and sixty-two marines from Camp Lejeune, North Carolina. The Coast Guard base was also drawn upon for food and other supplies. Navy lieutenant William Rigdon, FDR's traveling secretary, recalled spending only forty dollars of his boss's money during the stay: FDR never carried any cash himself.

By his fifth day at Hobcaw, the sun and quiet seemed restorative. The President and his White House assistants would remain at

Hobcaw from April 9 to May 7, raising speculation in Washington when FDR did not return for the funeral of Navy Secretary Frank Knox, who had died on the day of Lucy Rutherfurd's visit. Following the lunch with Lucy on April 28, Roosevelt had suffered unexpected abdominal pains, which Bruenn and McIntire, both in attendance, attributed to gallstones, yet neither physician followed up the supposition. Codeine relieved the symptoms enough that Roosevelt could talk with reporters about Knox, and the complaint soon receded. Three newspapermen representing the press associations had been restricted to a hotel in Georgetown. Frustrated by learning only what they had been told, and instructed to withhold even that until given clearance, one of them confronted Mike Reilly of the Secret Service, "Come on, Mike, stop trying to kid us. We know the Boss is not here. He's out in Chicago in a hospital. He's dying."

"You're nuts," said Reilly. "He's up at Baruch's, fishing. And having lousy luck." (He caught his first bass on April 21, off the Vanderbilt plantation at Arcadia.)

"Hooey," said a second reporter. "I just got a wire from my office. Our Boston man knows that FDR has had a serious heart attack and is under Dr. Lahey's care right now in Boston." The guess was premature. Lahey would be called in for consultation in early July.

Once Roosevelt spoke to newsmen "at Baruch's" about the services to the nation of Secretary Knox, the Republican vice-presidential nominee in 1936, who had contributed a nonpartisan dedication to the war effort, rumors that the President had undergone secret surgery at Hobcaw or elsewhere faded. And he did begin hooking some catfish, with a Coast Guard patrol boat cautiously following aft.

The President saw few official visitors, one of them Lieutenant General Mark W. Clark, who had returned briefly from the Mediterranean. FDR's only intervention in Washington politics from afar occurred after a strike began at the sprawling mail-order firm of Montgomery Ward in Chicago. Led by crusty Sewell Avery, management refused to recognize union activity or bargain with employees. On the recommendation of Attorney General Francis Biddle, Roosevelt ordered an end to the strike and a vote on unionization. Montgomery Ward's chief clientele, Biddle argued, in contrast to the more conservative Secretary of War, Henry Stimson, were farmers, who were crucial to supplying the troops. Ordered in, a few soldiers physically removed the stubborn and sullen Avery from his office, carrying him out to the delight of waiting press photographers.

The eviction aroused a profound, and largely negative, reaction throughout the country. Small businessmen well below "Monkey Ward's" size and status, according to a flood of mail to congressmen, wondered whether what happened to Sewell Avery, an instant free-enterprise hero, could happen to them. Republican politicos hoped that the Montgomery Ward intervention would cost the Democrats campaign contributions and votes.

On May 6, the day before the White House party left Hobcaw, the President convened Merriman Smith, Douglas Cornell and Robert C. Nixon for an informal press conference, after which they were free to release what limited news they had. One of them had already protested, "We could be outmaneuvered by that un-New Deal paper in Charleston. You know there's been a columnist for that Charlotte paper over at Fawley's Island for the past two weeks, too." Roosevelt gave them a review of his difficulties in finding "some government property near Washington where I could spend a holiday." He had no news for them other than his long-distance role in a court-martial proceeding at Guantanamo in which a marine lieutenant was convicted of ordering the shooting of a limping calf, ostensibly to put it out of his misery. However, the calf was then butchered and supplied three dinners of excellent veal. "It was all lined up to ruin this kid's life—to dismiss him from the service. . . . So I took the recommendation that had been prepared for my signature, reading 'Approved. The sentence will be carried into effect,' and instead of signing it I wrote thereon: 'The sentence is approved, but it is mitigated so that in lieu of being dismissed the accused will be placed on probation for a year, subject to the pleasure of the President. This man must be taught not to shoot calves. Franklin D. Roosevelt.'"

It was obvious that the message the pool reporters were to get out was that the President, now fully rested, was feeling very well and in old form.

Despite thirty-six articles in the press referring to Roosevelt's health in the first five months of 1944, largely ignored, a hint of what was to come that actually caused notice appeared as an editorial in *The New York Times*, which welcomed the President back to "the almost overwhelming burdens his office forces him to carry. He earned every hour of it." Roosevelt had not yet announced his candidacy for another four years at the White House, yet the lines seemed almost an endorsement. On the other side of the divide, the leading political columnist of the day, Walter Lippmann, advocated in his syndicated *New York Herald-Tribune* column a change in administration in Washington. Twelve years, or sixteen, he contended, was too long for any party or person to remain in power, for the government becomes "ossified" and strained by its inner contradictions.

Party politicians among the Democrats had called for a fourth term as early as the waning months of 1943. Missouri senator Harry Truman had suggested in February 1944 that no one else existed who could do the job. "To entrust the winning of the war and the framing of the peace into the hands of any man with a limited outlook and without the experience needed for such a job would be the sheerest folly." In January, at the Southern Governors Conference at the Statler in Washington, the President had not even been offered the courtesy of an appearance, and over their bourbon the conservative die-hards discussed possibilities they could support.

Finally, one of the more enlightened of the group, J. Melville Broughton, governor of North Carolina, emerged to tell reporters waiting in the hallway, "We go into meetings to cuss him out, but we just can't figure out any other answer than Roosevelt."

While no one in the United States, including Roosevelt himself, was certain that he would run again, propaganda minister Joseph Goebbels in Berlin had no such doubts. He employed a former Baltimore newspaperman, Douglas Chandler, who had embraced Nazism, to broadcast to America, on short-wave radio, diatribes against the President. To an introduction of shrill fifes and clopping hoofs, and in a cultivated voice, Chandler spewed hate as "Paul Revere." He called on Americans to repudiate Roosevelt, a traitor and charlatan, the agent of Jewish-Bolshevik subversion. Another presidential term for Roosevelt would lead to a Communist reign of terror: "Get that man out of the house that once was white!"*

Health concerns aside, partisans of the President recognized the controversial nature of a fourth bid for office, although that had been deflated in part, as war approached in 1940, by the third term. The not-quite-sacrosanct two-term tradition established by George Washington's example had been breached by Ulysses Grant's serious but failed attempt to secure a third-term nomination in 1876, and by Theodore Roosevelt's third-term—and third-party—candidacy (after William Howard Taft's single term) in 1912, a Republican split that had elected Woodrow Wilson. FDR had long talked of retiring to private life—to write and to travel. He loved the sea and dreamed of journeying long distances as a passenger on a slow freighter. Yet while there was still a war to be won, these were only dreams.

The President had not imagined a grueling further candidacy after his previous re-election. Although he would wear a brown

---

* Chandler was seized in 1945 and sentenced in Boston to life-imprisonment for treason.

Genoese "war bonnet" after Pearl Harbor, it was not the floppy felt hat under which he had stumped for office years earlier. The battered gray original had been auctioned off in Hollywood in March 1941 to benefit the Screen Actors Guild, and, according to Grace Tully, was purchased jointly by Melvyn Douglas and Edward G. Robinson for $5,000. When Roosevelt had offered it he had observed, "I won't need this again." But in 1944, when the new owners felt it necessary that he appear again in public with the trademark topper, they offered it back. It was with the President on all his campaign travels.*

Although FDR's train had made a two-hour stopover in Chicago on Saturday, July 15, four days before his scheduled arrival in San Diego, the president had no plans to remain for the Democratic Party convention which would renominate him. He had long resisted any announcement of his availability, yet there had never been any question of it if he felt that he had sufficient vigor to campaign again. Any alternative would be conceding the election. No Republican officeholder imagined anyone else. Representative John Taber of New York, a GOP dinosaur, characterized, in March 1944, every government directive as "partly drivel, partly insidious propaganda against Congress and for a fourth term." Since 1932 Roosevelt had been the overwhelming political personality in America. Under his enveloping shadow few of his associates had achieved electable visibility. Yet his renewed candidacy would come with the baggage of long incumbency. As Walter Millis, historian and editorial writer for the *New York Herald-Tribune,* put it about the FDR administration, "Everywhere the fate of Aristides is steadily overtaking it. It is sagging more and more visibly under the weight of the contradictory dislikes, dissatisfactions, cantankerous human recalcitrances, and rebellions which must inevitably be accumulated by any power called upon to perform such great social tasks as those

---

* Both hats are now in the FDR Library at Hyde Park.

which fell to its lot." (A dominant Athenian for years during the late-5th-century BC Persian wars, Aristides was reputed to have asked a farmer who did not know the identity of his questioner to vote to continue Aristides in office, and the farmer had responded, "I'm sick and tired of him.")

Curiously—and briefly—the President had thought of one off-the-wall possibility outside of party, and government, rare evidence that he had withheld his decision about another term not as a dramatic gesture but because he was aware of his fragility. As Daisy Suckley noted in her diary on May 5, from Hobcaw, FDR confided to her that "he discovered that the doctors had not agreed altogether about what to tell him, so he found out that they were not telling *him* the *whole* truth & that he was evidently more sick than they said! It is foolish for them to put anything over on *him*!"

On his return to Hyde Park, Daisy asked—it was May 22—whether he had decided on a vice president. "I haven't even decided," he claimed, "if I will run myself." Because whoever ran, he thought, whatever the party, should have a fair chance at being heard, earlier that day he had queried War Production Board chief Donald M. Nelson about portable radio batteries. Half the nation's farmers, he wrote, have no wired radio reception. Could more batteries be manufactured for civilian use so that "by this Summer . . . people can listen to the political debates?"

"What is going to decide you?" Daisy asked. "For you are practically nominated already."

"What will decide me, will be the way I feel in a couple of months. If I know I am not going to be able to carry on for another four years, it wouldn't be fair to the American people to run for another term."

"But who else is there?"

"I *have* a candidate—but don't breathe it to a soul—there is a man, not a politician, who, I think, I could persuade the country to elect. There would be such a gasp when his name was suggested, but* I believe he would have a good chance if he were 'sold' to the country in the right way."

He named West Coast shipbuilder and industrialist Henry J. Kaiser, also sixty-two, who had proven a phenomenon at war production. Among other achievements he had persuaded Roosevelt to override the Navy and put flight decks on cargo ship hulls to create, quickly, an armada of mini-carriers to escort convoys and inhibit submarine attacks. Kaiser could acquire the political and international experience quickly, Roosevelt claimed. Daisy asked how the already legendary builder of Liberty ships and escort carriers would get on with Churchill and Stalin.

"He's more like them than I am."

The private enthusiasm did not last. A dynamic businessman outside of party and with ideas of his own, and hardly known to partisan politics, Kaiser would have been a non-starter. And despite FDR's seeming irresolution, the party machinery was geared up to renominate him, and he had already cabled Churchill, on June 29, that "for purely political considerations . . . I should never survive even a slight setback in Overlord"—the massive landings in Normandy that had succeeded on June 6 and were moving forward despite stiff German resistance. The PM surely understood that Roosevelt did not mean surviving to be renominated, but to be reelected.

It took until a morning press conference on July 11 (his 961st) was concluding for the President to make his expected announcement and put the lid on aspirations and predictions that were entirely fanciful. "I have got something else," he said. Holding a sheet of paper in a hand that trembled noticeably, ashes from his cigarette scattering over his desk, he read a letter from party chairman Robert Hannegan confirming that an overwhelming number of delegates had already intended to cast their ballots for the President.

---

* The editor of Daisy Suckley's diary writes *that,* but the context suggests *but.*

Hannegan was asking him to run, to which FDR had replied affirmatively. The guessing game, long extended because of his own concerns about his health, was over.

Earlier, a White House reporter had inquired about rumors in the anti-Roosevelt press that because of the war, the election would be called off. The President asked how that could be done, and the newsman said, "Well, I don't know. That's what I want you to tell me."

"Well, you see," Roosevelt said, "you have come to the wrong place. . . . All these people around town haven't read the Constitution. Unfortunately, I have." There was no provision for postponing a presidential election. Asked at every press conference whether he would accept another nomination, he had usually answered, blandly, "There's no news on that today." As late as June 13 he was asked at a press conference, "Is there any place we could go, Mr. President, to find out about your fourth-term intentions?"

"My what?" He feigned lack of understanding as reporters laughed. "Well," he added, "I don't know. I want to be helpful . . . " but in truth he did not want to be helpful—yet. Like his physicians, and privately, he worried about his health. Yet his party had nowhere else to go, and he liked his job and felt that no one any better at running the country and the war was still out there. At every press conference the question came up, in different ways, to try to draw out FDR out. At his 959th press and radio conference it was, "Mr. President, is there anything that can be said about the Democratic candidate for President?"

What?" he asked the questioner, to much laughter. "They saddled it on you today?"

At the next news conference the question was, "Mr. President, have you found a candidate for vice president yet?"

"Well, that sounds like an unfriendly question," he joked, evasively. "I won't answer it."

Some in the Roosevelt circle—or once in it—had objected to a third term and now opposed a fourth term. One was former

Postmaster General James A. Farley, party chief in New York since 1930, and campaign manager for FDR in 1932 and 1936. Unrealistically, he had seen himself as the logical Democratic candidate in 1940, and had broken with FDR when no backing materialized. He was coming to Chicago to announce his retirement from New York politics in order to become the high-salaried chairman of the Coca-Cola Export Corporation. Reporters asked whether he would permit his name to be placed in nomination for the presidency. "No comment," Farley snapped. Whatever their dreams, other frustrated aspirants realized, they could not be nominated themselves. *The New York Times* observed in a headline, "Some Democrats Marked as Opponents Now See a Wartime Need." It was the premise under which the President would run.

Forty thousand convention attendees were expected. Bob Hannegan and Chicago mayor Edward Kelly came aboard the presidential train at the 51st Street coach yard to entreat Roosevelt once more to lend himself to a stop-Wallace movement. Vice President Henry Wallace, however admired on the Left, was seen by political pros as flaky at best. Kelly told party intimates that their task was "to replace Wallace with a fellow who stands for Roosevelt's program and who is also sane." No politician spoke directly to FDR about his health, and each realized that no other Democrat was electable, yet the vice presidency was now understood as a likely vestibule to the White House. When meeting with Roosevelt at the White House late in June, with Hannegan and presidential counsel and speechwriter Sam Rosenman, a former New York Supreme Court justice, FDR confided that he was "just not going to go through" dictating a running-mate choice as he had in 1940. The party divisions that would occur would "kill our chance for election in the fall." He was open to bringing harmony to the ticket, building up a successor to run in 1948. On July 5 he would even send Rosenman quietly to query the feisty Wendell Willkie, the President's opponent in 1940, about the second slot. Willkie finessed the feeler.

A dispatch by openly conservative *New York Times* columnist Arthur Krock, which would have long legs, was that in the Chicago Yards meeting the President told Bob Hannegan and Ed Kelly that whatever the eventual vice-presidential choice, they had to "clear everything with Sidney." To the Right, labor leader Sidney Hillman, a Wallace backer who had raised a campaign bundle and foot soldiers as head of the Congress of Industrial Organizations (CIO) Political Action Committee, was a leftist devil. Krock later claimed that his sources were two failed aspirants for the vice-presidency, one of them James F. Byrnes. Actually his confidant was his colleague Turner Catledge, who (as he owned up to in a memoir) had the story from Mayor Kelly. Catledge, who was close to both Kelly and Byrnes, did not want the story in *The New York Times* under his byline.

Byrnes, FDR's "assistant president," who had been handling the nation's domestic business efficiently if conservatively for two years, had been derailed by labor and urban Democrats who saw him as a loser in their constituencies. Conceding Byrnes's negatives while claiming support for him, Roosevelt had directed Hannegan, "There is one thing I want you to do, and that is clear [the nomination] with Hillman and Murray." (Philip Murray was ostensibly Hillman's boss as CIO president.) Since neither union official was likely to support a South Carolinian with old-line labor and racial attitudes, it signaled that Byrnes's aspirations were as defunct as Wallace's. In substance the charge was accurate. Republican advertising and speechmaking exploited the "clear it with Sidney" allegation throughout the campaign.

Democratic power brokers knew that Henry Wallace, with his utopian views, would drain allegiance from the ticket—possibly most states in the South, with its crucial electoral votes. His champions, some charged, included dangerous radicals in the labor movement, Communist sympathizers in Hollywood—and Eleanor Roosevelt. Considered eccentric despite his scientific background in agronomy, Wallace had long consulted an astrologer known as

Madame Zenda. Yet a cartoon by Eric Godal in the leftist New York
tabloid *PM* subtitled " . . . But the Guy Is Bulletproof" stubbornly
defended Wallace, showing him striding toward a rising sun labeled
POLITICAL DESTINY while armed villains perched in a tree labeled
on its branches SOUTHERN DEMOCRATS and MONOPOLIES fired
vainly at his back. One of the cartoon ruffians had a poison dart,
but the authentic venom was furnished by FBI director J. Edgar
Hoover, who was even farther to the right than Herbert Hoover.
FBI agents illegally tapped Wallace's phones, opened his mail and
made lists of recognizable listeners at his speeches. Quietly, Hoover
passed on derogatory allegations to Wallace's many political enemies. Republicans derided Wallace as a deluded idealist who
"wanted to give a quart of milk to every Hottentot." However false,
the label stuck. The Bushmen of southern Africa seemed code for
poor American blacks.

To party professionals, the President, who felt guiltily loyal to
the unelectable Wallace, had promised before leaving Washington
to keep his endorsement of the vice president tepid, and to accept
an alternative nominee. As nothing of William O. Douglas's sleazy
womanizing had reached Roosevelt, he proposed the impossible
alternative of the youngish and liberal Supreme Court justice, who
had never run for office and had disclaimed interest in 1940. Party
chieftains who understood the electoral burden of Douglas urged
someone more middle-of-the-road, like Hannegan's fellow Missourian, Harry Truman. The public knew little about the self-
effacing but tenacious Truman other than that he chaired a special
Senate committee to watchdog war expenditures and root out negligence, misconduct and waste. Washington was what newsman
David Brinkley would call a "bureaucratic shark tank." Oversight
was rare.

Truman had made some headlines but also knew when not to
make them. When his investigative committee wanted to look into
the unprecedented start-up expenditures for a huge and mysteri-
ous manufacturing installation to be managed by the chemical

colossus E. I. Du Pont de Nemours along the Columbia River at Pasco, Washington, Truman had to be diverted from the nuclear operation—part of the "Manhattan Project"—without exciting suspicions. Army chief of staff George C. Marshall dispatched his savvy Legislative and Liaison director, Brigadier General Wilton Persons, who was unaware of plutonium extraction and its explosives potential, to request that Truman and his committee "ask no questions whatsoever" about Pasco. Persons was to quote Marshall as explaining, "This is a matter of great importance and one in which I am exercising a direct personal supervision."

Once General Persons offered Marshall's terse comment to Senator Truman, the first $100 million for work at Pasco was granted without any proviso to account for it. Secretary of War Henry L. Stimson also asked Truman to trust him personally about the project, and the senator (according to Stimson's diary) "said that was all he needed to know." Although he inferred a good deal from his own sources, Truman would not learn the facts about atomic bomb development until April 12, 1945.

Unaware how serious the deal-making involving him was in the early summer of 1944, Truman had promised to nominate Byrnes, a former senatorial colleague who had accepted, and then relinquished, a lifetime Supreme Court appointment to assist Roosevelt with domestic affairs while FDR ran the war. Yet the efficient Byrnes, ambitious for the nomination but a lapsed Catholic and a Southern racist, was electoral poison in the North. Truman's reluctance to go back on his word would be difficult for convention managers to handle. Even when Byrnes was pushed aside and Hannegan showed Truman the president's note, Truman insisted that he didn't want the job. "It's all over; our candidate won't take it," Hannegan mourned to Frank Walker, "we have no candidate."

The presidential train had resumed its route westward, moving slowly so that it would not arrive at San Diego until early on the day when delegates were to convene. Chicago Stadium, a convention hall in the center of the city where the Republicans had already met, seated twenty-four thousand and could absorb ten thousand more as standees and in folding chairs. To stress FDR as a wartime leader, thirty-eight large wall posters featured service personnel in battle poses. From the balcony hung portraits of fourteen allegedly Democratic presidents, from Jefferson to Roosevelt.

An advance locomotive for the traveling White House chugged ahead, flying two white caution flags. At a siding in Arizona the presidential special halted to recharge its batteries. Only when it reached the San Diego rail yard on July 19 did Hannegan, in Chicago, resolve to appeal Truman's reluctant candidacy directly to Roosevelt. Early the next morning, Hannegan called for Walker, Flynn, Kelly—and Truman—to meet with him in a room in the Blackstone Hotel. When they arrived, the President was telephoned in his Pullman car. As planned, he asked, naming no names in case the line was insecure, "Have you got that fellow lined up yet?"

"No," said Hannegan, "he is the contrariest Missouri mule I've ever dealt with."

"Well, you tell him," Roosevelt said, as Hannegan held out the receiver so the others could hear, "that if he wants to break up the Democratic party by staying out, he can, but he knows as well as I what that will mean at this dangerous time in the world. If he wants to do it anyway, let him go ahead." And the cabal heard the President slam down his telephone receiver.

"I guess I'll have to take it," Truman said.*

A week later, the senator, now the nominee, visited Henry Wallace at his office in Washington. Never, said Truman, had he spent such an unhappy week as he did at Chicago. "You know, this whole matter is not of my choosing. I went to Chicago to get out of being Vice

---

* Other versions of the telephone dialogue exist, but without any substantive difference.

President, not to become Vice President." According to Wallace's diary, Truman worried that Republicans "would dig up all the dead horses which he thought he had gotten safely buried and throw them at him." Almost certainly he was referring to his early sponsorship by the corrupt Tom Pendergast machine in Kansas City, to which Truman had remained, but for local patronage matters, stubbornly independent. Yet there were other potential embarrassments. In a Missouri primary for a judgeship in the early 1920s, he clawed for further endorsements in Jackson County by paying ten dollars to join the Ku Klux Klan, soon discovering that the Klan was interested in preventing Roman Catholics from getting county jobs. Because many of Truman's army buddies were Catholic, he innocently asked for his money back—and, curiously, the Klan returned it.

Harry Truman never had much income. Another of his dead-and-buried horses was the bankruptcy in 1922 of the Kansas City men's clothing store he operated after the war with his field artillery friend Eddie Jacobson. It took Truman fifteen years to settle his share of the debt. His mother's Missouri farm in Grandview was heavily mortgaged for years, with payments long overdue, and portions sold off. In 1939 only a politically questionable loan arranged when he was strapped for funds saved what was left of the farm from foreclosure.

Truman's monthly senatorial after-taxes pay in 1944 (on an annual senatorial salary of $10,000) was only $687, and since he lived on the edge he had put his wife, Bess, on his office payroll as a drop-in-sometimes clerk. Her check, an annual pre-tax $2,400, not inconsiderable when the federal minimum wage was thirty cents an hour and a loaf of bread cost nine cents, made a difference in their unshowy lifestyle. He had arranged federal jobs for such relatives as his brother, Vivian. Worse than that, as of September 1, 1943, he had put his sister, Mary Jane, on the payroll at $1,800 a year although she lived in Grandview, where she cared for their aged mother full time, and had never been to Washington. *

Even congressmen with substantial private incomes did much the same. While he was vice president, John Garner thought nothing of having his wife on his office staff for two terms. Yet despite what Truman conceded was his "lack of worldly goods," his risky new visibility after two decades in politics left him open to questions from an unforgiving press about every transaction. He had, after all, made a public career out of exposing government waste.

As Pendergast, now convicted of tax evasion, languished in a federal jail, the *Des Moines Register* cartooned a hulking Boss Pendergast in bold prison stripes with a sheaf of papers labeled "A B C OF POLITICS" lecturing a puny student in oversized glasses named Harry Truman. The caption below was "The Political Education of a Vice Presidential Candidate."

---

* During the campaign Clare Boothe Luce would call Mrs. Truman "Payroll Bess," but the charge disturbed few voters. Representative Luce apparently did not know of Mary Jane Truman.

Two _____

The Missouri Compromise

T he keynote address at the Democratic convention was delivered by Governor—later senator—Robert Kerr of Oklahoma, an oil millionaire in his family's business. By radio he also reached a national audience. "Do you remember," he asked, "the twelve long years from 1920 to 1932 when America 'hardened' under Harding, 'cooled' under Coolidge, and 'hungered' under Hoover?" Both audiences did. Expecting listeners to imagine a match of their own, he did not attach a pejorative to Dewey. Since age and health issues were already central to the Republican opposition, Kerr asked what Churchill or Stalin would think of an aspirant for the White House who considered them, along with Roosevelt, as tired old men. Governor Kerr then went through a litany of military leaders, including Admiral King, sixty-six; General MacArthur, sixty-four; and General Marshall, sixty-four.

When an impromptu, if expected, parade of Roosevelt delegates began forming below the speaker's platform, hostile Texans tried to

tear away the FDR banners, while the sympathetic Virginia, Mississippi and Tennessee delegates remained stolidly in their seats. Con-
trarily, the Connecticut delegation marched with a WE WANT
WALLACE! placard affixed below their state standard. Finally, Kerr,
who had stopped as the tumult drowned him out, seized the microphone and continued, closing at 11:57 p.m. Chicago time, long
past bedtime in the East.

The next afternoon the delegates convened to rubber-stamp the
President's renomination. Although at odds with Roosevelt over
taxes, Alben Barkley, party leader in the Senate, delivered the ora-
tion. He had nominated Roosevelt for his third term in 1940.
Byrnes, burned by the President's reluctance to back him, urged
Barkley to make his speech only as a "duty, without being very
enthusiastic," as he, too, had been passed over for the second spot.
Exasperated by the President's deviousness—or slipping control of
the situation—Barkley, the veteran of eleven previous presidential
conventions, told a reporter sourly that he was sick and tired of
trying to figure out which shell the pea was under. He felt personally let down, as did every other aspirant. Radio newsman H. V.
Kaltenborn had predicted on no authority but his own that the popular senator from Kentucky would be the nominee.

Superlatives were the norm for nominating speeches. Barkley
put his defeated ambitions aside and described the President as
having demonstrated "the intellectual boldness of Thomas Jefferson, the indomitable courage of Andrew Jackson, the faith and
patience of Abraham Lincoln, the rugged integrity of Grover
Cleveland, and the scholarly vision of Woodrow Wilson." When he
finally mentioned the withheld name of the nominee—a device expected on such occasions—the thousands in the hall rose to their
feet, cheered, then marched with FDR placards while the house
organ and bands in the galleries added to the planned pandemo-
nium. Then Senator Samuel D. Jackson of Indiana, the convention
chairman, called for order and the music stopped for the seconding speeches and the less-than-serious courtesy nominations.

Although Roosevelt had wanted the political clout of unanimity, three defiant southern delegations—Mississippi, Virginia and Louisiana, rather than reluctant Tennessee—defected to unreconstructed Senator Harry F. Byrd of Virginia. Another, divided Texas, threatened emptily to do so. Nevertheless, on July 20 the President was overwhelmingly nominated on the first ballot, 1,086–89–1. (Jim Farley received a token vote.) Cheers again erupted; FDR-banded straw hats flew; the house organist played the Democratic anthem of 1932, "Happy Days Are Here Again." Transcontinental network radio carried the enthusiasm across the country. It was almost as if there had been authentic competition.

The real contest, long brewing, would be over the vice-presidency. Earlier, Senator Jackson as a courtesy had agreed to permit Vice President Wallace to give an additional seconding speech for the President. The chairman should have been forewarned of trouble, as on arriving in Chicago, Wallace had announced, "I am in this fight to a finish." In his characteristic rumpled suit rendered further shapeless in the heat and humidity of the hall, Wallace delivered his endorsement. Then he launched into an impassioned plea that his party in winning the war should not desert the post-Depression social gains of the New Deal. "The future," he challenged, "belongs to those who go down the line unswervingly for the liberal principles of both political democracy and economic democracy, regardless of race, color, or religion. In a political, economic, and educational sense, there must be no inferior races. . . . The Democratic party cannot long survive as a Conservative party."

Wallace's political liabilities left him with a diminishing delegate count, and he must have realized as he spoke that he was finished as a factor in his own party. Ever the pragmatist, Roosevelt counted upon the votes in Congress from the eleven states of the old Confederacy and expected the rising tide of democracy, in time, to lift all boats. The galleries, packed by young Wallace boosters impatient to accelerate the unfinished business of the New Deal, lacked sufficient votes to put him over, and he was a pariah to conservative Democrats who might walk out. Four years later, Dixiecrats would begin bolting the party anyway. And so would Wallace.

In San Diego, Roosevelt was preparing to embark for Pearl Harbor to confer with Admiral Chester Nimitz and General Douglas MacArthur on Pacific war operations. But for Navy photos, some of which had never been released to the press, FDR had not seen Pearl Harbor after the Japanese attacks during what he called, in asking Congress to declare war, "a date that will live in infamy." Two battleships remained as sunken relics of December 7, 1941—the *Arizona*, with more than a thousand seamen still entombed in its wreckage, and the *Utah*, an obsolete hulk that had been used for target practice but that enemy airmen mistakenly assumed, from the planks on its decks, was an aircraft carrier. The *Oklahoma*, which had capsized and was refloated with difficulty, was fit only for scrapping, and sank when being towed to the mainland.

Although the harbor now bustled with ships and planes and with thousands of troops preparing to storm enemy-held islands in the western Pacific, and Japan itself, a new post-disaster cleanup had just been completed. On June 14, having downplayed the embarrassment for three weeks, the Navy confessed that on May 21 explosions had occurred while loading ammunition onto "several" landing craft. Twenty-seven men were killed, 100 were still missing and presumed dead, and 380 were wounded—soldiers, sailors, Marines and civilians. The landing craft, similar to those the President had seen in the exercise at Oceanside, California, were destroyed. A further blast occurred at an ammunition magazine when torpedoes were being unloaded from a truck to a dock platform, resulting in ten additional men dead or missing. Power lines and rail tracks were also disabled. The services did not need a return of the Japanese to bring the war back to Pearl Harbor.

Another embarrassment closer to home would occur just before the President's departure and lead to politically damaging charges of service incompetence. Late at night on July 17, at Port Chicago on San Francisco Bay, a vast munitions depot, two fully fueled (and flammable) ships being loaded with thousands of tons of incendiary bombs, depth charges and torpedoes from standing rail cars detonated after an explosion on the pier. Seismographs at Berkeley registered the gruesome catastrophe and 3-mile-wide fireball as a 3.4 Richter scale earthquake. The highly visible disaster could not be kept from the papers. All the sailors on duty, but for white officers, were black, and accounted for 202 of the 320 dead. Only 51 of the shattered bodies were identifiable.

Fear of further explosions led to a mutiny by the survivors of the segregated ordnance battalion. Fifty would be court-martialed and sentenced to long prison terms, resulting in widespread adverse publicity for the Navy, which asked Congress for $5,000 for each deceased victim's family. When Representative John E. Rankin of Mississippi learned that most of the dead were black men, he insisted that the compensation be reduced to $2,000. Congress meanly settled on $3,000. The nation's capital was Jim Crow in attitude if not entirely in law, with formal segregation beginning as blacks crossed the Potomac into Virginia, where trains stopped so that "coloreds" could be herded together into segregated cars.

"To avoid any semblance of discrimination against negroes" after the Chicago episode, the new Secretary of the Navy, James Forrestal, reported to the President, white units would be added to the munitions-loading rotation. Knowing her sensitivity to such matters, as well as its likely impact upon the black voting public, FDR forwarded a copy to Eleanor. The NAACP campaign to appeal the convictions of the "Chicago 50" would be led by future Justice Thurgood Marshall.

Six weeks into the cross-Channel landings in France, the end-game for Nazi Germany seemed inevitable, but there was still another war across another ocean, and the President's sailing had serious implications for Pacific strategy. Islands on the Japanese sea periphery had to be seized and Japan itself invaded if its suicidal resistance could not be broken. Further, Roosevelt had to make a personal demonstration of his fitness to conduct the war to its conclusion. However downplayed, polio had long immobilized his legs. His triumphs over adversity had come at heavy cost. Although his muscular upper body was all most onlookers saw, the President was more helpless, physically, than the public realized. No one was permitted by his Secret Service escorts to photograph the President being lifted from his limousine. Few ever saw him, as at Bethesda Naval Hospital, seated in an armless kitchen chair fitted with two large wheels in front, smaller ones in back. He had campaigned in 1932, 1936 and 1940 from a raised platform in an open car, or standing with increasing difficulty on heavy locked braces painted black to match his shoes and socks, and now ill-fitting because of his loss of weight. He "walked" when supported under one or both arms by aides.

Despite the ordeal of the amphibious review immediately after his concealed medical episode, the President had visited, at the Camp Pendleton base hospital, Marine colonel Evans Carlson, severely wounded at Saipan, and others among the human wreckage of Pacific island landings. Then Roosevelt was returned to the rail siding to learn of his expected nomination and to radio a message of formal acceptance to the happy delegates in Chicago. Despite enormous casualties, the successful landings in the Marianas had been nearly as crucial as the expensive D-Day operations, almost at the same time, in Normandy. Japan's defensive perimeter had been breached, and the Navy's "Great Marianas Turkey Shoot" had destroyed hundreds of enemy aircraft and several irreplaceable carriers, including Admiral Jisaburo Ozawa's own flagship. By the time of the political formalities in Chicago, Saipan, Tinian and Guam were secured and the Commander-in-Chief had bragging rights on the path to Tokyo.

His battery of physical examinations by outside specialists now weeks in the past, the President had left Washington for Chicago on July 13, intending after a brief stop there for conferring with party officials to entrain slowly for San Diego, arriving in time for his speech from the train accepting his renomination. However slowly they traveled, Roosevelt insisting on a leisurely 40 miles an hour, arrival time seemed to be approaching too soon, and Dewey Long of the White House transportation office altered the routing lengthily through El Paso, Douglas (Arizona) and Calexico, on the border. Despite the official secrecy, no other train traveled so slowly or with more security personnel watching the trackage, and at every stop where the presidential Scottie, Fala, was permitted on the platform, security vanished.

In the convention hall in Chicago, spotlights focused on a huge portrait, from an earlier campaign, of a genial, robust Roosevelt, who was introduced as "speaking from a Pacific Coast naval base." In reality a far more frail Roosevelt spoke from the presidential railway train. Its communications car was cluttered with motion picture and press cameras and broadcasting equipment amid a tangle of wires. Largely it was a diesel-powered radio receiving and transmitting station in constant touch with the confidential Map Room in the White House. FDR's private car near the tail of the train, originally a luxury dark-green Pullman built in 1928, was one of several named for famous explorers. It had been thoroughly refitted for the President's wartime use with bullet-proof window glass and armor plate, and sold to the White House for one dollar by the Association of American Railroads.

As always, Dewey Long made the arrangements for trackage and security. No tickets were issued, and the railway staff had the numbers assigned to the nameless passengers and billed according to miles traveled. The White House paid six fares for the *Ferdinand Magellan,* which had a dining-conference room, four staterooms, galley, pantry and servants' quarters. An observation lounge with door led to the open rear platform. Two elevators could each lift the President's wheelchair on and off. FDR would clock 44,000 miles on it in 1944.

Behind the locomotive was an oversize baggage car once owned by the Barnum and Bailey Circus. It had been retrofitted for the President and his Secret Service escort to hold four automobiles—two large sedans and two convertibles. A second railway car carried communications gear, and a third housed radio operators and railway staff. Roomette cars as necessary were for the press, nearly empty this time as only a few pool reporters were to accompany Roosevelt on the Pacific voyage. A club car housed a bar and tables with armchairs in green plush, and a dining car was behind it. Then came a roomette car for presidential staff and the Secret Service, and, in the rear, the *Magellan* and the observation car.

Seemingly recovered from his morning episode, Roosevelt's familiar voice boomed from the *Ferdinand Magellan* into convention loudspeakers. He reiterated his long-postponed desire to retire to a quiet life at Hyde Park on the Hudson—but "you in this convention have asked me to continue." As a "good soldier" he would comply. "What is the job before us in 1944? First, to win the war—to win the war fast, to win it overpoweringly. Second, to form worldwide international organizations. . . . And third, to build an economy for our returning veterans and for all Americans—which will provide employment and provide decent standards of living." He would be, however, "too busy to campaign in the usual sense" and would press his case for re-election on "experience versus immaturity." (At forty-two, his Republican opponent, Governor Thomas E. Dewey of New York, was twenty years younger.) The President accepted his "draft" as a wartime duty. "Today Oklahoma and California are being defended in Normandy and Saipan,

A haggard FDR broadcasting his acceptance of a fourth-term nomination from his presidential train, San Diego, California, July 20, 1944. James Roosevelt and his wife are seated to his left. James Roosevelt had been the only witness to the cardiac episode. *FDR Library*

and they must be defended there—for what happens in Normandy and Saipan vitally affects the security and well-being of every human being in Oklahoma and California."

For a press pool photographer, Roosevelt posed, with Jimmy at his side, re-reading lines from his speech. A newsreel camera whirred. The nearest film-processing facilities were in Los Angeles, where the Associated Press arranged to provide prints for the media. From the negatives, the local AP editor chose one with the President speaking, and another with his mouth closed. For transmission from Los Angeles, Dick Strobel chose "the one with the open mouth, since it was more obvious that he was talking. I went into my office to write the caption while the darkroom technicians processed the print."

As soon as the cameraman, George Skaddings, saw the results, he rushed the picture back to Strobel. "Hey, you better look at this," he warned. Roosevelt's mouth hung slack and gaping; flash-bulbs had glazed his eyes and highlighted his haggard features. Yet there was no time to prepare a substitute image. The President was in San Diego, and in the East it was already two in the morning on the 21st. Final editions of the morning papers were being held for the wire photo. "I made the judgment," Strobel explained, "to go with what we had."

For the anti-FDR press, the photo was a gift. The image validated for the opposition that Roosevelt was feeble beyond his sixty-two years, and demonstrably unfit to continue in office. Eleanor Roosevelt, who had been on the train but had flown east from San Diego, would be "sick about the whole business." The President's press secretary, Steve Early, banished the innocent Skaddings from the traveling press corps. Even worse, the brief newsreel shot at the same time revealed more of the hollow cheeks, gaping mouth and loose shirt collar that evidenced serious weight loss.

Exploiting a whispering campaign about Roosevelt's health, which publisher Robert L. McCormick, long a conservative crank, had abetted, and the photos from San Diego had dramatized, the *Chicago Tribune* began publishing contrasting photographs of the contenders. Pictures at two-year intervals from an ebullient one in 1932 to the devastating newest shot showed a drastically deteriorating Roosevelt. A photo of Dewey on a golf course drew a protest from the governor's campaign manager as inappropriate, but Colonel McCormick defended it as "distinct evidence of vigor." A new Gallup Poll found that 34 percent of interviewees believed that Roosevelt's health, about which they knew nothing but rumor, would not permit him to perform his presidential duties in a fourth term. One of McCormick's star reporters in Washington recognized the reverse impact, nevertheless, of any portrait of FDR. "Although he couldn't walk," Walter J. Trohan of the *Tribune* recalled of the presidential image familiar for eleven years, "he had the face of a fellow who could march."

In Chicago, delegates fearing an unpredictable Wallace as a successor in the White House saw after his backers' attempt to stampede the delegates a middle-of-the-road vice-presidential nominee as increasingly urgent. As Roosevelt could not have been unaware, weeks had been spent in trying to fix on an alternative acceptable to all party factions. Barring presidential disability or death, the office of vice president, but for ceremonial duties, condemned its holder to political invisibility—so much so that most Americans could not have identified the vice presidents under Woodrow Wilson, or Ulysses S. Grant, or Andrew Jackson or James Monroe—all two-term occupants of the White House. Because Roosevelt, in his twelfth year in the White House, seemed indestructible, Harry Truman had told a Missouri friend who had urged him to run, "The vice president merely presides over the Senate and sits around waiting for a funeral." To former senator George Norris of Nebraska, Roosevelt had written, "I am honestly trying to keep out of the Vice-Presidential contest which includes a score of candidates and another score who have their lightning rods up and would like to be struck."

The lightning crackled through the convention. The crucial session would last nine anxious hours. As a consummate manipulator, Roosevelt in Byzantine fashion had assured several aspirants for the second slot that he was in favor of open electioneering, with the party's choice openly arrived at. In a White House meeting on July 13, the President had claimed, insincerely, to Wallace, who was just back from a trip to China intended to put him literally at a distance from politicking for himself, "While I cannot put it just that way in public, I hope it will be the same old team!" He wasn't talking politics, FDR said, cautiously: "I am now talking to the ceiling." But Roosevelt's parting message to Wallace was far less positive: "Even though they do beat you out at Chicago, we will have a job for you in world economic affairs." Deviously, the President also told Jimmy Byrnes that he was "the best qualified man in the whole outfit" and that he hoped Byrnes would "stay in." Although he recognized the tepidity of the recommendation, Byrnes determined to stay in contention.

Early in the morning of the day the convention was to begin, he telephoned Harry Truman from Washington—the senator was still in Missouri, a short train hop away from Chicago—that Roosevelt was about to endorse the "assistant President" and asked Truman to make the nominating speech. Despite rumors about himself as the choice of the power brokers, an outcome which both tempted and repelled him, Truman agreed.

At the White House a week earlier, Roosevelt, hardly disengaged, tried to persuade Bob Hannegan that Justice William O. Douglas, despite no perceptible interest in him, would be the best fit. He also proposed John Winant, ambassador to Great Britain, a liberal former Republican governor of New Hampshire who had international credentials but utterly no party following. Conceding that Byrnes was unacceptable to the convention, Roosevelt listened to a chorus of suggestions that he should settle for Harry Truman. As Ed Flynn, party boss in the Bronx, recalled (*alleged* seems more accurate), Roosevelt enjoined the party leaders to "inject Truman into the picture." FDR had actually confessed, "I hardly know Truman," and he wondered about Truman's age. (He had last seen him at the White House on March 5.) A copy of the *Congressional Quarterly* was fetched, then quietly ignored by the conferees, hoping that Roosevelt would forget that he asked for it. The Missourian was sixty—nearly as old as the President. Douglas was a vigorous forty-five. A month after Pearl Harbor, *TIME* had referred to "grey little Harry Truman," who had visited the White House as chairman of the Senate committee investigating the domestic war effort. "Senator Truman told Mr. Roosevelt that he was going to rip the whole defense organization up the middle," that war production "was an awesome mess." Criticizing the President's penchant for overlapping authorities and casual oversight, Truman, forthright as usual, was not out to make friends. The senator had not been invited to the Oval Office much thereafter.

The apparent dithering over the second slot dismayed politicians who worried that any anointed nominee might soon become Roosevelt's successor and control the party machinery as well as the country. Douglas had claimed no interest, but he had the insider backing of Harold Ickes, and to suggest disinterest he went off to a mountain retreat in Oregon, then slipped north to Whitman College in Washington, where he awaited word by telephone from Chicago. The informal rules of the Supreme Court were that a sitting justice could not run for political office without first resigning his seat.

With backstairs intrigue still unsettling convention preliminaries, Hannegan asked to have FDR's preferences in writing. On a handy scrap, Roosevelt wrote, postdating the memo July 19, two days before the convention opened, as would become obvious on its release,

Dear Bob,

You have written me about Bill Douglas and Harry Truman. I should, of course, be very glad to run with either of them and believe that either of them would bring real strength to the ticket.

Always sincerely,
Franklin D. Roosevelt

Reaching his car parked under the North Portico, Hannegan had leaned into the back seat to wave the paper at Frank Walker. "I got it," he said. But Hannegan felt that he needed to enhance the endorsement of Truman. At the White House again the next morning, Hannegan asked—as the President's handwriting was becoming shaky—whether the note could be typed by Roosevelt's secretary.

With that OK, Hannegan dropped by Grace Tully's office. "Grace," she recalled Hannegan as saying, "the President wants you to retype this letter and to switch these names so it will read 'Harry Truman or Bill Douglas.'" Tully had her assistant, Dorothy Brady, type it up on White House stationery. Roosevelt never saw it again, but Tully herself was also expert at her boss's initials. Complicating the endorsement situation, Henry Wallace would also arrive in Chicago with a cagily written presidential letter.

That morning, Walker had returned with Hannegan to see Jimmy Byrnes in his East Wing office. Walker had been tasked with relaying the bad news from the convention managers that Byrnes had no chance. Like Wallace, but for opposite reasons, the South Carolinian was too controversial. He had guessed as much, but sulkily stood his ground. Party boss Ed Flynn, although admiring Wallace, had already told the President frankly that despite support from organized labor, the incumbent vice president would be a drag on the ticket. Only Truman had no negatives. But to Jim Farley, who did not take Truman seriously, the senator lacked the requisite heft. When Truman dropped in at Farley's hotel room at the Blackstone to ask for his vote—very likely for Byrnes although Farley assumed it was for Truman himself—he warned bluntly, "Before you take it, you've got to ask yourself if you have the capacity to make a decision once the facts are put in front of you."

Truman realized that Farley was serious. Rumors swirled among the delegates that whatever was being revealed publicly, the unseen Roosevelt was failing, and that they were very likely going to nominate two presidents. A third president was also a possibility: Henry Wallace, whether or not the party's choice in Chicago, might even succeed in office before inauguration day on January 20, 1945.

To replace the iconic FDR seemed daunting enough. For Truman to do so with marginal executive experience during an ongoing world war was even more frightening. On July 9, as the opening of the convention approached and the pressure on him was building, he wrote to his daughter, Margaret, from Missouri, "1600 Pennsylvania Avenue is a nice address but I'd rather not move in through the back door." It suggested a small fissure in his studied obstinacy. "I am satisfied where I am," Truman had told his Kansas City friend Tom Evans, adding, while gesturing with his forefinger and thumb, "Just a heartbeat, this little, separates the Vice President and the President."

To party insiders, despite his own doubts, Truman had the right stuff. Other than being relatively unknown outside the Senate, making him hard to politically pigeonhole, he came from many-sided Missouri, a border state. To Flynn, Harry Truman "just dropped into the slot." Still, Roosevelt felt that he owed Wallace some form of endorsement, yet one without guarantees. Several days earlier, before the President entrained west, Wallace requested a written endorsement. On July 14, Roosevelt wrote to the permanent chairman of the convention that he liked Wallace, respected him, and considered the vice president a personal friend. "For these reasons I would vote for his renomination if I were a delegate. . . . At the same time, I do not wish to appear in any way as dictating to the convention." In Chicago, Wallace would release it as Holy Writ. In his journal, Allen Drury of United Press wryly rephrased the letter as, "If you want him, well, OK. If you don't, well, OK. Suit yourself. And so long, Henry." A cartoon on the *Philadelphia Inquirer* editorial page would show Wallace as a barefoot farmer in front of a closed convention door reading Roosevelt's letter of recommendation: "Here's a nice boy! But don't hire him if you don't want to! FDR."

Although realizing that the letter lacked fire, Wallace personally took it to Chicago and released it to the press. Flynn, Kelly, Pauley, Hannegan and labor stalwarts like Sidney Hillman, until then a Wallace man, had to forestall Wallace delegates from stampeding the convention on the first ballot. Hannegan released his own letter

from Roosevelt to the press. Emotions among delegates and spectators seeking seats suggested imminent drama, and a large cast.
The party cabal planned to encourage favorite-son nominations on
the opening ballot, to prevent Wallace, whose grass-roots support
remained formidable, from accumulating a winning majority of
529 votes. To head off Wallace, Hannegan wanted to rush through
the running-mate slot on the same steamy Thursday evening as the
presidential balloting, but that meant locating all the nominating
speakers and seconders, who had been counting upon doing their
duty the next afternoon. It meant doing the impossible.

While Roosevelt's disembodied voice from San Diego accepting
his renomination rumbled through the loudspeakers in Chicago,
the search went on to locate the vice-presidential nominators. The
key to Hannegan's strategy was Senator Bennett Champ Clark of
Missouri, who could be spellbinding when sober. He would be
located at the Hotel Drake toward midnight, too drunk to go on—
"cockeyed," according to Truman, whom he was to nominate. By
then, through Hannegan's bullying past convention rules, the tide
of the Wallace candidacy began imploding.

After the President's address and the inevitable cheering, shouts
of "We Want Wallace!" had arisen, abetted by his theme song,
"Iowa, Iowa, That's Where the Tall Corn Grows," pumped out over
and over again by the convention organist, who was only awaiting
instructions and filling empty space. A conference of floor leaders
worried about Wallace supporters stampeding the convention materialized on the podium. As Wallace die-hard Claude Pepper, the
New Dealing Florida senator, rushed up to exploit the vacuum and
renominate the incumbent, the convention chairman, Senator Jackson, on Hannegan's orders, banged his gavel and rushed an ad-
journment, later claiming fire laws about overcrowding.

Listening to the radio from his Pullman car, Roosevelt telephoned
the podium in Chicago to find out why the leadership had lost control. Mayor Kelly assured him that everything was set for the second

slot and that the roll call on Friday would be disciplined. Truman was aware that he would be nominated, and Byrnes had spared Truman a futile speech and his own embarrassment by calling off his nomination. Truman had even located, and rescued from the bottle, his ostensible sponsor, Champ Clark, yet his own misgivings remained.

What was scheduled to be the final session began as originally planned, at 4:30 on Friday afternoon, July 21. On the first roll call, alphabetically by states, sixteen names were placed in nomination. Champ Clark, now cleaned up and sober, put his favorite-son colleague, Harry Truman, forward with lines more prophetic than he realized. "In this year of destiny," Clark shouted over a stormy sea of waving Wallace placards, "it is more than ever necessary to select a Vice President possessing all the qualities and qualifications desirable and necessary for a President of the United States." A prewar isolationist and America First stalwart, and consistent critic of Roosevelt's policies, foreign and domestic, Clark was busy trying to obscure his past. A candidate for re-election to a third term, he would lose in the Missouri primary, blaming "the Communist-controlled CIO."

Wallace led after the first ballot with 429 votes. He seemed close to overturning the hard-won compromise of party chieftains, yet he was at the limit of his delegate strength. Truman followed with 319. By prearrangement, when Alabama was called, alphabetically, on the second ballot, its favorite son, Senator John Bankhead, announced his withdrawal in favor of Truman. State after state then announced switches to Senator Truman—but for Illinois, where Mayor Kelly, who had worked hard for Truman, forgot his instructions in the confusion and continued his state's support of favorite son Senator Scott Lucas. Ohio announced for Truman, but when a delegate protested and asked for a count, Massachusetts was again recognized and shifted its 34 votes to Truman. The charade culminated when more states switched and put the junior senator from

Missouri further over the top. Other nominal rivals melted away. New York's 93 votes for Wallace were diverted to Truman, and other delegations clamored for the chair's attention to ratify the winner.

No delegate, and no longer a candidate, Jimmy Byrnes was sitting in the reserved visitors' section with Bess Truman and her daughter Margaret. Excusing himself, he rushed down to the South Carolina delegation on the floor and urged that the state's 16 votes be switched to Truman. With the melancholy end for himself inevitable, he slipped out and went back to Washington, where he told an intimate bitterly that Roosevelt had "no backbone" and had "a jellyfish way of doing business." At the final gavel, Wallace was down to 105, then to 66; Truman had bulked to 1,031. Even so, Truman had done little to win other than to permit his name in nomination.

Hundreds of Wallace placards quickly vanished, and three large white tethered balloons labeled in blue "We Want Wallace" were cut loose and floated to the iron girders at the ceiling. Wallaceites would cry foul, and Republicans would charge Democratic bosses with rigging the convention. Republican chances had rested on making issues of machine politics, Roosevelt's impaired health and Wallace's political fragility. Urban political bossism was as American as apple pie: both parties played that game. (Philadelphia had been Republican for generations.) Republicans had lost Wallace as a target, but it would take much political spin for Democrats to overcome the imposition of Truman and the wire-photo vision of a ravaged Roosevelt.

Aware of the machinations in Chicago, although not of the scenario as it played out, the President had lost personal control of the party machinery. Nevertheless, he dictated a message to Truman from his railroad car, to be telegraphed when appropriate: "I send you my heartiest congratulations on your victory. I am, of course, very happy to have you run with me. Let me know your plans. I shall see you soon." In Chicago, Truman would hastily write a few lines about honor and his willingness to do his best. At the bank of microphones on the podium, he improvised from his jottings on a scrap of paper and declared in his flat Midwest manner, "You don't know how very much I appreciate the very great honor that has come to the state of Missouri. It is also a great responsibility which I am perfectly willing to assume." He had been dragged unwillingly to the nomination, as many knew, and he confessed as much—that he had expected only to continue in the Senate "to help shorten the war and to win the peace." Closing one of the shortest acceptance speeches in convention history, Truman added, "I don't know what else I can say, except that I accept this honor with all humility. I thank you."

As the Trumans, with their daughter Margaret, then twenty, left the tumultuous convention floor guarded by Chicago policemen, and exited to a waiting car,* Bess Truman, who would lose her job, and salary, and privacy, glared at her husband and asked, although anticipating the answer, "Are we going to have to go through this for the rest of our lives?" The most immediate change in the candidate's own life was relinquishing the Truman Investigating Committee, which he had chaired since early in 1941, when the burgeoning war build-up exposed gross malfeasance and profiteering in construction and industry contracts. Under-Secretary of War Robert Patterson, a Wall Streeter, had tried to get the committee disbanded after Pearl Harbor but failed. Billions would be rescued from improper billing and defective manufactures, from ships to aircraft engines. Yet candidate Truman could not wear both hats. Hugh Fulton, the committee's attorney, and committee members met him at Martinsburg, West Virginia, where he disembarked. "I had made up my mind on that," he wrote to Bess the next day, August 4, "when the nomination was forced on me. I have never in my life wanted to sit down and

* An alternative exit story via Edwin Pauley that seems unlikely is that a driver for Mayor Kelly also ferried Harry Truman (without his wife and daughter). Not realizing the other man's identity, the chauffeur related to Kelly fierce remarks about Truman by his previous passenger, Helen Gahagan Douglas, a Wallace die-hard, and candidate for Congress from California.

really blubber like I did when I told them I was quitting. I didn't do it—but they did. Connally, Mead, Kilgore, Brewster, Benton, [and] Ferguson were there." The committee, he later wrote to Bess, "passed a resolution that almost made me a close relative of Christ. [Senator] Arthur Walsh [of New Jersey] said he intended to give me a party and sell seats to the pool across from the Lincoln Memorial so they could watch me walk on it. (That's awful.)"

By the close of the convention the President was actively pursuing his wily win-the-war style of politics. Home-front matters had long been left to lesser hands. From his train he dictated a message to Josef Stalin on "leaving on this trip to the Pacific," praising the "amazing" advances of the Red Army, acknowledging "heavy losses" in taking the island of Saipan in the Marianas group and in continuing action in reoccupying nearby Guam. "We have just received news of the difficulties in Germany and especially [the failed bomb plot] at Hitler's headquarters in East Prussia. It is all to the good." But to Eleanor he wrote, "I might have to hurry back [from Hawaii] earlier if this German revolt gets worse! I fear though that it won't."

Although Roosevelt had acknowledged to Stalin that he had learned of the abortive conspiracy against Adolf Hitler, there was nothing to be done but observe the barbaric Nazi reaction play out. It was not "all to the good." A loose cabal of belatedly anti-Nazi officers led by Lieutenant Colonel Klaus von Stauffenberg had planted a bomb in a briefcase at Hitler's East Prussian headquarters, where the Führer dictated how the collapsing war in Russia should be run. When the briefcase was inadvertently shifted, the plotters were helpless to alter events, and the sturdy conference table partly shielded the blast. Although injured, Hitler ordered the plotters punished with bestial fury. The war would go on across both oceans.

As the July convention had neared, with Roosevelt's renomination assured, the press continued to focus on the President's health.

Any reported or even rumored travel, or postponement of a press conference—FDR had conducted more than nine hundred—reawakened concerns. Only after he had met with newsmen at Hobcaw on May 6 had the press been authorized to report where he had been. *Life* published a photo spread as "Roosevelt Returns," showing him in apparent good shape although more drawn than before, and *The New York Times* covered his return on its front page.

At Ross McIntire's request, Dr. Harry Etter, a retired rear admiral and a specialist in physical rehabilitation, examined the President in swimming trunks at the edge of the White House swimming pool shortly after his return from Hobcaw. Although FDR was no longer the robust presence of earlier years, Etter found him "alert, keen, and in a great mental state." He did not conduct a full physical and was not called in further. McIntire was protecting himself rather than FDR.

The more grim reality was set down in a memorandum on July 10, 1944, eleven days before the convention, which did not surface until 2007. Dr. Bruenn, who was with the President almost daily, never reported in his clinical notes a confidential return visit by Dr. Frank Lahey at the White House on Saturday afternoon, July 8, after which Roosevelt supposedly asked, "You have good news for me, Dr. Lahey?" His response, so Lahey told a group of physicians years later, was, "Mr. President, you may not care for what I have to say." The eminent heart specialist from Boston claimed that he was summarily brushed off. "That will be all, Dr. Lahey," Roosevelt said, dismissing him.

The exchange was an invention. Sworn to secrecy, Lahey had made his diagnosis and reported only to FDR's physician. Although chairman of the Navy's medical consulting board, Lahey was outranked by Vice Admiral McIntire.

Much later, according to Dr. Samuel Day of Jacksonville, Florida, Lahey claimed that Roosevelt had covertly traveled to Boston by special train—an impossibly hush-hush journey for the highly visible

Ferdinand Magellan and its security necessities—for an examination at the Lahey Clinic. The consultation, which never occurred, posited advanced stomach cancer. When Lahey advised FDR then not to run for reelection, he was told, firmly, "Well, I am running."

"Well, Mr. President," Lahey allegedly retorted, "I would suggest you take on a strong vice president."

Samuel Day's tale of a surreptitious rail journey seems little more than fantasy fashioned from hearsay. Yet Lahey apparently did break his silence years afterward in conversation with his friend Dr. George Pack of the Memorial Sloan-Kettering Cancer Center in New York, revealing that he had examined the President just before the nominating convention, and that he advised Roosevelt against a fourth-term campaign.

Lahey never advised Roosevelt about anything. As directed, he presented his findings only to Ross McIntire, typing protectively a cautious single-spaced, one-page memorandum on the Monday after the consultation, which he immediately locked away. According to Lahey's document, he warned McIntire that Roosevelt could not survive another term and should not run again, and that the admiral agreed to convey that blunt assessment to the President. McIntire not only never did, but apparently exploited his position to remove Roosevelt's clinical records kept at Bethesda.

"It was not my duty," Lahey wrote, covering himself, to advise [the President] concerning whether or not such a term was undertaken, but to inform Admiral McIntire, "as his family Physician[,] my opinion concerning his"—FDR's—"capacity to do it." Lahey secured the memo with his business manager, Linda Strand, a trustee of the Lahey Clinic, instructing her that should he "ever be posthumously criticized for his conduct in relation to his consultation . . . and his failure to make a public report thereof, the document was to be published if [Strand] saw fit." When Lahey died of a heart attack in 1953 the memorandum was deposited by Strand with her Boston law firm, Herrick and Smith. She did not show it to a physician until she offered a copy to Dr. Harry Goldsmith, a Boston

Frank H. Lahey, M.D., July 10, 1944, personal memo to cover himself about his having reported his views on President Roosevelt's deteriorating medical condition to Vice Admiral Ross T. McIntire. *McIntire papers, FDR Library*

professor of surgery, who told her that he had heard of the episode from George Pack. Goldsmith kept the copy to himself for almost twenty years, then reproduced it in a self-published book, *A Conspiracy of Silence.*

As hypertensive heart disease seemed insufficient to conspiracy theorists, rumors about Roosevelt's alleged variety of terminal and inoperable ailments persist. What Lahey did suggest to Ross McIntire was that FDR, with a history of high blood pressure, had experienced what seemed to Lahey to be a heart seizure "or something close to it" at Tehran late in 1943, at a conference with Stalin and Churchill. The President had come through then with no ill effects obvious to his staff and had returned via Cairo and Algiers. "With this in mind," Lahey told McIntire, "it was my opinion that over the four years of another term with its burdens, he would again have heart failure and be unable to complete it." In his covering memo Lahey confirmed that he had warned McIntire that he "felt strongly," if Roosevelt accepted another nomination, "he had a very serious responsibility concerning who is the Vice President." McIntire agreed to advise the President accordingly, but Lahey must have assumed—the private document is the evidence—that Roosevelt's personal physician would reveal nothing to his patient. Although McIntyre continued his cover-ups, Roosevelt could have had no illusions about his decline.

Despite Lahey's mordant memorandum of July 10, just before the President left for Chicago and the Pacific he remained, as chairman of the War Manpower Commission's Procurement and Assignment Service for Physicians, Dentists and Veterinarians, close to Admiral McIntire. Something about Leahy's consultation must have leaked. Writing to the Surgeon General of the Navy on the commission's letterhead on September 12, 1944, two months after his White House visit—and well after FDR's voyages to Hawaii and Alaska—Lahey reported to McIntire an inquiry from Charles Ross of the *St. Louis Post-Dispatch*, who had been directed by his editor

> to run down a rumor that following the collapse of Germany the President [assuming his re-election] would resign in order to handle a peace settlement. He asked me if I had discussed any such thing with the President or if he had given me such information.

OFFICE FOR EMERGENCY MANAGEMENT

WAR MANPOWER COMMISSION

WASHINGTON, D. C., 25

September 12, 1944

PROCUREMENT and ASSIGNMENT SERVICE for
PHYSICIANS, DENTISTS and VETERINARIANS

Vice Admiral Ross T. McIntire
Surgeon General of the Navy
Washington, D. C.

Dear Admiral McIntire:

I have to write you this letter to protect myself against
any possible mis-statement that may be made. A Mr. Charles
Ross of the St. Louis Despatch telephoned me that his editor,
Mr. Pulitzer, had commissioned him to come to Boston and see
me about something of a confidential nature which he could
not discuss over the telephone. I told him that it was a
long trip for him to make on such a vague basis, that I would
see him here, and I saw him this morning.

He stated that he had been confidentially committed to run
down a rumor that following the collapse of Germany the
President would resign in order to handle a peace settle-
ment. He asked me if I had discussed any such thing with
the President or if he had given me any such information.
I told him how ridiculous this was and that the only time
I saw the President was when I got in trouble with the
Procurement and Assignment Service, and that he had never
made a remark to me which had any political implication.

I told him that I did not see how an editor could send an
assistant editor on such a foolish mission. He asked me if
I had seen the President professionally and I told him that
that was something that I felt he had no right to ask, and
that the only answer I could make was that you had told me,
and it was my opinion, that he was now in excellent health.

If all of the above seems foolish, it is merely to state the
facts lest there be any distortion at any time. I suppose we
must expect more and more of this business as we get nearer
to election time.

With kindest personal regards, I am

Sincerely yours,

Frank H. Lahey, M. D.
Chairman, Directing Board

Frank H. Lahey, MD, letter to Vice Admiral Ross T. McIntire, September 12, 1944, reporting an inquiry from a reporter on FDR's medical
condition, and how Lahey parried the question to cover McIntire. *McIntire papers, FDR Library*

I told him how ridiculous this was and that the only time I saw
the President was when I got into trouble with the Procurement
and Assignment Service, and that he had never made a remark to
me which had any political implication.

In effect Lahey, who would never have been called in by the President about a trivial medical personnel assignment, was denying to a reporter that he had ever seen the President for diagnostic reasons or had ever discussed politics with him or had any concerns about FDR's ability to continue in office. A further irony in the deception would be left to history. Charles Ross would become press secretary to President Harry S. Truman, then newly nominated to the second slot on the Roosevelt ticket.

To newsmen, the President, in deflating allegations about his health, seemed his genial old self. Dr. Bruenn, who accompanied his charge to Hawaii and Alaska, could not effect a cure, but he had essentially stabilized Roosevelt's condition, and FDR's revived involvement in politics had also been upbeat. Convalescing from serious surgery at White Sulphur Springs, West Virginia, a former resort converted to an army hospital, Harry Hopkins, long the President's closest confidant, had earlier received a jovial and revealing pre-convention get-well letter. Roosevelt's message urged Hopkins not to attempt to return to work too soon and not to shake things up in his usual fashion. "If you do come back before then, you will be extremely unpopular in Washington, with the exception of Cissy Patterson, who wants to kill you off as soon as possible—just as she does me." More a wealthy society hostess than a newspaperwoman, Patterson was a cousin of "Bertie" McCormick, whose *Chicago Tribune* prejudices she reflected in the *Washington Times-Herald*, which she owned—and bossed over.* Her anti-Roosevelt, British-bashing editorials were usually written by Frank Waldrop, who once was seated at a posh dinner party across from Commander Roald Dahl of the RAF, then an embassy attaché and largely unknown as an up-and-coming author. After listening to Waldrop's vituperations, Dahl said, "Do you

* Also taking his cues from McCormick, Cissy's brother, Joseph Patterson, owner of the mass-circulation *New York Daily News*, was equally hostile to the administration.

realize that if you were to go to England today there are men in your U.S. Eighth Air Force who would tear you limb from limb for the things you write?"

"Well," said Waldrop, "I guess I won't go to England."

"It is a good thing to connect up the plumbing and put your sewerage in operating condition," FDR cautioned Hopkins. "You have got to lead not the life of an invalid but the life of common sense. I, too, over one hundred years older than you are"—Hopkins would be fifty-four in August—"have come to the same realization." What FDR was actually reporting was the Bruenn regime: "one and a half cocktails per evening and nothing else. . . . And I have cut down my cigarettes from twenty or thirty a day to five or six a day. Luckily they still taste rotten but it can be done." Without that information, the *Philadelphia Evening Bulletin*'s editorial cartoonist depicted a chain-smoking FDR (his ashtray contains the remains of his first- and second-term cigarettes) lighting a fourth-term cigarette from his third-term butt.

Hopkins replied with rumors from the hospital corridors that the President's unannounced post-convention Pacific trip had been canceled. "The underground is working overtime here," Hopkins reported, "in regard to your health." The rumors as well as the realities in early summer had focused Roosevelt's mind on the upcoming voyage and its possible consequences. "Grace," he remarked, abruptly, to his secretary, "if anything should happen to me while I am at sea, I want to be buried at sea. You know, it has always seemed like home to me." The mordant reflection was something new, as in a memorandum to Missy Le Hand dated December 26, 1937, he had specified in detail a Hyde Park rose garden burial under "a plain white monument—no carving or decoration."

"I'm sorry, sir," Miss Tully said, "but I think that is one wish that will not be carried out and I hope it won't. I personally do not like it or even the thought of it, and I believe the people of this country would feel as I do."

When Hopkins, still feeble, returned to the White House, he was only able to work two or three hours a day and remained in Washington, with diminishing responsibilities, as chief conduit to Prime Minister Churchill and his staff. "Things seem to be going really well in the war," Hopkins wrote to 10 Downing Street. Yet he knew little about Pacific theater planning, which Roosevelt intended to adjudicate. Service rivalries between Army and Navy, in part responsible for the failed preparedness at Pearl Harbor, had never really abated. Each branch still competed for priority in winning the war.

The President was piped aboard the 14,000-ton cruiser *Baltimore* at sundown on July 20, his wheelchair pushed up a specially built wooden ramp, with his Scottie, Fala, following on a leash. Already aboard were cases of bottled Saratoga Springs water and boxes of matches with long wooden stems—required supplies for a presidential trip. FDR would occupy the cabin of Captain W. C. Calhoun, the commanding officer, and Admiral Leahy was quartered in the flag officer's cabin. As Roosevelt had a seaman's superstition about embarking on a Friday, at thirteen minutes after midnight, Pacific time, the calendar having turned to Saturday, July 21, the *Baltimore* raised anchor and rendezvoused off Point Loma with six destroyers in escort, all taking zigzag courses to evade any lurking enemy subs.

The slow throb of the *Baltimore*'s engines was relaxing to the President, who slept well and in daylight enjoyed the sun, while watching land-based aircraft keeping vigil within their range from California. At his mess he delighted in telling stories beginning with "When I was in the Navy," referring to the Woodrow Wilson years when he was a very energetic assistant secretary of the Navy. As West Coast overflights were replaced by Navy patrol planes from Hawaii, Roosevelt's entourage, from Admiral Leahy to Lieutenant Robert H. Myers, Map Room Watch Officer, down to the eight Filipino stewards and sixteen-man Secret Service detail, knew they were closing in on Oahu. The cruiser maintained radio silence but received news and messages. With no writing assignments as yet, and the quarter-deck trimmed down for action, Sam Rosenman hauled up a straight-backed cabin chair for Roosevelt's reading. Lieutenant William Rigdon, FDR's traveling secretary, hovered in range of the President.

On the morning of July 26, the island of Molokai became visible, then Barbers Point at the entrance to Pearl Harbor. The five remaining destroyers (one had left after courier duty) moved away, and the *Baltimore* slowed to a stop at 2:25 p.m. and took on a harbor pilot. An admiral's barge with Chester Nimitz aboard pulled alongside, and the Pacific Fleet chief came aboard to the flag deck. "What a sight," Bruenn wrote in his diary in awe. His naval experience had been limited to hospitals. "Hundreds of ships from air[craft] carriers, battleships, cruisers to tugs—all with their crews in [dress] white—'manning the rail.' Bands playing. Men at attention. Our vessel moved slowly up the channel, bugle playing at intervals. The most impressive sight I have *ever* witnessed." At the dock was a greeting party of admirals and generals. Following them was burly Mike Reilly, chief of the White House detail of the Secret Service, with sailors carrying pouches of presidential mail. Despite the supposed secrecy of the departure and the zigzag course from San Diego, Reilly told Roosevelt, the voyage and arrival were big news in Hawaii, and Honolulu's harbor was decorated with pennants for the occasion. As the cruiser was warped to a berth behind the aircraft carrier *Enterprise*, Roosevelt was assisted to the starboard rail and doffed his fedora while horns blared and spectators cheered. Looking carefully over the array of brass, the President asked Nimitz, "Where is MacArthur?"

Three

Fighting the Fourth Term

Early in 1944 Douglas MacArthur, commanding forces in the Southwest Pacific from Australia, saw himself as the distant yet popular rescuer of the Republican Party from three terms of Rooseveltian attrition. The most unappreciated darling of the party's right wing remained dour Robert A. Taft, who had lost the nomination to upstart maverick Wendell L. Willkie in 1940. Senator Taft's delegate momentum now was imperceptible. General MacArthur's proved little better.

The general had not been home since 1937. He had twice offered (no one took him seriously) to come to the White House to press his Philippines-to-Tokyo strategy, yet backed off each time, perhaps concerned that he might be replaced. MacArthur was even reluctant to fly to Hawaii in mid-1944, suspicious that a conference with the President would only exploit a fourth term for Roosevelt. Yet the dream of returning in triumph to the Philippines (which MacArthur had lost) hung on the President's decisions about how American power would be positioned to close in on Japan. Island-hopping beyond the Marianas was Admiral Chester A. Nimitz's scheme, and the Army Air Forces sought coral platforms for launching heavy bombers toward Japan. If a case was to be made for a Philippines route to Tokyo, MacArthur had to make it in person.

By the time the Honolulu conference was set, MacArthur's presidential bid, which never had a chance from Australia, had vanished. Always on the edge of outright insubordination, he had kept his Southwest Pacific fiefdom because Roosevelt needed the wartime support in Congress of the general's vocal, if largely insincere, backers. MacArthur had a devoted fan or two in the House of Representatives and cultivated a former isolationist from Michigan, Senator Arthur Vandenberg—very timidly a candidate himself. The senator, who had received only one cautious letter from MacArthur, which he hailed as "supremely historic," had begun organizing an informal candidacy in 1943, enlisting retired General Robert Wood of Sears, Roebuck as moneybags and former president Herbert Hoover as facade. The covert campaign was so little a secret that in an issue of *TIME*, publisher Henry Luce, who once shared his wife Clare's former enthusiasm for MacArthur, included a sly fantasy, with a cartoon of Vandenberg as impresario. The senator was shown asleep in his office chair, dreaming of a procession in a great hall at convention time, led by prewar isolationist Hamilton Fish (ironically, the congressman formerly representing FDR's home district), "magnificent in khaki and gold" and on a white horse, celebrating the drafting of MacArthur on a "win-the-war" platform. Over the cheers of the convention crowd, Vandenberg hears the jaunty tune, "There's Something About a Soldier." The case for the general, *TIME* suggested, would be simple. No politician could defeat Roosevelt, "but the people will be voting for a Commander-in-Chief rather than for a President, and there are no credentials equal to MacArthur's upon that score."

MacArthur's declared willingness to be drafted as candidate had little impact at the Republican national convention in stifling Chicago Stadium (indoor temperatures above 100°F late in June), preceding the expected anointment of Roosevelt. The general remained useful, however, for barbs by partisans that the President was short-changing MacArthur in weaponry and manpower. Down from an anticipated eleven supporters on the first ballot, he received two votes. "I am a man, not a jellyfish," shouted Grant Ritter, a dairy farmer from Beloit, Wisconsin. "I vote for MacArthur."

Willkie also seemed a spent force. A former Democrat, he was too liberal and internationalist for a repeat nomination. Also, he drank too much, exacerbating his hidden health problems, and was considered so friendly to the President as to be little short of treasonable to his party. At a rally Willkie described his opponents, predictably praised at the Republican convention by Herbert Hoover, as "a bunch of political liabilities." The *Chicago Tribune* editorialized, "From today on, Mr. Willkie can be dismissed as a minor nuisance." Yet following the Democratic convention soon after, in a letter dated August 1, columnist Drew Pearson wrote to Willkie, "You would have been surprised at the number of friends you had there and the number of people who spontaneously expressed the hope and the wish that you might be on the ticket, even though . . . you might not have even considered such a proposition."

Quietly, as late as July 13—as Roosevelt was leaving for Chicago, San Diego and Hawaii—the President had been sounding Willkie out, through Sam Rosenman, to join a post-election realignment of parties, liberal and conservative. As the American body politic had a long history of being disengaged from reality, realignment was a hope without promise. Conservative Southern Democrats dominated Congress. Willkie was not on their agenda.

Ohio's Robert Taft, who since Pearl Harbor had only faintly supported the war, found his home state less warm on his behalf than in 1940. His peak in 1944 came as chairman of the convention resolutions committee, which, other than arguing for more efficient conduct of the war, and accepting some vague form of postwar international cooperation, largely repeated the party's repudiated positions in 1936 and 1940. Droning through a reading of the Republican platform, which the *Philadelphia Inquirer* praised as "forceful" and "progressive," took Taft fifty minutes. Governor John W. Bricker of Ohio, a Hoover clone with a Harding profile, was his state's nominee. Once Governor Earl Warren of California backed out in claimed "good conscience" as the expected second choice, Bricker parlayed his delegate strength into the vice-presidential nomination.

Taft was riled, as he wrote to an AT&T executive on July 13, by columnist Walter Lippmann's "ignorance, both of the platform and the problem before the country." Lippmann had been leaning in Thomas E. Dewey's direction, but "The truth is," Taft alleged, "that he is a confirmed Fourth Termer." The dapper, mustached governor of New York, forty-two, a racket-busting former district attorney with a mechanical smile, would be the easy winner on the first ballot. Ostensibly Dewey was not a candidate, as he had promised New Yorkers in 1942 that if elected he would serve a full four-year term, but a month before the convention his busy managers, led by savvy lawyer Herbert Brownell, had already locked up over 300 votes more than the 530 needed for the nomination. Bricker, a candidate of the Taft wing of the party, had never been a serious pre-convention threat. Brownell considered him little more than "an old-fashioned political orator—I could imagine him delivering the Fourth of July speech in the square of some Ohio town on the topic of 'God, Flag, and Country.'"

Having committed himself on few issues, Dewey had offended no factions in the party. Even in late May, when asked about his candidacy, he claimed, although he had already won the Wisconsin primary, "It looks like I have no control over that at all." Yet he had assigned wealthy "Listerine King" Gerald Lambert, recognized for his shrewdness in advertising, to arrange for polls of cross-sections of Republicans to identify which of a variety of policy opinions most nearly reflected party views. The majority outcomes went into his speeches. At the National Governors Conference in Hershey, Pennsylvania, the all-but-nominee urged fellow state executives to take the lead in opposing "that concentration of national power which would wipe out our republican system and substitute a disguised totalitarianism." Dewey had arrived with two speeches, one to be used to respond to the news of an expected cross-Channel invasion. In mid-May that hadn't yet materialized. He delivered the other one.

Also a speaker in Hershey, Governor Bricker, then a rival for the nomination from the paleolithic wing of the party, attacked spendthrift Democrats who were financing the war by bonds and other forms of borrowing. Despite admittedly elastic price and wage controls, the cost of living had kept rising and dollars bought less than ever. An ordinary woman's dress cost $2.98 and a high-fashion one $16.95. Men's suits approached $26 and topcoats $28. A cheap hotel on Broadway above Times Square was already $2.50 a night. Basic industrial wages were reaching a dollar an hour, and although corporations and farmers were doubling and tripling pre-war income, Congress was hostile to paying for the war through increased taxes.

Bricker urged an improbable balanced budget and warned against opening elective doors to the "absolutism and every form of demagogy" from Washington that would follow the creeping paralysis of state and local government. The Republican Party, he had claimed earlier in the year, "is the liberal party in America. The New Deal is reactionary. It reaches back for centuries to Old World devices for extending power and depriving people of their rights." Now Bricker warned, the "States' Rights" core of Republicanism (which Lincoln would not have recognized) was at a "crossroads." D-Day in Europe had not yet occurred, as it would by Democratic convention time, and the Japanese imperium in the Pacific was barely breached, but Republican leaders were opening their campaign as if the war were over and the nation could return to the inward-thinking 1920s.

With their governor a sure thing, supporters at the New York County Republican convention introduced a rather strained campaign song, "Yankee Dewey Dandy," promoting his acknowledged record as prosecutor:

> Oh, Tom E. Dewey came to town
> A-ridin' on a pony.
> He busted gangs and jailed the mobs
> And cleared out every phoney.
> Tom E. Dewey keep it up,
> You're swingin' sharp and handy.
> The White House is your home next year,
> Our Yankee Dewey Dandy.

The ditty was an improvement upon the absurd brass band number to be played in Chicago, "What Do We Do on a Dew, Dew, Dewey Day?"

Boarding a train for Chicago, Dewey's campaign managers, J. Russell Sprague, Herbert Brownell and Edwin F. Jaeckle, told the unsurprised press that their man would not spurn what they still called a draft. "My personal opinion," said Brownell of the charade, "is that the Governor will accept, if nominated. Any good American would." Sprague added that in his opinion Governor Dewey would come to Chicago to accept the nomination and would be elected in November. The governor already had his United Airlines ticket in his pocket.

As candidate, Dewey's self-righteous outrage at the state of the nation would be delivered in an energetic and resonant baritone belying his lack of height. Never at a loss for a put-down, Alice Roosevelt Longworth, socialite eldest daughter of Republican icon Teddy Roosevelt, described Dewey devastatingly as "the little man on the wedding cake." (A nonpartisan backbiter, in 1940 she had carped about her distant cousin, FDR, "I'd rather vote for Hitler than vote for Franklin for a third term.") Oswald Garrison Villard, a young liberal in Theodore Roosevelt's day who had become an America First conservative, deplored the unkind crack that Dewey was "that little man who has to sit on three telephone books in the Governor's chair in Albany in order to be photographed." The liberal *New Republic* cartooned the "Big Show" of the nominating convention with Taft riding a GOP toy elephant backwards and a childlike Dewey tugging on a balloon and chewing on a rag doll, while the maverick Willkie appears as the head on a Democratic donkey. The ultra-liberal New York daily *PM* would publish a bowler-hatted caricature of the Republican "Old Guard" coaching a diminutive Dewey atop the GOP elephant's trunk straining to reach the top of the mighty "Roosevelt Yardstick." "Stre-e-etch!" shouts the party manager.

A campaign ploy of Republican politicians leading up to the rival convention and beyond was a guilt-by-association linkage of left-leaning Democrats to the Communist Party. Robert R. McCormick of the *Chicago Tribune,* isolationist exemplar of the paranoid dimension in American politics, had long been both anti-British and anti-Communist and had charged in February 1944 that "some 410,000 Communists in New York State . . . hold the balance of power between the Republican and Democratic parties. Unless they vote with the Democrats, no Democrats can be elected and unless the Democrats accept their dictation they will not vote for the Democratic candidates." To defuse allegations that it was a disloyal political entity, at the Communist national convention at the Riverside Plaza Hotel on 73rd Street in New York City late in May the splinter Stalinist Party dissolved itself. Delegates allegedly from forty-four states participated in the four-day meeting, with Earl Browder, the general secretary, delivering the keynote address. Realistically, he conceded that the party had to shelve its goal to make the United States a socialist nation "because there does not exist now in our country an actual or potential majority support for such a program." Yet, reconstituted immediately as an organization not out to elect its own candidates but with a mission to promote "a democratic and progressive America," the "Communist Political Association" then played into the hands of Republicans by formally backing Roosevelt for a fourth term.

At the same time, in the Hotel Roosevelt at 45th and Madison, a newborn party left of center, and limited to the state of New York, materialized. The 2,500 delegates of the Liberal Party ratified a platform calling for an international organization to maintain postwar peace, while urging retention and expansion of the social gains of the past decade, and support of the President, "the shining symbol of American liberalism," for a new term. Obviously pointing at the certain candidacy of the diminutive Governor Dewey, Samuel Share, vice president of the International Ladies Garment Workers Union, told delegates that "small men cannot perform great tasks, no matter how big their ambition or how wealthy their backers." Although the party chairman elected was a Columbia University professor, John L. Childs, the leadership came primarily from labor unions. Republicans gained an additional "radical" target.

Emphasizing comparative youth and obvious vigor in his acceptance speech in Chicago, Governor Dewey excoriated "the men in the White House who have grown old, tired, stubborn and quarrelsome." He played up the radical fringe groups and parties which had attached themselves to Roosevelt's candidacy. Bringing his mass-circulation news magazines and his anti-Communism with him, Henry Luce, who had supported Willkie in 1940, reluctantly joined his spouse in the Dewey orbit. Anti-Roosevelt primarily because the President failed to share his devotion (as the child of China missionaries) to the futile regime of Chiang Kai-Shek, Luce was actually at the Republican convention not to cheer on the governor but to support by his presence his well-coiffed wife. Now a svelte forty-one, Clare Boothe Luce, a featured speaker and former playwright (*The Women*) who had parlayed her connections after a single term in Congress from Connecticut into a seat on the powerful Military Affairs Committee, followed Herbert Hoover on the program. While the former president maundered on the rostrum, Luce read, despite the obvious gaze of reporters, what was effectively the party organ, the *Chicago Tribune*. When Mrs. Luce was introduced, he put the newspaper down and listened as if he had never before heard her maudlin histrionics about how "GI Joe and GI Jim" were greater risks in battle because of the inefficiencies of the worn-out Roosevelt administration. In fact, the Christlike "Jim" she had righteously invented was already dead:

> Who is GI Jim? Ask, rather, who *was* GI Jim. He was Joe's pal, his buddy, his brother. Jim was the fellow who lived next door to you. . . . Jim did not complain too much about his government. . . . Jim figured that anybody can make mistakes. . . . If Jim could stand here and talk to you he might say, "Listen, folks, the past wasn't perfect. But skip it. Get on with the business of making this old world better." . . . And this we will do, for Jim's sake . . . the risen soldier.

Governor Thomas E. Dewey, in what became his trademark pose, accepting the Republican presidential nomination in Chicago on June 28, 1944. *Dewey collection, University of Rochester Library*

Well-wishers in Governor Dewey's hometown of Owosso, Michigan, raising placards and cheering his nomination. *Associated Press*

Disgusted, a writer for *The New Yorker* commented that Mrs. Luce's speech "made it difficult to keep anything on your stomach for twenty-four hours." Covering the convention, *New York Times* reporter Anne O'Hare McCormick noted how the party speeches, but for exceptions like the irrepressible Clare Luce, largely shelved attacks on the conduct of the war and emphasized undoing the Rooseveltian 1930s. Even Mrs. Luce, according to McCormick, could not resist charging that the fading New Deal was fumbling the future away:

> The party leaders and the delegates tried to convince one another that the campaign hinges on domestic issues. They kept insisting that the war would occupy only a part of the next term. The primary job of the administration taking over next January, they argued, would be to manage and to speed up the adjustment to peace. The dominant theme was that this process could be better

carried out under the fresh, eager, resourceful and harmonious direction of the Republicans than by the old, tired, bureaucratic and divided minds of the Democrats. The Republican Party grew younger and younger with every [convention] speech.

From Washington, political pundit Isaiah Berlin, a watchdog for the British embassy, described Luce's "sentimental gush" as "difficult to endure" even by her audience and viewed the GOP platform as a concoction of "ancient platitudes, the lowest common denominator of anti-New Dealism." In his weekly summary to London he concluded that as the Republicans did not expect to win, they lacked any incentive to appeal to the constituency which the New Deal had transformed. Opposing the liberal (for his time) William Ewart Gladstone, whose contemporary equivalent, Berlin noted, was FDR, the conservatives lacked a Benjamin Disraeli.

The Republican dilemma was that while counting upon a weary electorate losing confidence in a weary administration, and a Democratic Party divided between New Deal urban liberals and Southern throwbacks who were a continuation of the Confederacy by other means, events were rapidly bypassing the cavils of the opposition. The pre-polio Roosevelt, assistant secretary of the Navy under Woodrow Wilson, had dodged Republican shellfire for three terms, while his opposition candidate had no war record in any war. (Bricker was a lieutenant and assistant chaplain in 1918.) Henry Wallace would no longer be on the ticket to attack, and Harry Truman—an artillery captain in France in 1918—would prove difficult to target as the pick of big city bosses or as a sleazy Southerner. His record in the Senate was New Dealing yet nonpartisan. Despite his early support by the Tom Pendergast political machine in Kansas City, he owed nothing to anyone; and when he had run for re-election in 1940, he had told white audiences, "I believe in the brotherhood of man, not merely in the brotherhood of white men, but the brotherhood of all men before the law." The political process that would nominate him was cynical, but not the nominee.

Although far from won, the two-ocean war dominated newspaper
headlines. Only two weeks before the Republican convention convened in Chicago, American troops in Italy had seized Rome and
in France had landed under heavy fire. Nazi Germany, however
much fight remained in the colossus, seemed doomed. In two
nationally broadcast radio addresses one day after another, the
allegedly tired Roosevelt had celebrated the capture of Rome, then
offered a brief, moving prayer, front-paged everywhere, for the
success of the D-Day invasion. A resident of Newtonville, Massachusetts, wrote to the President that his radio message about Rome
"gave heart to Italians everywhere," while another, from Braintree,
Massachusetts, wrote, with dubious capitalization, grammar and
spelling, "What nerve you had to make a Political speech to get Ital-
ien votes, when at the same time you were sending our boys across
the English channel to be murdered. . . . Got help you on Nov 7th [I]
hope you can take the humiliation without committing suicide." A
week later, when FDR urged Americans to buy war bonds, a lady
from Atlanta, Georgia, wife of a retired sergeant, wrote to him that
she put her money for clothes into war bonds and "bought some
material to make a dress, the material was four printed feed sacks . . .
the cost was 20 cents each." She vowed to wear the colorful "feed
sack dresses . . . to speed Victory. So our boys can come home and
the world be at peace once again." The White House preserved all
such mail, pro and con. As an election albatross the war had not
quite vanished. An expensive end seemed in sight in Europe, but
Japan still clung to the Pacific rim and beyond and was fighting
regardless of casualties to keep the Home Islands distant from attack. Whether the war remained an election factor at all seemed to
depend upon when the voting public saw its end as imminent.

Although the Pentagon on May 4 had ordered that "a policy of
strict impartiality in the dissemination of political information" be

enforced, news was news, and citizens in uniform would not easily forget their effective disenfranchisement. Twelve million Americans were in uniform. Those twenty-one or older would be eligible to vote only if technically acceptable under widely differing state laws. Politicians expected that relatively few federal ballots, authorized by Congress but rigged with technicalities, would be mailed overseas and returned in time.

Republicans again faced the disadvantage of opposing an incumbent with overwhelming name recognition. The President had the opportunities of a national stage—the White House—and a public forum, the press conference. A Republican nominee would not be heard on the radio automatically whenever he wanted an audience (that restriction would be modified somewhat) while Roosevelt could exploit his "fireside chats." Portraying the unseen, radio encouraged the imagination. The immensely popular CBS comedy show "Amos and Andy," supposedly set in a taxi office in the South, portrayed two ostensibly black men played by whites. Other programs used sound effects that seemed real to listeners, from train whistles and car crashes to the crackle of lightning and the rumble of thunder. The President's microphone was usually not by a fireside, nor were his listeners' radios.

Similarly, Roosevelt could tell homely stories to White House reporters—and thus to newspaper readers—that sounded plausible enough but were no more real than the weekly tumbling of derelict household effects in Fibber McGee's imaginary radio closet. The ordinary Americans who allegedly came to see the President in the White House about their problems, always without an appointment, were no more authentic than the denizens of "Allen's Alley" on Fred Allen's Sunday show, or the hooting of Jack Benny's imaginary and unreliable vintage Maxwell automobile. One citizen who dropped by, the President told the press corps early in June, two weeks before the Republican convention, had a mighty good job out on the Pacific coast. I don't know what he was—a welder or something like that. I said, "What are you doing back home?"

"Oh," he said, "the war's over. I am going to try and get a permanent job before everybody quits working on munitions." He just walked out, quit his job—and he was a good man; he was a munitions worker. . . . Now that's the thing we have got to avoid in this country. The war isn't over by any means. This operation isn't over. You don't just land on a beach and walk through—if you land successfully without breaking your leg—walk through to Berlin. And the quicker this country understands it the better.

Earlier, on May 30, the President had addressed widespread concerns about the increasing cost of living, noting that some purchases—like fruit and vegetables out of season—were not necessities. This time the squire of Hyde Park identified a supposed "friend of mine,"

who was a foreman in one of the substantial trades, [who] came in last January, and said to me, "My old lady is ready to hit me over the head with the dishpan."

I said, "What's the trouble?"

"The cost of living."

"Well," I said, "what, for instance?"

"Well, last night I went home, and the old lady said, 'What's this? I went out to buy some asparagus, and do you see what I've got? I got five sticks. There it is. A dollar and a quarter! It's an outrage.'"

Well, I looked at him, and I said, "Since when have you been buying asparagus in January—fresh asparagus?"

"Oh," he said, "I never thought of that."

"Well," I said, "tell that to the old lady, with my compliments."

A reporter jumped in, asking, to much laughter, "Mr. President, is that the same foreman you mentioned in a press conference some time ago who bought the strawberries in the winter?"

"It happened to be a different one," said the President, "but it's all right." Issues to him were not matters of legislation or politics or policy. If they impacted people, they were all three.

On June 22, 1944, only a few days before the Republican convention, another powerful reason for servicemen and their families to vote for a continuation of the Roosevelt mandate came when the President signed the Servicemens' Readjustment Act of 1944, already labeled popularly the "GI Bill of Rights." Much renewed and updated, it is still that. "A sound post-war economy," he declared, "is a major present responsibility." An editorial page cartoon in the *Toledo Blade* depicted far away cheers for "war heroes" while "over there" across the water a GI shouldering a rifle and full pack shouts

FDR signing the GI Bill at the White House with members of Congress looking on, June 22, 1944. *FDR Library*

back, "Hey Buddy! Ask 'em to save all that applause for all of us [until] *after the war!*" In 1919, after the earlier world war, veterans received sixty dollars and a train ticket home from their points of discharge, and could keep their uniforms.

In 1924 the Adjusted Compensation Act offered veterans a small additional sum, but payable only in 1945—a mean-spirited piece of legislation which disgruntled ex-soldiers called a "tombstone bonus." In the depths of the Depression, in 1932, a "Bonus Army" marched on Washington to petition President Hoover for early payment. His maladroit response, which helped elect Roosevelt, was to have his zealous Army chief, General MacArthur, rout them. Yet Roosevelt's Economy Act the next year, recognizing the deep fiscal hole he had inherited, further cut veterans' benefits as well as service salaries, and, speaking at the American Legion convention in October 1933, Roosevelt declared, "No person, because he wore a uniform, must thereafter be placed in a special class of beneficiaries over and above all other citizens." Another and greater war, and its likely consequences, had produced his complete about-face.

Grumblers in Congress on both sides when the controversial GI Bill was introduced in January 1944 carped that the law would diminish incentives to work, and that reassimilating into private life was a personal matter into which the federal government need not intrude. The legislation almost died when, for months, the two chambers could not agree on common language, and deadlocked on its hardly munificent unemployment provision—twenty dollars for a maximum of fifty-two weeks. (It was quickly derided as the "52–20 Club.") In the House of Representatives, an absent member from Georgia, John Gibson, had to be rushed in on June 13 to cast the tie-breaking vote.

The bill combined aspects of several messages that Roosevelt had sent to Congress since July 28, 1943, authorizing veterans' unemployment and job-training benefits, loans for buying homes or establishing businesses, support for living expenses and tuition for college and other post-secondary education, job counseling, hospital care, and other benefits FDR considered earned by wartime military sacrifice. Signing it ceremonially in the Oval Office, the President declared, "It gives emphatic notice to the men and women in our armed forces that the American people do not intend to let them down." Yet *emphatic* and *American people* overstated broadly the will of the people's representatives. Passage was a close call in a divided and clamorous House and Senate, yet in terms of impact upon social mobility for generations of Americans, the GI Bill would be the most far-reaching legislation ever enacted by Congress. Although its first draft had been written by Harry W. Colmery, a former national commander of the American Legion and a former Republican national chairman, it became the climactic measure of the waning New Deal.

The discordant and quarrelsome mid-war Congress of 1943–1944, elected in November 1942 after a year of defeats and withdrawals—the Battle of Midway excepted—was largely the result of a week's delay in *Torch*—the invasion of Vichy-French North Africa. The post–Pearl Harbor enthusiasm of "Praise the Lord and Pass the Ammunition" had evaporated, and there would never be popular successors to the frothy rhetoric of "We'll Rally Round the Flag, Boys" or "Over There" of earlier wars. Wartime malaise seemed pervasive. Roosevelt had hoped for a stirring military success before the congressional elections. When Dwight Eisenhower, commanding his first combined operation, informed the President that he could not ready the landings on schedule, FDR had conceded that success outweighed haste. During the hiatus, with troops already at sea, electoral failure for the Administration ensued at ballot boxes across America. Absent helpful headlines, both the House and the Senate came under the control of dissident Southern Democrats and resurgent Republicans, some of them prewar isolationists.

Recognizing that many of the Rooseveltian measures that Republicans had opposed for twelve years were too essential to daily

life and too desirable to rescind, and would be here to stay, Dewey
in 1944 attacked, instead, "unnecessary" government "bigness"
and "bureaucracy." Without mentioning the loaded term New Deal,
he pledged to keep substantially all of it. "Much of this growth and
complexity," he conceded in addressing a youth group sponsored
by the American Legion (Womens') Auxiliary, "is utterly in-
escapable. It is a natural outgrowth of our American social and
industrial life. It is a natural outcome, also, of the fact that today we
expect many things of government, State, Local and Federal,
which our grandfathers did not expect . . . and which, I imagine,
some of them probably thought, government ought not to meddle
in at all. Now, we cannot go backward. . . . We would not want to if
we could." To many conservatives that seemed apostasy, although
Germany under Otto von Bismarck had established Old Age and
Disability Insurance in 1889, and David Lloyd George pushed
through parallel legislation in Britain in 1910. A Helen Hokinson
cartoon in *The New Yorker* showed a comfortable lady complaining
to her husband over her newspaper, "I think it's a shame the way
they're pushing poor Mr. Dewey against his wishes." What was
pushing Dewey was reality.

While GI Bill legislation proved beyond party, broadly covered even
in the service journal *Stars and Stripes*, Republicans in Congress
sought to keep troops from alleged partisan contamination by the
press. (Always over the edge, Robert McCormick of the *Chicago
Tribune* denounced *Stars and Stripes* as "an out and out Communist
New Deal paper.") Senator Taft sponsored a fussy amendment to
the Soldiers' Vote Act that would keep publications with "political
content" from being available to servicemen. As Bernard DeVoto
put it in an "Easy Chair" column in the September 1944 *Harper's
Magazine*, "With the help of the Southern Republicans who vote
Democratic, the bill was passed and became Public Law 277, 78th
Congress." Longevity in Congress had made many of the ostensible
Democrats legislative power brokers, and they "had grown con-

cerned about the gullibility, as they saw it, of our fighting men. Their most strenuous efforts had not sufficed to prevent Mr. Roosevelt from being a candidate again, or even to set up an opposition candidate who could inspire confidence in Mr. Taft."

Some of the impetus for safeguarding the military from "political propaganda masquerading as legitimate military stuff" may have come from MacArthur's small cabal. His Lilliputian presidential boom had struggled into 1944. Henry Luce as publisher of *Life* had sent a correspondent to Australia to assess MacArthur's chances. He returned without a story. A Gallup Poll credited MacArthur with only 15 percent of the likely Republican primary vote. In the January 1944 issue of the liberal *American Mercury*, John McCarten, once an editor for Luce, harshly evaluated MacArthur's military record since the war began and described his presidential hopes as literally misguided. "It may not be his fault," McCarten wrote, "but it is surely his misfortune that the worst elements on the political Right, including its most blatant lunatic fringe, are whooping it up for MacArthur."

Although dispatches critical of the general from his Southwest Pacific domain had been quashed before by censors, probably because MacArthur's name turned up in the titles, McCarten's article was automatically listed by the Army War College's library service in its monthly bulletin to service libraries as relevant reading. On the Senate floor on March 9, 1944, Arthur Vandenberg attacked the Army for recommending "smear" literature to troops. MacArthur cabled the War Department that the article was "scandalous in tone and libelous in essence." Although Secretary of War Stimson and Chief of Staff Marshall were guiltless, they apologized for an administrative oversight many rungs below their purview, and ordered the endorsement expunged. The month before, the Army had prevented *Harper's Magazine* from publishing an article critical of MacArthur by the London *Daily Express* correspondent in Brisbane, Walter Lucas, under the dubious claim of security. "The article as written," a local spokesman explained, "undermines the confidence of this country, Australia, and particularly the troops in this theater, in their commander and his strategic and tactical plans." *Harper's* editors charged that MacArthur was "protected by censorship from adverse criticism." Later they would protest, "No candidate for the Presidency, tacit or otherwise, should be hidden behind a veil of censorship."

Uncensored, twelve adulatory books on MacArthur, some resembling campaign biographies, had been published and available since 1942. MacArthur would peak in the polls in mid-April 1944 at 20 percent, the same month in which early primaries gave him three delegates in Wisconsin (which he claimed as his home state) and a cosmetic victory in Illinois against negligible opposition. Unfortunately, an obscure Nebraska congressman, Arthur L. Miller, trying to keep the modest boom going, chose to release two letters from the general in response to a letter from Miller that promoted the general as "Commander-in-Chief and President of a free America." MacArthur had responded, coyly, that Miller's denunciation of the New Deal was "sobering" and his suggestion that the general let his name be placed in nomination was "flattering"— and deserved "the thoughtful consideration of every true patriot." The *Washington Times-Herald*—often an echo of the *Chicago Tribune*, and run by McCormick's rancorous cousin, Eleanor "Cissy" Patterson—had already editorialized that if MacArthur were not the Republican candidate, the successful nominee, to win in November, would have to "promise that MacArthur would be appointed Secretary of War."

Patterson ranted in an editorial that, unlike the general, FDR had "no first-hand knowledge of war. . . . He stayed far away from the battlefield[s] of the first World War. Although at the time a young man, and in perfect physical condition, he did his bit as Assistant Secretary of the Navy here in Washington." Cissy was often remote from reality. Roosevelt did sail for England in early July 1918 on the destroyer *Dyer*, traveled to the Western Front, visited blasted Verdun, and British and American units, coming under artillery fire and enduring air raids. After inspecting a Marine artillery battery he had been instrumental in sending to France, he drafted a cable to Secretary of the Navy Josephus Daniels asking to resign to become a Marine lieutenant colonel with the battery and do his "proper duty." The destroyer on which he recrossed the Channel en route back was bombed twice by the Germans.

Returning via Scotland, where he visited Navy anti-submarine defenses on the Firth of Forth, he collapsed aboard the *Leviathan* with double pneumonia and at New York had to be removed on a stretcher. It took a month before he was back at work. Woodrow Wilson had turned down his request for uniformed service.

MacArthur's indiscretions to Representative Miller were fed to the press, where service personnel, wherever they were, could not help but see them by mail from home or in newspapers. Despite Vandenberg and Taft, military chiefs recognized that election year or no, Congress appropriated its funds, and the political neutrality of the armed services had to appear above reproach. The Army announced a policy of "strict impartiality" short of banning all "information and entertainment from the armed forces." Federal funds or sponsorship could not be used to influence voting in federal elections—but what did *sponsorship* mean? Did federal delivery of mail apply? The liberal weekly *The Nation* soon reported that the Army had relented and issued a revised list of 189 magazines "which may be distributed without scrutiny for political content. The majority of these are comics, westerns, and story magazines, but in the list are included all the mass-circulation magazines, most of which discuss and analyze news." Absent were political weeklies like *The New Republic* and *The Nation*. On the safe list were 37 comics, 26 romance and adventure magazines, 13 detective magazines and 13 movie magazines.

Postmaster General Frank Walker banned others from military mail, like *Esquire*, for its girlie cartoons, as unfit on grounds of obscenity. Although attacked by some chaplains, the racy strip

Male Call, by Milt Caniff of *Terry and the Pirates,* intended for
and received with pleasure by armed services publications, survived, but a CIO pamphlet presenting the case for a steel workers'
pay increase was returned by Army censors as inappropriate for
soldiers. The U.S. Armed Forces Institute, which produced aca-
demic correspondence courses, fell under the ban for economics,
political, and social science texts, which GIs could read now only
from British Army equivalents. Catherine Drinker Bowen's biography of Oliver Wendell Holmes, *Yankee from Olympus,* could not
be sold at post exchanges because her subject was a Supreme
Court justice, and thus political. The year's bawdiest novel, *Forever Amber,* Kathleen Winsor's tale of seventeenth-century sex and
social climbing, although banned by fourteen states and condemned for indecency by the Catholic Church, was more easily
available, as it sold 100,000 copies the first week of publication.
Army post theaters could not show Darryl Zanuck's *Wilson* as it
was too political—but GIs could see it off-base. Fibber McGee's
comedy *Heavenly Days* was banned because he goes to Washington celebrated as the Gallup Poll's "Mr. Average Man" and is
expelled from the Senate for trying to make a speech. The period
musical *Meet Me in St. Louis* and the sentimental *Going My Way*
were acceptable.

To his brother Stanley Hart White, *The New Yorker* writer E. B.
White wrote that his book *One Man's Meat* was denied an Armed
Services Edition because it contained "political implications." That
gave him, he confessed, "more pleasure than anything that has
happened in a long time, although it costs me 90,000 copies at
approximately nothing per copy. At least the . . . boys can pick up
their presidential preference from the comic strips and other reliable sources."

Soldiers who would manage to secure a ballot would not be devoid of reading or viewing matter, but the politically correct charade
did not reach its acme of absurdity until the late summer of the
campaign, when the *Official Guide to the Army Air Forces* (525,000

copies printed) was banned from sale at post exchanges because it contained a frontispiece portrait of President Roosevelt—a candidate—as "Commander-in-Chief," which, indeed, he was.

Curiously, complaints about the suppression of political comment also emerged from the Right. "One is reluctant to believe," David Lawrence, editor of *United States News*, editorialized unhappily,

> that the War Department is trying to elect Mr. Roosevelt to a fourth term. Yet the narrow view taken of the existing provisions of the law prevents a wide dissemination in the Army [of] the news of the political campaign, which, of course, means that the Roosevelt candidacy will benefit. For it is obvious that between a well-advertised personality like President Roosevelt and a less advertised personality like Governor Dewey, the net effect of keeping all information from the troops during the campaign is bound to be beneficial to the man in office.

Government bureaucrats, Lawrence charged, had "blundered" by suppressing published political comment. Yet by law and by practice, troops themselves could subscribe to anything and have it delivered if addressed personally to them. It was nevertheless not that simple. Ships at sea and troops on the move were not always available for mail call.

Some publications on a favored list even received special treatment. Among them was the Luce newsweekly *TIME*, which published a thinned and miniaturized "pony" edition, without advertisements, for servicemen. Many home-town newspapers were similarly miniaturized, in four-page fold-ups, with emphasis, beyond the carefully neutral news page, on local events, sports, pin-up beauties, and comic strip favorites like "Blondie," "Winnie Winkle," "Jiggs & Maggie," "Mutt & Jeff," and "Gasoline Alley," in which young Skeezix had enlisted, unlike "Li'l Abner," who might not have passed a literacy test for the draft. One applied for pony copies at the newspaper offices, and mailed them to service personnel. Troops overseas could even do their own campaigning at Uncle Sam's expense, mailing V-mail letters on any matters not subject to censorship to friends and family. Such V-letters—forms available to home folks and troops—were microfilmed for lightweight transport, then enlarged to 4 x 5½ inches and printed and mailed at stateside facilities. By 1944 one-third of all service mail used the "V" system.

Since military votes could be crucial, Republicans chided FDR for "playing soldier." Dewey's handlers offered the press his statement that "Mr. Roosevelt is the first of thirty-two Presidents of the United States to claim that the title of Commander-in-Chief makes him a soldier and to use that title as a pretext to perpetuate himself in political office." The charge bent the facts, but another line attributed to Dewey did not. The president on re-election for a third term in 1940 had assured the American people, "You will have a new President in 1944."

"When he said that," Governor Dewey predicted, "he was right."

At a press conference in Albany, Dewey also charged, a week before Roosevelt announced that he would run again, that the President, in his military guise, would make some headline-grabbing campaigning gesture on a battlefield abroad. "The American people will understand that [pretext] pretty well," he said, "without my assistance." The issue had emerged when the *New York Herald-Tribune* alleged that Roosevelt would make his acceptance speech to the Democratic convention from reoccupied Normandy—a good guess, probably from a White House leak, but adjacent to the wrong ocean. Although the government could not have rejected a request from Dewey to make a battlefield tour of post–D-Day Europe, to establish some military credentials—a proposal by one of the candidate's campaign managers, New York state party chairman Ed Jaeckle—Dewey rejected the idea. It would only call attention, Dewey felt, to his lack of a war record. After taking his time to register his disappointment, Jaeckle resigned.

Two weeks before the Democratic convention, and FDR's voyage to Hawaii in his role as commander-in-chief—also a thinly covert campaign trip as candidate—the war news from all fronts remained a plus for the President. Even a laconic dispatch from the Pacific from Admiral Nimitz contributed. Three enemy admirals had been killed in the fighting at sea around Saipan. One was Chuichi Nagumo, who had led the strike force that had attacked Pearl Harbor.

Four _____

Commander-in-Chief

At Pearl Harbor, his arrival set for July 26, FDR intended to deal with the devious General MacArthur without the top Pentagon brass. Admiral Ernest J. King and General George C. Marshall, the service chiefs, remained in Washington to oversee the war. Since Governor Dewey had already hammered at the allegedly geriatric leadership in Washington from the White House on down, the President planned to dramatize that nothing had hampered his durability. Seconding that, columnist Dorothy Thompson observed waspishly on her regular nine o'clock Monday evening NBC broadcast,

> They say he is tired. And I say you *bet* he's tired. Churchill is tired; Stalin is tired. Marshall, Eisenhower and MacArthur are tired; Admiral King is tired. And G.I. Joe is tired—so damned tired that he has red rims around his eyes and premature lines in his young face. . . . Every mother of a man overseas is

tired—tired from that never-ending worry. . . . And if in the President's face, printed like scars of battle, is the record of crises endured and overcome, could anything better become the leader of our nation? . . .

Mr. Dewey was not tired, she added. "Why should he be?"

In response to a flood of requests after the broadcast, a half-million copies of Dorothy Thompson's remarks were mailed to listeners.

Roosevelt's busy White House pulpit, cultivated for frequent press conferences and radio talks, was also his command post as chief of government and of the armed services, and in those helpfully political capacities he had welcomed the irascible Charles de Gaulle earlier in the month. A brigadier general (he would not promote himself) towering an imposing six-foot-five who was the

FDR greeting General Charles de Gaulle, July 6, 1944, at the White House. Anna Roosevelt Boettiger as hostess for the day stands behind her father. *FDR Library*

presumptive symbol of still-feeble French resistance, de Gaulle bore his Gallic pride, the President thought, impatiently, imagining himself a reincarnated Saint Joan. The general had even volunteered that association. "I am the Joan of Arc of France at the present moment," he had told Roosevelt the year before, at Casablanca, after which FDR had referred to him privately, to Secretary of State Hull, as a willful bride, "the temperamental Lady de Gaulle."

A MacArthur in the making, the difficult de Gaulle was needed to secure the cooperation of the liberated French, by authority vested in him by himself. *Le grand Charles* arrived at the White House on Thursday afternoon, July 6, a month after D-Day, from which he had been barred in landing—to his unconcealed insult—as he had no troops involved. He wore "an air of arrogance bordering on outright insolence," presidential press secretary Bill Hassett recalled, "his Cyrano de Bergerac nose high in the air." Roosevelt required de Gaulle's clout with French civil functionaries who would run local affairs (as many had done under the Nazis), and with rising resistance forces who could make trouble for retreating Germans.

At Casablanca the President had observed that Georges Clemenceau, premier of France at the end of World War II, was a tough, single-minded politician. "I am a Clemenceau," said de Gaulle.* After D-Day he had become even more imperious. Their testy business over for the day, early that evening Roosevelt presided over a lavish state dinner for the "Free French" leader. He was struck, the general wrote later, by Roosevelt's "glittering personality," never realizing that the occasion was being hurried through not only because his host wanted to get rid of him but because FDR was expecting Lucy Mercer Rutherfurd that evening. The press widely covered de Gaulle's parleys with Roosevelt, an opportunity not available to mere aspirants like Governor Dewey,

---

* De Gaulle's fantasies were reported after a meeting at Casablanca in early 1943, when FDR had written to his son John, "General de Gaulle was a thoroughly bad boy. The day he arrived, he thought he was Joan of Arc, and the following day he insisted that he was Georges Clemenceau."

but reporters, whatever they knew, prudently wrote nothing about
Mrs. Rutherfurd. (On earlier visits she had been concealed as
"Mrs. Paul Johnson.") Lucy disappeared as anticipated in the
continuing clamor over de Gaulle, who reappeared on Saturday,
departing that afternoon just before the President had himself
driven quietly to 2238 Q Street, where Lucy was waiting at the
home of her sister, Violetta. She returned with FDR, emerging at
the more obscure driveway between the White House and the
State, War and Navy Building, for a quiet dinner with Anna and
her husband, Major John Boettiger. No guest list was prepared.

The next morning at eleven, a sunny Sunday, Roosevelt was
again driven to Q Street to escort Lucy for the day to "Shangri-La,"
his retreat in Maryland's Catoctin Hills, now (since Eisenhower)
Camp David. The security escort kept its distance until summoned.
In that far more discreet era, personal lives usually remained private from press accounts. The ostensibly happily married Wendell
Willkie, for example, had a devoted mistress, Irita Van Doren, editor of the *New York Herald-Tribune*'s book review. Even when she
openly hosted political gatherings for Willkie, the more intimate
relationship never reached print.

General Marshall's travel orders to MacArthur (flying via New
Caledonia and Canton Island) code-named him "Mr. Catch"—
possibly Roosevelt's sly nomenclature—and specified that he was
to bring with him no staff to meet with "Mr. Big." "Purpose,"
Marshall radioed to Brisbane, "general strategical discussion."
No panjandrum of MacArthur's stature actually traveled with utterly "no staff." On his four-engine C-54 (the civilian DC-4)
MacArthur brought along Brigadier General Bonner Fellers as
his military secretary. Fellers, an underling from Manila who had
risen to total obscurity under his boss, signed the self-serving
communiques MacArthur penned. Also aboard was Colonel
Lloyd A. Lehrbas, a former journalist who developed promo-
tional stories for MacArthur and was described as military aide,

and the general's second-string Army doctor. (MacArthur always traveled with a personal physician but seldom needed so much as an aspirin.)

Attempting with little confidence to inhibit MacArthur from any political theatrics, Marshall warned Lieutenant General Robert C. Richardson Jr., commander in Hawaii, "I wish you to see that no reference is permitted regarding General MacArthur's presence . . . except in strict accordance with the President's instructions."

As Roosevelt asked Nimitz whether MacArthur had arrived, a bright red convertible, its siren blasting, pulled up at dockside with a motorcycle escort. In leather flight jacket, scrambled eggs cap, Ray-Ban sunglasses and corncob pipe, all familiar appurtenances from press photos, the general sat jauntily in a rear seat awaiting correspondents' cameras. The President had not seen him since 1937. MacArthur had borrowed the vehicle from the Honolulu fire chief through Richardson, an old friend. The President had instructed his traveling Secret Service chief, Mike Reilly, to locate an open touring car for the visit, but the only appropriate one turned out to be owned by the madam of a well-known bawdy house. The Commander-in-Chief appropriated MacArthur's vehicle.

Arriving earlier, MacArthur had visited briefly with Richardson at Fort Shafter, where he would stay during his brief visit. Marshall had arranged to borrow what Leahy described as a "palatial" Waikiki area villa at 2709 Kalakua Avenue, not far from the Royal Hawaiian Hotel, for the President. The estate of the late Chris R. Holmes had been a rest home for carrier pilots as they rotated between missions, and it would return to that use. For the President's stay, access was blocked off by marines, with patrol boats offshore.

Two years earlier, when MacArthur needed a general for I Corps in New Guinea, Marshall and Stimson had offered the plum assignment to Richardson, once MacArthur's West Point colleague, but Richardson found evasive excuses to avoid glory. (New Guinea was too humid and messy and hazardous.) The combat command went to Robert Eichelberger, who would take an instant dislike to MacArthur's style, especially to his taking credit in communiques he wrote for everything positive the military accomplished and permitting almost no press coverage of anyone else. Eichelberger was even threatened with being sent home after flattering reports about him appeared in *Life* and *The Saturday Evening Post*. Richardson lobbied Stimson, also an old friend, for the posh Hawaii posting, where the general received a third star for being there and enjoyed his leisure. Nimitz and the Navy controlled what went on in Hawaii.

When MacArthur's borrowed convertible, with a chauffeur in khaki, screeched to a stop at the gangplank, FDR shouted from the quarterdeck, "Hello, Douglas! What are you doing with that leather jacket on? It's damn hot today." (The press would cautiously use "darned," which was outside Roosevelt's vocabulary.)

"Well," MacArthur shouted back, "I've just flown in from Australia. It's pretty cold up there." At about the same distance below the equator as Palm Beach is above it, Brisbane was down rather than up, and had never seen a snowflake. The general may have meant that it was cold when traveling airborne at high altitudes, but the flight jacket at Honolulu's surface climate in the nineties was obviously for show.

Halfway up the gangplank, MacArthur paused to acknowledge an ovation from dockside. Then he formally greeted the President, and the VIP party proceeded to debark. That FDR's military chiefs were nowhere to be seen and had remained in Washington suggested to the wary MacArthur that he had been summoned only for a political extravaganza; however he had already managed one of his own. Yet there was also serious business to conclude, and in Rooseveltian fashion both Nimitz and MacArthur would get much of what each wanted. The President had already made up his mind about where to attack next in the Pacific. MacArthur would propose a Philippines route toward Japan, and Nimitz a coordinate path already begun with Saipan and Guam. Crucially for Roosevelt, MacArthur was to attack well before election day. In November

1942, Eisenhower's push into French North Africa, hobbled by logistics until just after midterm elections, had cost Roosevelt crucial seats in Congress. He was not going to have *this* operation delayed beyond the balloting.

MacArthur had spelled out his Philippines case in a radiogram to General Marshall on June 18. The President had reviewed it but withheld approval. Now he would go over the details with MacArthur—and also range over wartime Oahu. "Douglas," he announced, "I'm taking that car"—and for six hours in the fire-red convertible the next morning, with security vehicles fore and aft, the President and MacArthur, with Nimitz also squeezed into the back seat, would tour sites already in place to train troops for assaults on Japan.

It was late afternoon when the docking and greeting formalities were over. The principals assembled for dinner at the President's Waikiki oceanfront spread that evening. Roosevelt began, as if he did not already know the answer, "Well, Douglas, where do we go from here?" Huge maps were posted on the walls of the spacious living room, and Leahy wielded a long bamboo pointer as locations were identified. Given sufficient naval and air cover, MacArthur proposed landing in the Philippines in three months and completing the reoccupation in six months. He would isolate Japan from its sources of oil, rubber and other strategic materiel in the occupied Dutch East Indies, strangling the enemy without the bloody frontal assaults on island approaches in the central Pacific planned by Chester Nimitz. Further, MacArthur contended, a proposed strike toward Formosa (Taiwan) that bypassed the Philippines would leave American invasion forces nakedly open for assault from occupied China and Malaya.

Already on track to create long-range bomber bases close to the Japanese home islands, Nimitz conceded that he could support either operation. He knew that a Philippines invasion was an expensive publicity stunt for the general who had vowed "I shall return," but MacArthur had a lock on the conservative press and on Republicans in Congress. Pleased, MacArthur recalled that Nimitz "displayed a fine sense of fair play," and that Roosevelt, steering the discussions, had remained "entirely neutral."

Although MacArthur later wrote that he was shocked by the President's pallor and frailty, their talks went on briskly and amiably until nearly midnight, then resumed in the morning. Yet the general would tell his wife, Jean, that Roosevelt "is just a shell of the man I knew. In six months he will be in his grave." In his memoirs, MacArthur quoted himself from memory certainly colored liberally by fiction—not an unusual autobiographical strategy for him. No one, not even the imperious MacArthur, would have spoken to his president and commander-in-chief as he later reconstructed his argument. "Mr. President," he quoted himself (forgetting the intimate "Franklin" and blaming Roosevelt personally for the loss of the Philippines),

> the country has forgiven you for what took place on Bataan. You hope to be reelected President of the United States, but the nation will never forgive you if you approve a[ny] plan which leaves 17 million Christian American subjects [Filipinos] to wither in the Philippines under the conqueror's heel until the peace treaty frees them. You might do it for reasons of strategy or tactics, but politically, it would ruin you. . . . The American people would be so aroused that they would register [the] most complete resentment against you at the polls this fall.

The non-churchgoing MacArthur exploited religion only when politic—as when he would quote *The Lord's Prayer* in a ceremony in 1950 flamboyantly and personally restoring reoccupied Seoul to the South Koreans. (A few months later the Americans and the Koreans in Seoul would both flee Mao's Chinese.) It is hardly likely that MacArthur tried his religious threat on Roosevelt, who in any event came prepared, if necessary, to argue MacArthur down on Philippines guilt. FDR had aides document the general's vulnerabilities, which were many, including the transcript of a conversation MacArthur had with Pacific Fleet Commander Thomas Hart a week before Pearl Harbor. The general had been alerted by George Marshall on November 27, 1941, in a "war warning" that a Japanese attack on American soil somewhere seemed imminent, and MacArthur boasted that he could defend the Philippines without further reinforcement. "My greatest security," MacArthur told Hart, "lies in the inability of our enemy to launch his air attack on our islands." Ten days later, and nine hours after the general learned of Pearl Harbor, a Japanese raid on Clark Field, north of Manila, destroyed much of MacArthur's bomber strength *on the ground*. Four weeks after the conversation with Admiral Hart, MacArthur had evacuated Manila and fled with such troops as could get there to the forlorn, unsupplied Bataan peninsula and the fortress island of Corregidor.

The general had grandly exploited Bataan as his symbol, even christening his personal four-engine C-54 *Bataan*. On Coney Island an amusement park wax museum displayed MacArthur on Bataan—not totally a fiction, as once in early January 1942 he had boarded at PT boat and visited there for an hour.

Roosevelt did not interrupt with readied rejoinders. MacArthur knew he had said, and done, many outrageous things, yet he had a Teflon public aura he cultivated assiduously. Much of what he remembered about the Oahu sessions seems invented long after the fact.

In their more believable chatter, MacArthur recalled asking Roosevelt, "What chance do you think Dewey has?" The President quipped that he was too busy with the war to think about politics— and both laughed at the bald untruth. Then FDR apparently confided, seriously—and here MacArthur seems utterly genuine, as pithy repartee often lodges in the memory—"If the war with Germany ends before the election, I will not be reelected." The remark strikingly prefigures the electoral fate of Winston Churchill in mid-1945.

MacArthur added politely that he understood that Roosevelt was the overwhelming favorite with troops, and the President, taking that as a cue, added about Dewey, "I'll beat that son of a bitch if it's the last thing I do!"

Touring in the red convertible on July 27, MacArthur, happy with the way the strategic business appeared to have begun, again called the President, as if a close friend, "Franklin." Earlier, when the general thought he had a chance for the nomination that had evaporated, MacArthur confided impulsively to Eichelberger, "The only reason I want to be President . . . is to beat that S.O.B. Roosevelt." Writing then to his wife, "Em," Eichelberger added, "I can see he expects to get it, and I sort of think so, too."

The scale and scope of the V.I.P. tour of the island—shipyards, airfields, barracks, training sites and ordinary villages—surprised civilian and military observers. Sam Rosenman thought that the President was taking unnecessary risks, for Hawaii's mixed population included many of Japanese ancestry, alerted by villagers whom the shiny convertible and security vehicles had already passed. Although West Coast Japanese had been ordered to "relocation" camps just after Pearl Harbor in a paranoiac frenzy employing phony legalism only then beginning a reversal, no equivalent measures had been employed in Hawaii, and there had been no inimical incidents in either place. Roosevelt and his companions—Admiral Leahy sat in a front seat with the driver—waved to cheering crowds with no evidence of anxiety.

When the cavalcade wheeled through the naval air station at Kaneohe Bay on Oahu's northeast coast, Aviation Machinist's Mate Tom Pitoniak, formerly a Westfield, Massachusetts, farm boy, looked up to see several of the most famous men in the world tool by in one of the most unlikely vehicles for their status. Few other sailors bothered. "It was payday," he remembered, "and the guys playing craps on the Quonset hut porches didn't even bother turning around to see."

FDR seated between General MacArthur (foreground) and Admiral Leahy, as Admiral Nimitz explains on a large map his planned Pacific strategy. Waikiki, Hawaii, July 28, 1944. *U. S. Navy/ FDR Library*

Another planning session after a late lunch at Roosevelt's Waikiki villa continued the talks as they pored over maps, and a further session convened the next morning. Arriving for the first meeting, Nimitz had been astounded by the license taken by the President's security chief, Mike Reilly. He had ordered a company of Seabees to uproot palms and make Roosevelt's access easier. Even Nimitz's own headquarters bathroom was widened for the President's wheelchair in case of need. The hasty makeover was repainted and speed-dried with a blowtorch.

The Navy scheduled a closing evening of Hawaiian entertainment, but MacArthur declined, taking his leave after some private words with Roosevelt. MacArthur was confident that FDR's go-ahead was imminent. Back in Brisbane, he would offer confidants variant versions of what had occurred. Although he had no confirmation yet of any Philippines plans, Leahy, who had been at FDR's side, had assured MacArthur, "I'll go along with you, Douglas."

After hearing his boss's spin, Eichelberger wrote home that "Sarah," having returned from a visit to "Cousin Frank," was "on top again. . . . He will capture the Philippines."

Sam Rosenman and others not privy to the Waikiki conferences could only sit under the palms, where from their beach chairs they could peer into the parlor where the talks were taking place. After hours one evening Rosenman and Bruenn sampled Honolulu night life. Not of sufficient rank among forty admirals and generals, neither was at a martini-laced luncheon given by Nimitz for the President before MacArthur flew off in the *Bataan*. Few brass had been privy to the real business.

Rosenman was with the President when, before leaving Oahu, FDR asked to visit a military hospital. They paused at Hickam Field to observe the unloading from a transport a group of wounded GIs who thirty-six hours earlier had been in action on Saipan. Several were brought on stretchers to the President's car, where he chatted with them. At the Aiea Naval Hospital, crowded with five thousand patients, a Secret Service man accompanying the party pushed Roosevelt slowly through wards occupied by casualties who had lost, or lost the use of, arms or legs.

> He insisted on going past each individual bed. He had known for twenty-three years what it was to be deprived of the use of both legs. He wanted to display himself and his useless limbs to those boys who would have to face the same bitterness. This crippled man on the little wheel chair wanted to show them that it was possible to rise above such physical handicaps. With a cheery smile to each of them, and pleasant words at the bedside of a score or more, this man who had risen from a bed of helplessness ultimately to become President of the United States . . . was living proof of what the human spirit could do to conquer the incapacities of the human body. . . . Here, in the presence of great tragedy, he was doing it on a grand, heroic scale. The expressions on the

faces on the pillows, as he slowly passed by and smiled, showed
how effective was this self-display of crippled helplessness.

Ordered as always not to file stories before the completion of a
trip where security was an issue, correspondents reported later on
his visit to the wounded, but carefully made no mention of Roosevelt's own disability.

The President also spoke to war workers at the Navy yard,
sailors at the submarine base, and troops of the Army's Seventh
Division, which included veterans of operations against the Japanese on Kwajalein Atol in the central Pacific. At Schofield Barracks
(hit on December 7, 1941) he spoke to long double columns of
Japanese American soldiers who would soon be fighting in Italy. He
visited the Marine station at Ewa, the naval station at Barbers
Point, the ammunition depot at Lualualei, the Seabee camp at
Moanalua Ridge, Marines training at Camp Catlin, the Army's
jungle training center at Kahana Bay, the Navy's air station at Kaneohe Bay (where the first Japanese attacks began on the morning
of Pearl Harbor), the amphibious base at Waimanalo and the Coast
Guard base at Wailupe.

Before departure on the evening of July 29 the President held a
news conference at Nimitz's harbor headquarters for Hawaii-
based newsmen and the pool reporters who had traveled with him.
He told of his inspections of bases and hospitals, his conferences
with military leaders, and his pleasure at his reception by the
people of Hawaii. He took questions but brushed aside politics.
Asked whether unconditional surrender demanded of Germany
applied also to Japan, he turned the page back to Lee's surrender
to Grant at Appomattox in 1865. It approximated unconditional
surrender, he claimed, but with implied magnanimity. Lee knew
that if he did not ask for softer conditions, Grant would offer some
on accepting the surrender. On ordering that enemy weapons be
parked or stacked, and other property formally given up, Grant
offered parole to their homes to Confederate soldiers if they

agreed never again to take up arms against the Union. Also, soldiers were to keep their horses and mules for the spring planting. "There," said the President, "you have unconditional surrender." Although it was, effectively, unconditional surrender then humanely modified, nit-picking critics would claim that FDR did not know his history—that only Lee's Army of Northern Virginia was involved, and that the only actual unconditional surrender demanded by Grant had been that of Fort Donelson on the Cumberland River in 1862. What the President was doing, however, was planting a seed within the Japanese hierarchy, hoping that it might take root before the troops he had seen on amphibious maneuvers in California and Oahu would have to storm the beaches of Honshu and Kyushu.

Later that day, Roosevelt, wheeled up the gangplank and reboarded the *Baltimore*. The cruiser weighed anchor for Alaska, its destroyer escorts plowing ahead on a northwest course. Pool reporters and Roosevelt's aides Sam Rosenman and Elmer Davis would fly back to California. As the lines were cast off, FDR sought out Fala, who had been kept aboard ship. By Hawaiian regulations, even the presidential Scottie had to serve out a four-month quarantine—here limited to the days aboard. At 10:35 p.m. the cruiser, moving out of the Kaiwai Channel, picked up speed to 22 knots, its destination the craggy outpost of Adak in the Aleutians.

On the second day out, a Navy patrol plane came into view. It was challenged by the *Baltimore*'s blinker signal, and responded with the code of the day. A flotation pouch with presidential mail was dropped, and a destroyer in the escort group picked it up and came alongside the cruiser, which, by harness, hauled the pouch aboard. At a small table in the captain's quarters, assisted by Admiral Leahy and Lieutenant Rigdon, who unsealed the envelopes, Roosevelt pored through the messages.

Most of the news was bad. The President's long-time secretary and intimate, Marguerite (Missy) LeHand, had been with him even before he was stricken with polio. She had suffered a paralytic stroke at forty-three in 1941, and had died in Boston. Missy had devoted her life to Roosevelt, encouraging him in adversity and exercising a proprietary interest in him that went beyond family. (Privately the President had called her, as he did Grace Tully, "Child.") She had lived quietly at Hyde Park and the White House, and had the license to offer unpleasant truths and criticize unworkable prose. Close enough to events, yet slipping slowly away, she had written, in a shaky hand, to Grace Tully on July 16, just before the Democratic convention opened in Chicago, "Who is getting the Vice Presidential nomination? I have been beside myself trying to figure it out. Shall it be (Barkley) Douglas, or Wallace (?) or whom?" She postscripted urgently "R.S.V.P. P.D.Q."—but Miss Tully was en route to California on the President's special train when the note reached the White House.

On Sunday evening, July 30, while the President was proceeding toward Alaska, Missy, seemingly recovering by inches from her stroke but enfeebled by rheumatic heart disease, was in a theater in Harvard Square, escorted by her sister, Ann Rochon, with whom she lived, and her friend Maydell Ramsey. The main feature was *The Man from Down Under*, with Charles Laughton as a World War I veteran who smuggles two orphans into Australia. Shorter features included the usual newsreel—which this time included takes from Roosevelt's special train in San Diego.

Shocked by her boss's haggard appearance—she remembered him as vigorous at their last meeting—she had returned home at eleven and began sorting anxiously through old pictures in her bedroom of the Roosevelt she knew in better, even pre-polio, times. Soon after midnight, her sister heard strange noises coming from Missy's room, and looked in. Trembling violently, Missy fell. She was unconscious when an ambulance took her to the Chelsea Naval Hospital, where she died that morning of a cerebral embolism.

Grace Tully had assumed Missy LeHand's office duties, but could not fill the personal void. Roosevelt had paid every expense of Missy's hospital and follow-up care.* As he worried that on his own death she would have nothing, he amended his will, authorizing half the income from his estate (the other half left to Eleanor) "for the account of my friend Marguerite LeHand" to cover "medical care and treatment during her lifetime." On her death the income would go to Eleanor, with the principal eventually to be divided among their daughter and four sons. As eldest son and executor, James would ask his father to alter the bequest. FDR refused, noting that the clause had become inoperative. "If it embarrasses Mother, I'm sorry. It shouldn't, but it may. . . . Missy didn't make it." Roosevelt would order a Navy transport named for her. When it was launched on March 27, 1945, he sent a message "in the hope that a craft which bears so honored a name will make a safe journey and will always find a peaceful harbor."

Two other deaths were reported to him. Manuel Quezon, exiled president of the Philippines, and Joseph Kennedy Jr., eldest son of FDR's one-time associate and appointee, had been lost aboard a bomber laden with explosives that had detonated prematurely over the English Channel. The elder Kennedy had hoped to spend millions making young Joe postwar governor of Massachusetts and then president. Now he had to bank on the next son, Jack, a Navy lieutenant who had been invalided after a PT-boat crash in the Solomons and might not survive.

News from Europe was also grim. The German conspirators who had failed to kill Hitler had been caught, tortured and hanged, but for two generals who had been—one forcibly—suicides. The Russians had blocked the Polish government-in-exile, in London, from entering reoccupied parts of Poland, and set up in Lublin its own

---

* In a cheap canard in his memoirs, *Tribune* sleuth Walter Trohan wrote that Missy LeHand "was provided for by [William] Bullitt, [Bernard] Baruch and Joe Kennedy, [so] . . . they confided to me. They took turns in making monthly deposits to her account and told me FDR never contributed a red cent." Each had his own reasons for badmouthing FDR.

puppet government of Communist Poles it had been nurturing in Moscow. In the United States, the President also had a no-win political dilemma playing out in Philadelphia. The union of transit workers serving nearly a million shipyard and industrial workers had struck when eight black employees had been promoted to trolley motormen. Although neither a liberal on race nor a friend to unions, war mobilization director Byrnes recommended presidential action, and William Rigdon sent a message for FDR, who was risking labor support in November, ordering the Army to seize control of Philadelphia Rapid Transit. Union leaders were to be arrested, armed soldiers were to accompany motormen, and strikers refusing to return were to lose their jobs and have their draft deferments cancelled. On August 3 a black protester against the strike—an arsenal employee unable to get to work—walked into Independence Hall and hurled a quartz paperweight at the Liberty Bell, ringing it with a deep thud that sent guards after him as he shouted, "Liberty Bell, oh, Liberty Bell—liberty, that's a lot of bunk!" (At least the local press printed "bunk.")

The Crisis, the national magazine of the NAACP, had been critical of the President's timidity on racial issues, and would observe, despite his intervention in Philadelphia, "Four more years of Roosevelt will mean four more years of control of the government by the Solid South. . . . This, unquestionably, would throttle the hopes and aspirations of Negroes, and bind tighter about them the noose of racial prejudice, segregation, and discrimination." Yet the NAACP had no realistic hopes that a Republican administration would do more.

On August 5, as the President continued through the cold, rainy Aleutians, the imprisoned union leaders urged their men to return to duty. Few strikers failed to report. The black motormen kept their new assignments.

Labor unrest suggested that much more trouble from that sector would come as the nation began reverting toward postwar employment. On Tuesday, August 1, Dewey spoke on nationwide radio from the Hotel William Penn in Pittsburgh, with an audience of fifty newspapermen prepared to ask questions afterward. "We will elect a President," he said—it was a constant theme—"most of whose term will be in peacetime. And as I see it, the United States simply cannot face another period like the Roosevelt depression, which lasted for eight years, continuously from 1933 to 1940. . . . We do not need to surrender our liberties to a totalitarian New Deal." Since it remained wartime, with much more still to be contested, a reporter asked about the Democrats' warning of changing horses in the middle of the stream. Dewey was ready with a riposte. "I should say that argument was demolished at Chicago. They changed half of the horse." The quip about dumping Wallace—rare humor for the usually cold candidate—may have been Dewey's best shot over the President's bow. Although FDR was still at sea, he must have learned of it as dispatch bags came to him. He would have to ready his own rejoinders.

"Why Not Change Horses?" by Jerry Costello in the *Brooklyn Eagle*, September 1, 1944.

The President's campaigning dilemma was whether it was more useful, in seeking both civilian and service ballots, to claim that the war was nearly won on his watch, perhaps playing into Republican strategy that way, or to insist that it had a long way to go, particularly with regard to Japan. Symbolic of the quandary would be the official restoration to the Library of Congress of the Declaration of Independence and the Constitution on September 19, when the Librarian, Verner W. Clapp, handed the Chief Clerk of the Fort Knox Bullion Repository a receipt for the documents safeguarded since Pearl Harbor. Two weeks later the Marine Band would play at widely covered restoration ceremonies in Washington. Was the nation now safe for Dewey?

Although the Aleutians were gray, dismal and forgettable in the short Alaskan summer, the islands had their special political overtones. While the Japanese were being crushed off the pinpoint of Midway in the central Pacific in June 1942, the hinge of the Pacific war, a smaller enemy strike force had occupied the distant Aleutian islands of Attu and Kiska. The only parcels of North American soil seized by the Japanese, they were only a minor strategic threat—a possible jumping off point for something more. Early in 1943 the army established a garrison on Adak, to the east, to block further encroachment, then, in June retook Attu. That August, with the Americans unaware in the sub-Arctic gloom, the Japanese abandoned Kiska. Expecting a battle, and augmented by Canadian troops, the Army reoccupied the barren rock. As FDR wrote to Canadian Prime Minister Mackenzie King, soldiers "found the only Japs on the island—two inoffensive dogs. They captured the dogs and then all of them marched down again."

Despite the wretched weather through the Inland Passage overlooking the towering peaks of mainland Alaska, the President predicted to King, "I believe that the scenery of one good day will compensate the tourists who will go there in increasing numbers." The long Aleutian chain stretched westward toward northern

Japan. Roosevelt had not traveled as a premature sightseer but to turn national focus toward the inevitable battle for the Japanese Home Islands—and to remind the voting public once more that he was the commander-in-chief of a two-ocean war.

Under low clouds and rain, the Alaskan coastline remained miserable. On his return train journey, though North Dakota on August 14, Roosevelt penned a facetious memo about it:[*]

> Shortly after leaving Honolulu, clear blue sky, calm sea, no wind, there appeared over the horizon a cloud as small as a man's hand. It saw us and approached slowly.
>
> It turned out to be one of those rather rare animals known as a "low." . . . We cannot shake it off. It smiled all over, circled us several times and took a position just off the stern. It followed us all night and the next day and the next.
>
> After three more days, we reached Adak, where it went ashore and played happily.
>
> . . . With it came wind and rain and fog. . . . Its presence became so persistent that the tug boats were prevented from pulling us off the dock.[†] . . . When it went off to gambol on the horizon for a few minutes, we got under way and had only been heading for Kodiak for an hour or two when the little "low" turned up again from nowhere and accompanied us. All the way to Kodiak it hovered around us and while it was kind enough to run away while we caught a fish, there it was back again the rest of the day and all the next day and accompanied us into Auke Bay [north of Juneau].

Although the President visited such Army and Navy installations as he could, the voyage through the chill, choppy waters around the

---

[*] He read it the next day to a press and radio conference held on the train en route east.
[†] Because of severe crosswinds, the efforts of five tugs were insufficient to loose the *Baltimore* from its moorings, delaying departure by an entire day.

southern fringes of Alaska had only symbolic military value. With FDR's whereabouts after Hawaii unknown, Representative Charles Halleck, the chair of the Republican Congressional Committee, with Herbert Brownell, Dewey's choice as chair of the Republican National Committee, at his side, charged to the press that the absent Roosevelt was only titular commander-in-chief—a "myth" rather than a reality. The President was not "in effect the actual leader of the armed forces." Matters of training, planning and strategy were handled by "trained officers." The title granted in the Constitution, Halleck contended, was written in because George Washington, widely expected to become the first president, had been head of American armed forces. Senator Taft chimed in, writing to Norman Cousins, editor of *The Saturday Review*, "For the first time in history we have a Commander-in-Chief running for re-election himself"—a gross historical blunder by Taft, as Abraham Lincoln had run for re-election in wartime 1864, and was a hands-on, if controversial, commander-in-chief. Every president in any case, war or peace, possessed the title.

Roosevelt used it, radioing MacArthur from shipboard on August 9, "As soon as I get back I will push on that plan [of yours], for I am convinced that as a whole it is logical and can be done. . . . Some day there will be a flag raising in Manila—and without question I want you to do it." He added, warmly, that it was "a particular happiness" to see MacArthur again. "I wished very much in Honolulu that you and I could swap places—and personally I have a hunch that you would make more a go as President than I would as general in the retaking of the Philippines." Thanking Nimitz for the arrangements in Hawaii, he noted that "we have been able to carry out all that we set out to do."

By August 25, MacArthur was preparing for a powerful landing on Leyte in the mid-Philippines, bypassing the big southern island of Mindanao, where the Japanese were waiting. He radioed Roosevelt for further confirmation, and the President wrote that "though there seem to be efforts [by the Navy] to do a little by-passing which you would not like . . . I still have the situation in hand."

On treeless, chilly Adak on August 3, draped in a heavy coat, Roosevelt had toured, by jeep, a submarine base, airfield and muddy new baseball diamond. Out of the cold, slanting rain in the Quonset hut mess hall, he lunched with enlisted men from a regulation GI aluminum tray, then told them, although they had little appreciation for the lonely mountainscape to which their orders had taken them, "You don't realize the thousands upon thousands of people who would give anything in the world to swap places with you." The men laughed. Ross McIntire recalled the President's asking servicemen what they missed the most. "Girls," said a marine from Arkansas. There were more such exchanges, which the President told a news conference (on August 15) "you cannot print."

FDR in the distant background at a mess hall in Adak, Alaska, August 3, 1944, as army and navy personnel are seated for lunch and to listen to the President. *FDR Library*

Twenty-two thousand soldiers and sailors crowded bare Adak, where formerly there had not even been a native village. Seabees had constructed all-weather roads, and preparations were being made, in concert with the projected invasion of lower Japan, to attack the crescent chain of the Kurile Islands, the northernmost appendage of the home empire, a thousand miles to the southwest. Seeming fit, although gaunt, Roosevelt transferred to a motorboat in the fog and rain, and with a borrowed rod he swept the choppy water for salmon.

Hemmed in by crosswinds, the *Baltimore* could not unmoor on schedule, and the President went forward after dinner and from the forecastle fished over the side, catching several small trout. Although the weather abated the next morning, Dutch Harbor, once a Japanese target, and next on the presidential schedule, was closed in by heavy fog, as was Kodiak Island, but after four hours of slow zigzagging, the cruiser found Kodiak. Docking, Roosevelt was motored to Buskin Lake, where from an open flat-bottomed boat he, with Admirals Leahy and Brown, and General Watson, fished for trout, only the President catching any. The other three, uninterested in fishing, dutifully held their rods in position. At Auke Bay, off Juneau, the small, bleak town that was the Alaskan territorial capital, the *Baltimore* anchored at the foot of Mendenhall Glacier. Waiting at Juneau, Governor Ernest Gruening—a Democrat—took the President, despite driving rain, close to some timber-covered small islands for more fishing. The two caught five salmon, two flounder, a halibut and several cod. Rather than keep hundreds of GIs standing in the rain, inspections of outdoor installations to follow were canceled.

To traverse the narrow Inside Passage of the Aleutians toward Puget Sound, the President and his party were transferred to the far less comfortable *Cummings*. The 1,465-ton destroyer had been at Pearl Harbor when the Japanese attacked but had sustained only minor damage. (By late morning that day it was at sea, heaving depth charges at a suspected enemy submarine.) The *Baltimore*

filled its bunkers with fuel and, accompanied by two destroyers, the
Dunlap and *Fanning*, headed southward for further action. In continuing rain and fog, the *Cummings* plowed slowly southeast toward the Bremerton naval base in Washington.

In an earlier wartime summer—he was more mobile in 1914,
when Assistant Secretary of the Navy—FDR sailed on a destroyer
commanded by a young lieutenant, William F. Halsey Jr. In 1944
Halsey would be an admiral familiar on the front pages. Young
Roosevelt was to look over naval installations on the Maine coast.
When in Passamaquoddy Bay, near the family summer home at
Campobello Island, Roosevelt suggested that because he was familiar with the narrow channel, he should guide the destroyer to
navigate the stronger tides. Aware of the differences in skill required to "sail a catboat out to a buoy" and "to handle a high-
speed destroyer in narrow waters," Halsey feared career-ending
trouble for himself but yielded to his civilian superior, a "white-
flanneled yachtsman." To the lieutenant's relief, Roosevelt "knew
his business" and took the ship through easily.

On the *Cummings*, after several frustrating attempts to throw
fishing lines from the quarterdeck, the President remained below.
While the destroyer trembled in choppy waters, he sat by a small
table in the captain's quarters, drafting a radio address he planned
to deliver on arrival in Bremerton. He discarded one shaky paragraph after another as unsatisfactory. Mike Reilly of FDR's Secret
Service detail, who had flown to the mainland after making security arrangements for the stops in Alaska, was to find a place and
time for the talk. "Is there a baseball park in Seattle?" Roosevelt
had asked. Reilly said that the Seattle team in the Pacific Coast
League had a good stadium. "Fine," said the President. "Make
arrangements for me to speak at the ball park." Advance planning
for that, Reilly advised, might disclose the destroyer's movements
to any lurking Japanese submarines. "Why not Bremerton Navy
Yard?" He recommended the deck of the *Cummings*. "All right,
you win," Roosevelt conceded. "Have Anna meet me."

A day short of Bremerton, a mail pouch was dropped for the President, with newspaper headlines about the Hawaii phase of the trip: "President Meets MacArthur and Nimitz in Hawaii"; "President Reviews Battle-Tested 7th [Division]"; "Roosevelt Chats with Wounded." Lieutenant Rigdon also typed out war bulletins from the radio shack and a draft of the Bremerton speech to be distributed to the press.

Thousands of shipyard workers lined the harbor as, late in the afternoon on August 12, the destroyer was warped into a flooded dry dock by Navy tugs. The President was to deliver his address to the nation from the foredeck of the *Cummings* at 6:00 p.m.—nine in the evening in the East. To prepare, he was assisted in his cabin into the leg braces he had not worn for a year. As he had lost more than nineteen pounds since then, they felt heavier, and awkward. The braces were not the only aspect of preparation to go awry. As daylight began to fade, the gusts out of Alaska picked up, causing the destroyer, held by mooring lines, to tremble. While the throng at dockside alerted by radio cheered vigorously, thirty thousand workmen just off duty crowded in. Clinging to the makeshift podium with both hands, Roosevelt fumbled at the pages of his speech as he waved to the crowd while awaiting the signal to go on the air.

His voice rumbled weirdly from loudspeakers, the echoes affecting unhelpfully what radio listeners heard. As he struggled to keep his balance, he veered from his prepared script, dropping syllables and even words. Chest tremors racked his body and he broke into a sweat. Bruenn would note "substernal oppression with radiation to both shoulders." Gamely but haltingly, ad-libbing when he failed to find his lines, the President reviewed the maneuvers he had witnessed, the massive activity at a renewed Pearl Harbor, his visits to hospitals and bases in Hawaii and to fog-shrouded outposts off Alaska. He did not believe, he declared, that Japanese warlords could be trusted to make a durable peace, and he vowed that Americans would continue on until total victory.

After thirty-five minutes he was exhausted, and millions of radio listeners were alarmed. The planned tour of the Navy yard was
scrubbed. While clutching his papers and hanging on to the forward gun mount, he waited agonizingly for assistance to the captain's cabin, where he collapsed into a chair, confessing to "one
hell of a pain in my chest that lasted half an hour." Dr. Bruenn
recognized angina symptoms, a constricting of the heart muscle.
Bruenn arranged immediately for an electrocardiogram, and took
a blood sample, neither of which evidenced any adverse changes
to the President's obvious heart disease. Yet "it scared the hell out
of us," Bruenn remembered.

At a radio in the White House, Sam Rosenman was appalled at
the "dismal failure," and wondered how the rest of the listening
public took the fuzzy, wandering talk. He did not have long to wait.
"It looks like the old master has lost his touch," the *Washington Post*
observed the morning after, knowing nothing of the circumstances.
"His campaigning days must be over. It's going to look mighty sad
when he begins to trade punches with young Dewey."

At a siding close to where the *Cummings* was moored, the waiting
presidential train, poised eastward, left quietly shortly after nine. To
Anna Boettiger and her father's secretaries with her, Grace Tully
and Dorothy Brady, Roosevelt looked worn but resilient, radiating
confidence. He had come through. In a notebook Lieutenant Rigdon wrote, "Total miles traveled by sea this voyage, 7248."

The President's notes from the *Ferdinand Magellan* on the
"low" that had followed them to Alaska and then to Puget Sound,
further parodying Mary and her persistent lamb, jauntily made no
reference to the medical incident which could have aborted his
campaign:

> In the late afternoon, we went to Seattle and boarded the train
> and to our horror the next morning after we woke up across the
> Cascade Mountains there was the little "low" following us. It kept

on going all the way into Montana and the following day across Montana and into North Dakota. . . .

So here we are approaching the Twin Cities and we have got the bright idea that Admiral Brown should continue to feed his little "low" and bring it with us all the way to Washington.

After an absence of thirty-five days and a rail-and-sea journey of 13,912 miles, the presidential party returned to Washington briefly on August 17. Barring the unexpected, the course of the Pacific war had been determined. Visiting Roosevelt at Hyde Park on August 21, Daisy Suckley loyally wanted to have it both ways. "The P has a good colour, & every one thinks him looking very well," she began in her diary. "He does, except for a sort of pallor and a strained look about the mouth which you see in sick people. He says he feels pretty well, but *tired*, most of the time. He has to save his strength to appear a few times in public before [the] election. . . . [Bremerton was] pretty exhausting. He says the muscles are 'just not there.'"

As the President's standing in the polls declined, a conference on forming a United Nations organization had convened on the 21st at the Dumbarton Oaks estate in Georgetown. Dewey quickly attacked its goals, allegedly to establish a superstate under the "coercive" domination of a few big powers. To diminish such fears, Secretary of State Hull met with Dewey's foreign policy adviser John Foster Dulles. At least one concern was real. Stalin wanted to assure veto power over most issues, and through his stubborn young ambassador to Washington, Andrei Gromyko, demanded that all sixteen Soviet republics be seated in the new peacekeeping body. Back in the White House, FDR was told about Russian maneuvering by Undersecretary Edward Stettinius. "My God!" Roosevelt exclaimed. The President, Stettinius explained to him, was his "biggest and last remaining gun." Would he talk to Gromyko?

Roosevelt was still drained after his Bremerton ordeal. Would the ambassador be offended by being received in the President's bedroom? Stettinius thought that Gromyko would be impressed by Roosevelt's extra effort in coping with the impasse, and the next morning FDR, in an old bathrobe, and Gromyko, in a severe dark suit, chatted pleasantly without an interpreter. When a husband and wife brought a dispute to court in the United States, Roosevelt observed in his press conference mode, they were permitted to testify but not to vote. That was fair play. Unyielding, Gromyko explained that only Stalin could alter policy, and that the President should cable him—which Roosevelt did, to no effect. The Dumbarton Oaks meeting would adjourn in early October with signatures on an anodyne agreement. Compromises going Stalin's way to assure his participation remained to come.*

Seeking ways after Roosevelt's return to get free radio time, Norman Thomas, the feisty presidential candidate of the Socialist Party, applied to the War Department for equal radio time to address fighting men everywhere on grounds that the President's Bremerton speech was "political." Under the Service Men's voting law, the Socialists contended, they were owed a response. When John J. McCloy, Acting Secretary of War while Stimson was away, agreed, and then, eight hours later, changed his mind, contending that the speech was within the "reporting" privileges of the Commander-in-Chief, Thomas objected. On August 26, the Republicans joined the Socialist protest, Senator Conrad Aiken of Vermont observing, "The President can't make a speech that doesn't have political implications."

The next day, August 27, the War Department gave in— somewhat. Equal time on the Army's short-wave radio facilities to

---

* Ironically, the two subordinate Soviet republics eventually awarded voting status, Belorussia (now Belarus) and Ukraine, would achieve real independence on the breakup of the Soviet Union.

"the armed forces overseas" would be made available on request each week to all qualified political parties for "re-broadcast" of "political addresses." Listed (in alphabetical order) were the Democratic, Prohibition, Republican, Socialist and Socialist-Labor parties as qualifying by fielding candidates in at least six states. Equal time would be given until November 1, by which date "overseas voting should be completed."*

Roosevelt's campaign would shift into low gear, as he planned to meet with Winston Churchill in Quebec in mid-September to discuss future war and peace issues. Presidential campaigns traditionally accelerated after Labor Day early in the month. Still, on August 29 he did have a political announcement to make. Although he was "too busy to make a swing around the country," on September 23 he would open his campaign with an address in Washington at the dinner meeting of the annual conference of the International Brotherhood of Teamsters. Although the Democratic National Committee was paying for his air time, it would not be "very political," FDR predicted to newsmen—"just a tinge."

---

* In his memoirs, Herbert Brownell claimed "an acrimonious discussion" with the networks, which "turned us down." He makes no reference to armed forces broadcasts, which were authorized.

Five

"Roosevelt's dog and Dewey's goat"

Quickly assuming an activist role for the Democratic ticket, Harry Truman spoke in Cadillac Square, Detroit, on Labor Day, September 4, to an enthusiastic CIO rally. As Truman's banker (and military reservist buddy) John Snyder, recalled, "The AFL [American Federation of Labor] and the CIO weren't getting along too well; . . . he had to address one group in the afternoon and another in the evening. . . . He delivered very much the same speech to both of them and came out with good support from both sides." To each gathering he sounded like one of their own, out of the working class. Blue-collar Americans, Truman asserted, had furnished the tools for victory. Recognizing, nevertheless, that an epidemic of strikes and slowdowns anticipating forthcoming peace would only lengthen the war, he offered "a word of warning from a friend. Labor has duties as well as rights." As a candidate he would not stray from the straight-talking image that had characterized his senatorial career.

After Roosevelt's Pacific journey, the President had quickly kept his promise to meet with Truman, having him to lunch hosted by Anna Boettiger—and a carefully arranged photo session—on August 18 under a large magnolia on the south lawn of the White House. Truman followed "old man [Cordell] Hull," the secretary of state, who left the President's office at 12:55. Recognizing Roosevelt's blend of guile and charm, Truman wrote to Bess, who was back in Missouri, later in the day, "You'd have thought I was the long lost brother or the returned Prodigal. I told him how much I appreciated his putting the finger on me for Vice President and we talked about the campaign, reconversion, China, postwar employment, the [Walter] George and [Harley] Kilgore Bills." Once lunch was announced, Truman accompanied Roosevelt as he was wheeled "into the back yard of the White House." The afternoon heat was oppressive, and the President suggested that they peel off their jackets and dine in shirtsleeves. "Then the movie men and the flashlight boys went to work." A photographer for *Life*, George

Truman and FDR at lunch on the White House lawn, August 18, 1944. *Truman Library*

Tames, framed the pair looking like old friends, with Roosevelt appearing much more vigorous than in the damaging shot, a month earlier, from San Diego.

It was not a meal for the newspaper front pages—sardines on toast and coffee—yet whatever the fare, Truman had to look like a confidant of the President, which, as newsmen realized, he was not. But Roosevelt had already considered the kick-off to their electioneering. "He gave me a lot of hooey about what I could do to help the campaign and said he thought I ought to go home for an official notification and then go to Detroit for a labor speech and make no more engagements until we had another conference. So that's what I'm going to do."

The President offered little background to his possible successor about domestic, military, diplomatic or administrative matters. Nor would he do so later, which suggests that any intimations of mortality FDR had were few and personally unconvincing. He was more concerned about losing than about dying. On one trip to Hyde Park he brought along his aide George Elsey to look over the library. "The President thought it was conceivable that Dewey could beat him," Elsey recalled, "and wanted me to inspect the library and recommend what security measures would be necessary to protect his classified papers."

From Left to Right, the press did not take Harry Truman seriously. Although the charge was unquestionably false, Governor Dewey would refer to him as "my opponent's hand-picked running mate." The liberal Richard Strout—later the "TRB" of his *New Republic* column—gently dismissed Truman as "a nice man" who will make "a passable Vice President," but questioned him as a possible President "in times like these." *TIME*, which had put Truman on its cover for running his effective investigating committee on the war effort, now reclassified him as a mediocrity, "the mousy little man from Missouri." *The Kansas City Star*, his home-town newspaper, faint-praised him as having "unusual capacity for development." Forgetting Woodrow Wilson's running mate Thomas Marshall, known since only for his quip, "What this country needs is a really good five-cent cigar," the *Pittsburgh Post-Gazette* described Truman as one of the weakest vice-presidential candidates his party had ever nominated.

After the war, the haggard FDR told Truman, post–New Deal initiatives would be on hold during a peacetime transition. The president who came next would have to be "slightly right of center." The implied message was that only a pragmatist in the White House would get things done. Nevertheless, Truman was not invited into the decision-making process in which veteran New Dealers, some aboard since 1933, and newer wartime appointees, many of them Republican, remained. FDR's other injunction to Truman was to avoid campaign travel by air. "One of us has to stay alive," he remarked.* The President's four-engine DC-4, *The Sacred Cow*, had a clean flying record, but rail trackage was on solid ground.

Reporters caught up with Truman as he left the White House and queried him about the meeting. "The President looked fine," he fudged, "and ate a bigger meal than I did. . . . He's still the leader he's always been, and don't let anybody kid you about it. He's keen as a briar." Returning to his Senate office, Truman apparently confided to his all-purpose assistant, Major General Harry Vaughan, "I had no idea he was in such feeble condition. In pouring cream in his tea, he got more cream in the saucer than he did in the cup. There doesn't seem to be any mental lapse, but physically he is just going to pieces. I'm very much concerned about him." It is possible, Robert Ferrell has written, that in his recollections, Truman "read the future into the past." Secretary Ickes lunched with the President a month later, perhaps under the same magnolia tree. Ickes kept a diary, which made no mention of a presidential lapse, yet he noted dark patches under Roosevelt's

---

* Later, in1962, Truman re-remembered FDR's injunction as "Oh, Harry. You mustn't fly. It's too dangerous, and we both must be careful." Truman's response to Eddie McKim (some lines later) is also slightly different than the 1962 recollection.

eyes and a thinning face—but "he seemed keen and alert and unless something should strike pretty hard I suspect that he is good for four years more."

Truman took his long-time friend and Army buddy Edward McKim, now a prosperous businessman, to a White House reception for the cast of the film *Wilson,* which most attendees had not yet seen. A month earlier, at its widely lauded premiere in New York (*Life* loved it), Wendell Willkie as chairman of the Board of Twentieth Century-Fox, as well as the Woodrow Wilson Foundation, had hosted a buffet supper for the players and surviving politicians of Wilson's era. It was Willkie's last major public appearance. Despite attempts to humanize the dour Wilson, Darryl Zanuck's production was an expensive 150-minute bore. Having Wilson root for Princeton football, sneak away to Broadway musicals, and preside at family gatherings around the grand piano to sing, at different times, eighty-seven bits of period songs, failed to soften his cinematic nobility. Ignoring its tedium, the Leftist tabloid *PM* had featured (on August 2) an eight-page picture spread, "*Wilson* Wartime Wisdom May Help Win for FDR." Late in the film, as in Wilson's life, a postwar stroke in October 1919 disables the President for the remainder of his term. Sitting near Roosevelt and Churchill at a showing later, in Quebec, Dr. Bruenn heard FDR mutter to himself, "By God, that's not going to happen to me."

Eddy McKim, of Harry Truman's small campaign staff, was so appalled by the President's fragility that as they left the East Wing he told Truman to look back at "that house" because that was where he would soon be living. "Eddie, I'm afraid I am," Truman confessed. "And it scares the hell out of me."

Pre-empting Labor Day, Truman had initiated his campaign symbolically on August 31, under a full moon on the steps of the Barton County courthouse in Lamar, the southwestern Missouri town where he was born in a white clapboard five-room house four blocks away. In the audience was his mother, Martha Truman, ninety-one. The event was billed as his formal acceptance of the vice-presidential nomination, tendered to him there by Senator Tom Connally of Texas, chairman of the notification committee. Connally also predicted—the ceremonies were being carried by all four major radio networks—that the American people "would not cashier the Commander-in-Chief" on the field of battle. To that, Truman contributed the familiar Lincolnian adage about swapping horses in midstream. "You can't afford to take a chance. You should endorse tried and experienced leadership."

Lamar was an outsized village unprepared for an outpouring of Missourians who had rarely before boasted a national candidate of a major party. Gallons of frugally hoarded gasoline rations were expended to get there. According to Margaret Truman, "Toilet facilities and the sewerage system broke down." The parking field was turned into a huge mud hole by a heavy rainstorm the previous

Speakers and part of the crowd at the courthouse in Lamar, Missouri, where Senator Harry S. Truman was formally notified, by custom, of his nomination for vice president, August 31, 1944. The portraits of the candidates seem years younger than the reality. *Truman Library*

Senator Truman reaching out to shake hands with well-wishers, Lamar, Missouri, August 31, 1944. Hatted and dark-suited is Senator Tom Connally of Texas, who made the formal notification of Truman's nomination. *Truman Library*

day. Truman's friend Harry Easley, frantically coordinating events, conceded, "All I can say is never have a big affair in a small town."

Forecasts by worried Democratic pollsters on Labor Day suggested a strong "outbound tide" in the Midwest, from Nebraska to Ohio, and including Missouri and Michigan, toward the Republican ticket, accounting for 155 likely electoral college votes, three-fifths of a victory margin. The reason seemed to be public perception of imminent peace. Newspapers printed optimistic headlines about Allied troops in France reaching the German border and the Spanish frontier, and Russians overwhelming Romania and plunging deep into Poland. Finland, a reluctant German ally, was about to quit the war. Press reports had it—they were erroneous—that Nazi troops would be evacuating Denmark in order to protect German soil. General Eisenhower declared that his troops were five days ahead of schedule, and unhelpfully kept to his Christmas Day

1943 forecast that the Germans could be beaten before the close of 1944. General Omar Bradley's army group approaching the densely forested Ardennes had its infantry "charging in trucks," with its "sweep" becoming a "romp." American forces had broken into Belgium. The British in Italy had "breached" the Gothic Line and were threatening the Po Valley. And as the sixth year of the European war began, the long and dismal blackout in Britain was to be "nearly banished"—but for some coastal areas—when double summer time ended on September 17.

Much of the giddy spin about the war on the Continent was misleading or wrong, and there would also be tenacious island-by-island fighting to come in the Pacific. Troops approaching Germany, with supply lines lengthening and few Channel ports open, would run out of rations, fuel, shells and even good weather. Infantry riding in trucks, a peculiarly American method of making war with foot soldiers, was becoming an ineffective anomaly. Eisenhower had boasted to Marshall that his forces "can advance almost at will," but added self-protectively that they were "subject only to the requirement for maintenance," and in that "we are stretched to the limit."

Marshall had warned Eisenhower not to put all his replenishment hopes "into the Antwerp breadbasket," and when the crucial Belgian port, taken by the Wehrmacht in May 1940, was finally reoccupied on September 4—Labor Day in the United States—its harbor demolished and clogged with scuttled ships, supply routes to the German border remained backed up all the way from Normandy. Holding out in the lowlands of the Scheldt Estuary, Nazi troops kept Antwerp unusable while protecting launch sites for V-1 robot aircraft and longer range V-2 terror rockets. Although isolated and besieged, even the big Atlantic port of Brest remained in German hands, and the armies-on-wheels of Courtney Hodges and George Patton would become fuel-starved and stalled. Americans at home were only faintly aware of the slowing down of the mighty war machine.

En route from Washington to Hyde Park for a private Labor Day weekend, the President's train made an unreported stop at a siding near Allamuchy, New Jersey, early on the morning of Friday, September 1.* With FDR was Daisy Suckley, in charge of Fala. In the House of Representatives the day before, bitter exchanges had erupted about the cost to the war effort of the President's voyages to Pearl Harbor and the Aleutians. Among the complainants was Congressman Harold Knutson, since 1917 representative from the 6th district of Minnesota, succeeding Charles A. Lindbergh, father of the aviator then a decade away from fame. "The President," Knutson railed, "had been accompanied by a flotilla of battleships, cruisers and destroyers that should have been out in the far Pacific fighting the Japs." Even beyond that, Fala, "that little Scotty dog, had been inadvertently left behind at the Aleutians on the return trip, and . . . they did not discover the absence of the little doggie until the party reached Seattle, and . . . it is rumored that a destroyer was sent a thousand miles to fetch him."

As Roosevelt's train reached Allamuchy in New Jersey, close to Rutherfurd House, and Lucy, on the following day, John McCormack of Massachusetts was responding to Knutson's charge about Fala, which had become a bigger news story than the fiction about battleships and cruisers. "A lot of people in this country have dogs that they love," he countered, "and a lot of people admire the President for his affection for his dog." McCormack had checked with Admiral Leahy about Fala: "The story about the dog is made of whole cloth. The dog was never lost. The dog was never sent for."

Knutson backtracked that he was "happy" that there was "no foundation to the doggie story." But he continued his charge "that

---

* Jim Bishop in *FDR's Last Year* (1974) alleged that months earlier, en route to Hyde Park before leaving for Chicago and San Diego, the President's train made an unscheduled and unreported stop to visit Mrs. Rutherfurd, but his Washington departure and Highland, New York, arrival times, and Daisy Suckley's diary, suggest that this was impossible speculation.

the President's trip cost the American taxpayers $20,000,000." Few seemed to care about the cost of a wartime conference between Pacific commanders and the President. No one would forget Fala. Much later. Eleanor Roosevelt guessed that the allegation had originated "with some bright young man in Republican headquarters."

Lucy Mercer Rutherfurd's estate, in the English manorial fashion, had been built for her late husband's first wife, daughter of Levi Morton, vice president when Benjamin Harrison occupied the White House. (Aiken in South Carolina was the Rutherfurds' second home.) "She came on the train hatless and stockingless," Daisy noted in her diary, "in a black figured dress, & black gloves—she is tall and good-looking, rather than beautiful." With Lucy, Eleanor's social secretary during World War I, at his side, Roosevelt in his wheelchair descended in the small elevator built into the rear platform of the *Magellan*. Secret Service men moved him into a waiting automobile, which would take him to Tranquility Farms. The three pool reporters aboard hardly looked up from their cards and magazines. Under their "voluntary" wartime restrictions they would not be reporting what they were not authorized to know about. The President had many acquaintances in big houses, and press vigilance was in suspension until he returned.

Lucy privately asked for advice from Franklin about how to cope with her 1,300 acres of farmland and woods with a widow's diminished income and wartime shortages of servants. At a lavish lunch with a plethora of guests, most of them her step-family, no evidence of financial strain surfaced. Mrs. Rutherfurd had laid out a bedroom for the President if he wished to rest, but he wanted to miss nothing of Lucy's company. At 3:35 the Roosevelt party, with Fala, rushed off to the presidential train, scheduled to depart at 3:45. Then FDR was wheeled into his stateroom for a nap. At 6:45 the *Ferdinand Magellan* arrived at Highland Station, where Eleanor, who had been at her Val-Kill cottage at Hyde Park, waited, apparently unaware of the interlude at Allamuchy.

During the Labor Day holiday the Roosevelts drove to Henry Morgenthau's home at Fishkill. There the Treasury secretary reviewed for the President his draft of a punitive plan to turn postwar Germany, in peacetime the economic engine of Europe, into a weak agricultural throwback. Although it was practically and politically unsound, both Roosevelts liked the idea at first hearing, and FDR promised to support it when meeting with Churchill in Quebec. When critics leaked the "mad scheme" to the press, Nazi propaganda minister Joseph Goebbels declared, hoping to spur waning war fervor, that Germany could not afford to lose and become Europe's potato patch.

As the Morgenthau scheme suggested that the President was out of touch with reality, the proposal dramatically illuminated Dewey's charge that the Democratic leadership had become aged and quarrelsome. Although discarded, the Morgenthau "plan" would not go away. Early Republican poll ratings rose, as Dewey kept charging on radio and in person that Democrats could not be trusted to manage the peace. Reminding the electorate that millions were still unemployed in 1939, the governor asked, "Do we have to have a war in order to get jobs?"

Dewey's campaign began in Philadelphia on the evening of September 7 with a rally scheduled to be the first of seven major appearances scheduled across 6,700 railway miles and twenty-one states. As his long campaign caravan slowly negotiated Broad Street en route to Convention Hall, irritated motorists presumably on meager "A" ration cards shouted, "Where did you get the gas?" It would remain an all-purpose political gibe.

A near catastrophe for the Roosevelt administration had occurred five days earlier in Philadelphia. As scientists at the Navy Yard were testing a cylinder of uranium hexafluoride for the high-secret "Manhattan" atomic bomb project, the corrosive compound exploded. A white radioactive cloud drifted over South Philadelphia, explained by the Navy to local newspapers as an unanticipated release of "steam." Douglas Meigs and Peter Bragg died instantly; a third chemist in the transfer lab suffered severe acid burns. Before losing consciousness he refused last rites from a priest. Pfc. Arnold Kramish's mother traveled by train from Denver—a three-and-a-half-day ordeal—to visit her hospitalized son, carrying with her a large jar of a miraculous medicinal liquid known as chicken soup. She arrived in Philadelphia the day before Governor Dewey. Kramish, then blinded, survived, regained his sight and would work on the hydrogen bomb in the early 1950s. The episode would not surface during the campaign. On June 12, 1993, it became public when, forty-nine years later, Kramish was belatedly awarded a medal.

Sixty-three reporters, including photographers and radio newsmen, had boarded the well-provisioned "Dewey Special." One restricted car carried speechwriters and political researchers, and another was for the governor and his wife, Frances. His spartan lunch, delivered daily at a scheduled stop, was, as always, a chicken sandwich, an apple and a glass of milk.

Dewey's Philadelphia radio address at ten, in a taut baritone, was also recorded for transmission to troops overseas. Although radio audiences could not see the 1,500 empty seats in Convention Hall's second balcony, newspapermen noted them. (His staff would improve its audience-gathering expertise.) He would lead a peacetime administration, Dewey stressed, for he would assume office late in January, by which time the war might be over. The big issue would be full peacetime employment. As the prosecutor he had been, he mastered facts and repeated points for emphasis, and to signal pauses for cheers. In Pittsburgh, supporters rang cowbells. But Richard Strout in *The New Republic* deplored "the sonorous, cold perfection of the Dewey delivery night after night . . . , running the gamut of emotion from A to B and possessing all a speaker should have except warmth, humor, and fellow feeling."

Dewey would campaign strenuously from his air-conditioned special train for three weeks, emerging for motorcades, local speeches, and meetings with politicians, officeholders, labor and business leaders, war veterans and influential blacks where there were any. To insert local color and identify local bigwigs in his speeches, he had advance men deliver to his staff on the train six copies of newspapers from the day before for each scheduled appearance. On the "Dewey Victory Special" copies of his speeches were distributed twenty-four hours in advance; coffee and sandwiches were always on call, reporters' laundry attended to, baggage handled and bridge partners arranged. (Turner Catledge recalled a reporter's description of the chaotic Willkie campaign train in 1940 "as resembling a bawdy house when the madam was away and the girls were running the joint.") On the Truman train, Richard Rovere told *The New Yorker* readers, "If you wanted anything laundered, you did it yourself in a Pullman basin."

Governor Dewey acknowledging greetings from supporters in Louisville on September 9, 1944. Kentucky governor Simeon Willis is at his side. *Associated Press*

Changing one of his three new pin-striped suits, ordered from
the Duke of Windsor's Manhattan tailor, once a day, Dewey carried, for effect, a gray homburg in his hand, careful never to have it
approach his head. When given a broad Western hat en route by an
admirer, he told a press photographer, "I'll hold it but I won't put it
on." He considered it "absolute torture" to wade into crowds, or to
shake hands, as he was anxious about germs. Like FDR he often
clenched a cigarette holder, but remained unsmiling, even at press
conferences. One of his assistants called him "cold as a February
icicle." Traveling pressmen referred to him privately as "Mr.
Warmth." One described him as the only man he knew who could
strut sitting down.

A *Philadelphia Evening Bulletin* cartoon showed an energetic
young Dewey jumping into the ring to confront a flustered FDR. It
illustrated a syndicated column by John Cummings which claimed
that while Roosevelt had become bigger than the Democratic Party,
it "has become the handy tool of miscellaneous interests and equally
miscellaneous characters. . . . It is openly charged and by no means
successfully repudiated that . . . the leadership in the campaign to
re-elect Roosevelt has been taken over by Sidney Hillman, chairman
of the [CIO] Political Action Committee, and Earl Browder, head of
the Communist outfit, which was the first to call on the President to
seek a fourth term." A "Hillman-Browder Axis"—the noun was
loaded—was allegedly in charge. "We face the threat of a behind-
the-scenes government dominated by Sidney Hillman and Earl
Browder, the former being as fine a citizen as ever came out of
Russia, the latter as fervent a patriot as ever emerged from jail."*
Perhaps to draw service voters to the page, the shrunken "pony"
edition of the *Bulletin* for mailing to troops abroad also included a
photo of four Miss America candidates in swimsuits.

---

* Browder was jailed in 1917–1918 for protesting the draft, in 1920 on "conspiracy"
charges during the postwar "Red Scare," and again in 1940 for using a false passport. He
was released in 1942 as a good-will gesture a year after the Soviet Union was attacked.

Worried about her re-election chances as Connecticut congress-woman despite the support of her husband's publishing empire, Clare Luce also played the patriot card. If her glamorous head rolled in the basket on election day, she declared, voters could be certain—unlike that of the opposition—that it was an "American" head.

Although most newspapers were outspokenly Republican, their reporters covered the Dewey-Bricker political odyssey largely "straight"—with direct quotes and precise local facts. In Owosso, Michigan, Dewey's birthplace, a "WELCOME HOME, TOM" sign hung on the facade of the city hall. Dewey emphasized that he was their own small-town boy who had made good in the big city. Wherever Dewey went, a band would strike up the University of Michigan football anthem, "Hail to the Victor."

"This is a campaign," he exhorted from the rear platform of his train at Des Moines, "against an administration which was conceived in defeatism, which failed for eight straight years to restore our domestic economy, which has been the most wasteful, extravagant and incompetent administration in the history of the nation, and worst of all, which has lost faith in the American people." Journalists quoting the candidate and assuring the inevitable morning-after headlines seemed confident that readers, and radio listeners, could compare Dewey's charges to their Depression memories and their present wartime prosperity, as well as to the headlines about victory upon victory after years of isolationist defeatism.

At a whistle-stop in Valentine, Nebraska, where Dewey greeted two thousand ranch hands and fifty Sioux Indians, he turned to the unfinished war. To connect his candidacy to the war, he had aboard, in full uniform with his three stars and four rows of service ribbons, retired Lieutenant General Hugh Drum, commander of the New York National Guard, who emerged from his Pullman car on occasion. The disappointed Drum had expected to be army chief of staff in 1939, but the President had jumped a one-star general, George Catlett Marshall, over dozens of more senior aspirants. Marshall gained three extra stars overnight and had run the war since. Demanding a greater role for General MacArthur in the Pacific, Dewey was unaware that was already underway on a grand scale. MacArthur's "magnificent talents," he declared, needed to be better employed, "now that he is no longer a political threat to Mr. Roosevelt." Dewey had to be doubly careful in his attacks on the war effort, as in decrying waste and inefficiency he had to limit his fire to the Washington civilian bureaucracy. Leading businessmen, most of them Republicans, had been making billions, for better or worse, from the war—and Roosevelt's running mate, Senator Truman, was the animating and widely respected force on the congressional committee investigating industrial corruption and fraud.

"The Doctor Needed" by Jerry Costello in the *Brooklyn Eagle*, September 23, 1944.

When Governor Dewey reached Spokane he pledged, while referring to the massive Bonneville and Grand Coulee dams, early New Deal projects that were bringing power to the Northwest, a Cabinet position for that "neglected area." In Seattle, turning to labor issues in a national radio broadcast, he castigated the New Deal "system of overlapping agencies and conflicting regulations," which left labor's rights "subject to political favoritism." There would be, in a Dewey administration, "no backdoor entrance to special privilege." Helpfully, on the labor front he had a voluble new ally in John L. Lewis, head of the United Mine Workers, and long a Roosevelt enemy, whose UMW adopted a resolution attacking "the fiat of governmental agencies." While lauding Dewey, Lewis claimed in his memorable, rumbling bass that the union was not specifically endorsing Republicans.

En route to Portland on the final northern legs of his cross-country campaign, Dewey's special, fortunately at low speed, smashed into a halted train at Castle Rock in Washington, 60 miles to the north. One reporter, Esther Tufty, was rushed to a hospital. In the bedroom of his private car, the governor was shaken and Frances Dewey struck her head, without injury, against a wall. Undaunted, the Dewey party continued on to Portland in rented vehicles, where he asserted to Oregonians that no man, not even FDR, was "indispensable." Afterward Dewey telephoned Miss Tufty's hospital room to inquire about her condition, and in an insensitive and widely quoted failure at a political joke, told her that she wasn't indispensable either.

Quickly refitted, the Republican special took Dewey to San Francisco, where in a speech broadcast from the Civic Auditorium he surprised Republican die-hards by defending government intervention in economic matters. "We are not going back," he declared, "to the days of unregulated business and finance." Still, he added vaguely, having it both ways, "We are not going down the New Deal Road to total control of our daily lives. We are going forward on the better road." In Los Angeles he went even farther down the

New Deal road. In an address from the huge Coliseum, with 93,000 loyalists in the audience, Dewey proposed broadening Social Security—decried by many Republicans since 1935 as Communist, or at least Socialist—to provide pensions for all citizens. "What kind of security is it," he asked, sweepingly, "which leaves all these [ineligible] people unprotected and yet puts the high-salaried officials of large corporations in the system, whether they need it or want it?" His realism bordered on Republican heresy. It was a hugely popular New Deal program.

The fireworks in the Coliseum came less from Dewey's civics-primer speech, which was directed toward a national radio audience of 164 stations than from the local faithful. Brownell deplored it as "rather boring," but the Hollywoodian spectacle was a success. What listeners could hear about but not see, and what brought in the crowds, was the extravaganza produced by Cecil B. De Mille. Movie stars like Cary Grant and Ginger Rogers were introduced. Circus elephants performed "paw stands," as Roosevelt would recall on nationwide radio, turning the big top trick into a partisan gibe. At the Coliseum microphone Dewey was dwarfed beneath a fifty-two-foot De Millean American flag.

Addressing the Hollywood Democrats for Roosevelt at the Ambassador Hotel soon after, Secretary of the Interior Harold Ickes joked that De Mille had left out one item of sure-fire spectacle, for "as I remember it, [he] enhanced his reputation by including in every movie that he made a scene of the heroine taking a bath. Imagine the enthusiasm if De Mille had rolled his candidate onto the platform in a bright and shining tub." One Hollywood personality promoting FDR was Bob Hope. Since 1941 he had made a career trademark of taking his comedy show to the troops at home and abroad. The experience led him to voicing support for the President, which evoked cheers from his service audiences. Yet his popular weekly broadcasts were sponsored by Pepsodent, which reminded him cautiously that "Republicans brush their teeth, too."

Despite the inevitable errors and accidents, Dewey's campaign-by-rail was drawing positive results. A poll published in *Fortune* claimed that Roosevelt's anticipated early lead had dwindled from nine points to five. A servicemen's edition of the *Philadelphia Evening Bulletin* later in the month, covering the governor's return to Albany after his coast-to-coast attacks on the Roosevelt regime's failings, included another Red-baiting Cummings column prefaced by a jingle,

> Clear everything with Sidney,
> And if Sir Sid ain't near,
> Clear everything with Browder,
> Sid's fellow buccaneer.

This time the accompanying "Angelo" cartoon showed a dapper Browder happily leaving the federal prison in Atlanta, as if 1942 were yesterday, remarking, "Franklin is a great guy." It was "unlikely," Cummings wrote, "that in our day we shall see the country restored to the Indians. But there is a chance of it's being turned over to the kind and gentle mercies of Sidney Hillman and Earl Browder." The "soft on Communism" theme would be repeated with variations in seven successive presidential campaigns.

Had Cummings known it, he could have written a follow-up column on FDR and the Red Chinese. The President had sent Patrick J. Hurley, once secretary of war under Herbert Hoover, to China in a nonpartisan attempt to adjudicate relations between the increasingly ineffective and unreliable Chiang Kai-Shek and American general "Vinegar Joe" Stilwell, whose attempts at propping up Chiang were failing. Because Chiang was more interested in attacking Mao Zedong's Communist rivals, who were gaining in South China, than in fighting the Japanese, Hurley also went to see Mao, who seemed to represent China's postwar future. Mao turned out to be more interested in the American election than in Chiang's inevitable collapse. Republicans, he realized, would be more likely than Democrats to pour resources into Chiang's eroding China to stall the outcome. Would Roosevelt win? Hurley didn't know. "We will wait," said Mao. "We have had long training in patience." As long as the Japanese remained in the war, Mao counted on attrition to exhaust them. "We will retreat and retreat across China. But what will Chiang do?"

The jobs issue worsened politically for the administration when General Lewis Hershey, the director of Selective Service, re- marked, on his own, that men in uniform might have to remain on active duty after the war, and be released slowly, to prevent the labor market from being swamped by competition with laid-off

Governor John Bricker of Ohio as vice presidential candidate leaning down from his campaign train's rear platform to shake the hand of a pleased boy. *Ohio Historical Society*

war workers. Dewey alluded to Hershey's boner (without identifying him) in nearly every speech, creating a boon for billboard
advertising in which Republicans charged, "IF YOU WANT TO BRING
THE BOYS HOME SOONER VOTE FOR DEWEY AND BRICKER." In his
syndicated column (*New York Post,* September 15), Samuel Grafton
observed that the "mobilization of discontent" was always one of
the campaign strategies of the "outs." Dewey "stroked . . . the
deepest possible discontent, the longing of wives for their hus-
bands, of parents for their sons, . . . and Mr. Dewey has invited a
discharge of this unavoidable nation-wide unhappiness into the
form of votes for himself."

Otherwise, the governor's foreign policy largely echoed Roosevelt's in accepting the idea—somewhat watered down—of a postwar peacekeeping organization. Robert R. McCormick, still an
isolationist at heart, sent a *Chicago Tribune* reporter, Hal Forest, to
Dewey to suggest that he shouldn't cut his political throat—his
conservative base—by courting voters of an internationalist bent.
"I'm keeping my neck in," Dewey told Forest. "If Dewey is elected,"
McCormick grumbled, "it will be in spite of his campaign."
Stumping the East, John Bricker was assigned to belittle the little-
known candidate of the Missouri compromise of 1944. "Truman?"
Bricker would say to appreciative audiences. "That's his name,
isn't it? I can never remember that name."

Through Maryland, Pennsylvania, Connecticut, Massachusetts
and Maine, Bricker continued to raise, for the committed and the
undecided, the Red herring of an alliance between Communism
and the New Deal. "Subversive forces of class hatred and pressure
politics under the leadership of Sidney Hillman and Earl Browder," he charged, "must be driven from high places in our American political life. Insidious and ominous are the forces of
Communism linked with irreligion that are worming their way into
our national life." Demonizing Hillman by false association with
Browder blurred the reality of Communist subversion. Browder,
from whom leading Democrats stayed clear, was indeed a source,

however minor, for the NKGB spy network based in New York. The FBI had installed wiretaps on every Soviet organization in the United States and knew the code names of many agents, often feeding them false or obsolete material. By August, 386 alleged government documents had reached the NKGB station during 1944, few of them of any significance. J. Edgar Hoover suspected—correctly—that among Soviet informants were Alger Hiss in the State Department, Harry Dexter White at the Treasury and Lauchlin Currie, an aide at the White House.

Before leaving for the Quebec conference with Winston Churchill, FDR had confided to Daisy Suckley disconsolately that he felt "like a boiled owl." He complained of being chronically unwell,

FDR and Eleanor (second from right), with Churchill and Clementine (center) at the Citadel during the second Quebec Conference, September 12, 1944. Canadian PM Mackenzie King is to the far right and Governor General, the Earl of Athlone, with his wife, Princess Alice, are to the far left. *FDR Library*

talked of possibly losing to Dewey, who was running "a very good campaign," and pondered the lifestyle retrenchments he might have to make if no longer in the White House support system. To lead off press accounts, Roosevelt wanted the *Ferdinand Magellan* to arrive in Quebec on September 13, before Churchill's train bringing him from Halifax, where the *Queen Mary*, now converted to a troop transport, was to dock. The President was able to greet the PM with "Well, Winston, welcome to Quebec."

Bigwigs were put up at the Citadel, the Governor General's summer residence and site of the talks, the second Two Power conference in Quebec in two years. Other conferees, including the 150 members of the press, were housed one minute away at the venerable Chateau Frontenac, which was closed to the public during the sessions. The government of Canada took up the tab—but for bar bills—for everyone.

The purpose of the meeting was announced as planning for knockout blows against Japan, but that ultimate response to Pearl Harbor had already been determined in Hawaii as largely an American affair. Politics and prestige more than strategy required involving Britain and its associated nations once Germany was defeated. Britain and the Commonwealth would be assigned to recover Southeast Asia. Overruling Admiral King, Roosevelt offered to have the Royal Navy, although a very minor factor, participate in the strangling of the Japanese home islands. Both the President and General Marshall were unenthusiastic about Churchill's obvious intent to restore restive European colonies in Asia to their prewar status. As they realized, even before the shooting stopped, reality would intervene.

While in Quebec, Churchill asked Admiral McIntire to his rooms in the Citadel. Would the admiral, the PM asked, concerned about Roosevelt's frailty, please tell him, in confidence, the true state of the president's health? Churchill was alarmed. So was the PM's personal physician, Charles Wilson, now Lord Moran, who noted later of Roosevelt, "You could have put your fist between his

FDR and Churchill at the Citadel, Quebec, September 12, 1944. *FDR Library*

neck and his collar—and I said to myself then that men at his time of life do not go thin all of a sudden just for nothing." McIntire offered Churchill the alleged results of "our June checkup." If the President "does not overdo, there is every reason to believe that he can win through." Howard Bruenn had noted to McIntire that Roosevelt's blood pressure was up, especially after he and Churchill had viewed the lengthy *Wilson*, which brought back to the President both good and bad memories. Bruenn increased FDR's dosage of phenobarbital.

The "winning through" remark disturbed Churchill. "With all my heart I hope so," he told McIntire. "We cannot have anything happen to this man. His usefulness to the world is paramount during these troubled times." The PM hoped for a continuing American postwar presence in Europe and did not envision that coming from a party still encumbered by prewar isolationists, however reborn after Pearl Harbor. When asked about the election, the President had confided to Churchill that he was "far from sure of the results." The PM, who would be rejected by his own electorate in mid-1945, thought that a Roosevelt defeat "would be ingratitude itself."

A reporter with Republican sympathies covering Quebec reached Dewey to claim that Roosevelt appeared to be a dying man, and that the governor had "an absolute duty" to bring the state of the President's health into the campaign. Surrogates were already doing so. From the far right, John O'Donnell in his syndicated column "Capitol Stuff" (September 20) raised the issue of the pre-election death of a candidate, noting that the party national committee members from each state "would vote the strength of their respective states" based upon the nominating conventions. "In the event of F.D.R.'s death, for example, the national committeemen from Vermont would have only three votes as against the 47 votes of New York."

Closeted with his advisers, Dewey debated how to handle the issue. Should they seek out damning medical evidence? With little or no investigative reporting on the matter available, Herbert Brownell's publicity director Steve Hanigan prepared an elaborate document proposing that Roosevelt's failing health become an issue demanding full disclosure by the White House. Dewey promised to study the possibilities, and Brownell wrote that not "a single night" went by without a discussion about how to deal with Roosevelt's health. Their charges could backfire. As it was not a winning issue unless proved, the idea was dropped. Steve Hanigan resigned.

FDR had invited the prime minister to visit Hyde Park after Quebec, and they proceeded there in the *Ferdinand Magellan*. On September 17 Roosevelt telephoned Daisy Suckley to report that "much was accomplished" at the conference, but, she told her diary, "he wanted to *sleep* all the time." While Winston busied himself into the morning hours, Clementine Churchill wrote to their daughter, Mary, from Hyde Park that the President "with all his genius does not—indeed cannot (partly because of his health and partly because of his make-up)—function round the clock, like your Father. I should not think that his mind [at Quebec] was pin-pointed on the war for more than four hours a day, which is not really enough when one is a supreme war lord."

When Harry Hopkins came to Hyde Park, Churchill assumed it was "only to please me." Hopkins's role at the White House had diminished. He had been away, and weakened, by severe illness and drastic follow-up surgery. "You must know," he explained, "I am not what I was." He was under a medical death sentence that would finally play out in January 1946. But for two days "it seemed to be like old times." Churchill thought, later, that Hopkins's "greatness of spirit [had] broke[n] under his variegated activities" for Roosevelt, yet despite increasingly failing health, Hopkins would undertake more missions for the White House, even to Moscow, and Stalin.*

Privy to both men's relations with Stalin, Hopkins was probably present on September 19 when Roosevelt and Churchill agreed in a secret memorandum to exclude the Russians from access to the ongoing development of an atomic bomb. Because Danish physicist Niels Bohr, long at work on the bomb, had quietly urged that Roosevelt and Churchill negotiate with Stalin on international control of atomic energy before the Russians achieved their inevitable nuclear successes, the President and the PM nervously included the proviso, "Enquiries should be made regarding the activities of Professor Bohr and steps should be taken to ensure that he is responsible for no leakage of information, particularly to the Russians." Soviet spies, however, had already penetrated the "Manhattan Project"—and an FBI watch on the impeccably loyal Bohr would be useless.

For one afternoon the President and Eleanor invited the Duke of Windsor to lunch, as his duchess had been undergoing medical treatment in New York, where they kept, in addition to their home in the Bahamas, Suite 28A in the Waldorf Astoria. Roosevelt, who

---

* Churchill published his reminiscence as if it were post-Quebec in August 1943. When corrected, he published it again, not acknowledging his error, this time as September 1944.

had little regard for the ex-king but felt sorry for him, knew that Churchill in 1936 had championed the former Edward VIII. The press publicity of having the prime minister and royalty of a sort as his house guests was politically useful. Americans had rejected a king in 1776 yet continued to have an insatiable appetite for royals. Churchill, however, with his late-to-bed and late-to-rise habits, and his endless capacity for brandy and cigars, taxed the stamina of any host, especially that of the obviously frail president. Happily, the PM and his party left Hyde Park early on the evening of September 19, to board the *Queen Mary* at anchor in Manhattan, with 9,000 American troop replacements already below. Exhausted, Roosevelt went to bed and slept for twelve hours.

As Dewey's campaign train turned eastward, and FDR returned to the White House, Sam Rosenman was called for consultations with the President. He found FDR in his bedroom, and in his underwear. He was leaning on the arm of Admiral McIntire and, despite the experience of Bremerton, trying to re-learn walking in his heavy steel braces. As he tottered in the ill-fitting leather harness holding up the old braces, while leaning on McIntire, he vowed to Rosenman, "I am going to walk again." He meant the appearance of walking, at the upcoming Teamsters dinner, and if necessary, standing before crowds at the rear platform of the *Ferdinand Magellan*.

The exercise failed. "I just can't stand up and make that speech," he confessed to Daisy Suckley. Harry Hopkins observed that there was no reason for him to speak standing up. Still, he appeared in good form at the White House for his 969th press and radio conference, on the morning of September 22, when a reporter asked him to comment on Governor Dewey's charge that under Roosevelt's administrations America had slipped "past its prime."

Disagreeing sharply, the President asked his questioner, "*You* think so?"

"No, Sir," the newsman said sheepishly.

Returning that day from a two-day trip escorting Arthur Hays Sulzberger, publisher of *The New York Times* since 1935, and his wife Iphigene, daughter of Adolph Ochs, Sulzberger's predecessor, through TVA installations in the Tennessee Valley, David Lilienthal thought FDR was making progress in converting attitudes resistant to change. *The Times* remained "out of sorts with the President on domestic issues," Lilienthal noted in his diary, but as Mrs. Sulzberger explained, "We can survive another four years of bad management on the home front but we can't survive another war." *The Times* would concede editorially late in the campaign that Governor Dewey was weak on international issues, and the war, and come out "reluctantly" for a fourth term.

On Saturday evening, September 23, Roosevelt, in black tie and dinner jacket, was wheeled into the Presidential Room of the Statler Hotel in Washington from behind draperies which opened onto the table for bigwigs on the platform. Screened by Secret Service men who then discreetly vanished, he was lifted, rather than walked, into his seat near the dais. Another Bremerton would have been a catastrophe. When the crowd of about a thousand, 700 of them Teamster union members, saw him behind the array of microphones and roared its greetings, the President clasped both hands and raised them in acknowledgment.

Flanking him were Teamster president Daniel Tobin and AFL president William Green. At a table near that of Henry Kaiser, whose bald dome gleamed in the bright lights, Anna Roosevelt Boettiger sat with Sam Rosenman. She remembered Bremerton, and what she knew of San Diego. "Do you think Pa will put it over?" she asked. "If the delivery isn't just right, it will be an awful flop." The radio networks expected to go on the air at 9:30.

The President toyed with the contents of his dinner plate, preferring to work further, with a fountain pen, on the draft of his speech, cutting several paragraphs. On the half-hour, Tobin introduced him with a metaphorical union label as "a great world leader of courage, experience, and real statesmanship, whom a band of avaricious manipulators of wealth" would replace with someone lacking all of Roosevelt's qualities.

As diners erupted in applause, Roosevelt reassembled his sheaf of papers, looked over the top of his reading glasses at the audience, and flashed his signature grin. The room went silent as his political adrenalin kicked in. "Well," he began, "here we are together again—after four years—and what years they have been. You know, I am actually four years older, which is a fact that seems to annoy some people." He mentioned no names, and throughout the campaign he would never refer to Governor Dewey or Governor Bricker. "In fact," he went on, " . . . there are millions of Americans who are more than eleven years older than when we started to clean up the mess that was dumped in our laps in 1933." His mellifluous voice was in working order, as it had not been aboard the *Cummings*. Diners cheered and pounded their tables, setting knives, forks and spoons bouncing.

"We all know," he went on in a mocking tone, "that certain people who make it a practice to deprecate the accomplishments of labor—who even attack labor as unpatriotic—keep this up usually for three years and six months in a row. But then, for some strange reason, they change their tune—every four years—just before election day. When votes are at stake, they suddenly discover that they love labor and they are anxious to protect labor from its old friends. I got quite a laugh, for example—and I'm sure that you did—when I read this plank in the Republican platform adopted at their national convention in Chicago last July." As he quoted from it he swung his head from side to side to emphasize the absurdity of the predictably quadrennial turnabout. The Republican Party, he read, accepted all the recent federal statutes that promoted the welfare of working people. Yet, said the President, Republicans "have personally spent years of effort and energy—and much money—in fighting every one of those laws in the Congress, and in the press, and in the courts."

The attempt to "switch labels," he asserted, would not work. "The object is to persuade the American people that the Democratic Party was responsible for the 1929 crash and the depression, and that the Republican Party was responsible for all social progress under the New Deal. Now, imitation may be the sincerest form of flattery—but I am afraid that in this case it is the most obvious common or garden variety of fraud. . . . No performing elephant could turn a handspring without falling flat on its back." Applause and cheers cascaded across the hall.

He went on to note the record of labor in building weapons, ships, and planes, mentioning that a champion of war industry, Henry Kaiser, "is here tonight"—and castigated the rival party for headlining strikes, which "since Pearl Harbor [have cost] only one tenth of one percent of man hours." Most working people, he continued, remember "what things were like in 1932, . . . the blank despair of a whole nation. . . .You remember the long, hard road, with its gains and setbacks, which we have traveled together ever since those days."

Turning again to alleged Republican falsifications of the record, such as blaming his administration for the Depression, he noted the adage about "never speak[ing] of rope in the house of a man who has been hanged," and ridiculed small and large campaign lies, including charges about postponing demobilization. Then he added a personal thrust which he had written into the draft text as "just a happy thought," and, via Grace Tully, sent to Sam Rosenman and Robert Sherwood from Quebec. "These Republican leaders have not been content with attacks on me, or my wife, or on my sons," he noted in mock sorrow. "No, not content with that, they now include my little dog Fala." The audience did not wait for the punch line before beginning to roar.

Well, of course, I don't resent attacks, and my family doesn't resent attacks, but Fala does resent them. You know, Fala is Scotch, and being a Scottie, as soon as he learned that the Republican fiction writers, in Congress and out, had concocted a story that I had left him behind on the Aleutian Islands and had sent a destroyer back to find him—at a cost to taxpayers of two or three, or eight or twenty million dollars—his Scotch soul was furious. He has not been the same dog since.

The cheering was so sustained that it took some time before the President could continue. "I am accustomed to hearing malicious falsehoods about myself, such as that worm-eaten chestnut that I have represented myself as indispensable," he conceded. "But I think I have a right to resent, to object to, libelous statements about my dog."

Several years later, Robert Sherwood recalled, "Whenever the Hearst-Patterson-McCormick Press referred to my activity as a

FDR at the microphone (center) addressing the Teamsters Union dinner at the Hotel Statler, September 23, 1944, and referring to Republican attacks on his dog, Fala. William Green is to his right, Daniel Tobin to his left. *FDR Library*

'ghost writer,' they always spoke of my background as a Broadway playwright and the one play invariably identified with my name was 'Idiot's Delight.' It was often suggested that my function in the White House was to stud the President's speeches with wisecracks. . . . I was generally given credit for the famous reference to Fala—and I should be able to claim this credit, but I had never even heard of the rumored episode in the Aleutian Islands until I read the paragraph."

There was more from the familiar, fighting FDR, now triumphantly resurrected, but radio listeners nationwide, and diners at the Statler, remembered little of what followed about finishing the war, reconverting the economy, and assuring a continuing peace. Roosevelt seemed in his old form, and newspapers on Sunday, however Republican, made Fala page one. Leaving the ballroom, Richard L. Strout saw one of the last of the "brotherhood" lingering at the table "battering a tablespoon against a silver-plated cake-holder in an ecstasy of enjoyment."

Reporters with Governor Dewey's campaign train from California into New Mexico and on toward Oklahoma City listened to FDR's address in the candidate's new lounge car for newsmen, and asked James Hagerty, Dewey's press secretary, whether there would be a rebuttal for Monday-morning papers across the country. Of the sixty-three in the group, a dozen had covered the President's previous campaigns, and all had covered Roosevelt at one time or another. According to *The Times*, "Some said they had never heard him make a better political speech." After one further stop they discovered that hecklers at the station, perhaps radio listeners ("the Roosevelt underground," one joked), had pasted red, white and blue FDR stickers to the train windows. According to *TIME*, hardly a supporter of the President, "even the stoniest of Republican faces around U.S. radios [had] cracked into a smile. . . . The Champ had swung a full roundhouse blow. And it was plain to the newsmen on the Dewey Special that the challenger had been hit

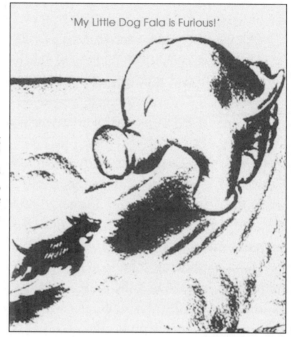

"My Little Dog Fala is Furious!"

"My Little Dog Fala is Furious!" Tom Little's cartoon in the October 2, 1944, *Nashville Tennessean*.

hard—as plain as when a boxer drops his gloves and his eyes glaze." Tom Little in the *Nashville Tennesseean* (October 2) cartooned a small black Scottie chasing a ponderous Republican elephant, seen only from his rear end, down a dusty road.

Dewey called the speech "snide" and ratcheted up his attacks for Oklahoma City's Municipal Auditorium. Jim Hagerty hastily stenciled a statement for distribution: "Roosevelt has dropped the mask of a non-political campaign . . . , designed that speech to make me angry, and he has. The result is that I will now campaign all the harder." Letting loose, Dewey told Oklahomans, and listeners elsewhere on radio,

> Let's get this straight. The man who wants to be President of the United States for sixteen years is, indeed, indispensable. He is indispensable to Harry Hopkins, to Madame Perkins, to Harold

Ickes, . . . to America's leading enemy of civil liberties—the mayor
of Jersey City. He's indispensable to those infamous machines in
Chicago, in the Bronx, and all the others. He's indispensable to Sidney Hillman and the [CIO's] Political Action Committee; he's indispensable to Earl Browder, the ex-convict and Communist leader.
Shall we, the American people, perpetuate one man in office for
sixteen years? Shall we do that to accommodate this motley crew?

Countering Dewey's indictment of ageing New Dealers, city
bosses and labor leaders, and supporters whom Democrats did not
want, Roosevelt would continue to go after isolationists, the business elite, and the radical Right, and wring political juice out of
such obvious partisan nonsense as the Fala accusation. Eric Godal
in *PM* would portray a hooded muse of History, quill pen in hand,
noting in a large ledger the qualifications for the presidency of the
candidates. Dewey was cited as "well groomed" and a friend of
publishers "McCormick, Patterson, Hearst, [and] Gannett."
Added after them was isolationist Gerald Nye. The bottom line for
Dewey was "kind to big dogs." Roosevelt's list included "winning

"I Will Never Divide America!" by Eric Godal, satirizing Dewey,
in *PM*, New York, September 28, 1944.

"Thanks, Frank, But He Had a Book" by Harold M. Talburt in the New York *World-Telegram*, September 28, 1944.

war in Europe and Asia, Social Security, Creation of Jobs, Selective Service, Lend-Lease," and "World Organization to Secure Peace." The bottom line was "kind to little dogs."

Perhaps not understanding what dogs do, Clare Luce would offer the press her nonsense that her cocker spaniel, Mr. Speaker, could lick Fala. Leaving the Statler with Anna Boettiger after the Teamsters dinner, Sam Rosenman, who had been a writer for FDR for seventeen years, chortled, "I think it's the finest speech he ever made." Journalists began joking that the campaign had become a contest between a big man with a little dog and a little man with a big dog. (Dewey had a 125-pound Great Dane named more symbolically than he realized, Canute.) New Dealer Paul Porter, director of publicity for the Democrats, would tell Rosenman that the election had become a contest between "Roosevelt's dog and Dewey's goat." Roosevelt was back.

Six

Misremembering Pearl Harbor

"How can you challenge a will-of-the-wisp?" Governor Dewey wondered to Colonel McCormick, the *Chicago Tribune*'s obsessively anti-British and isolationist publisher. McCormick wanted the Republican nominee to challenge Roosevelt to a public debate, where Dewey's precision-tool platform tactics might embarrass a weakening president. "Roosevelt won't debate anything with anybody," Dewey responded, "and [he] will laugh at the proposal from his positions at Pearl Harbor, Guadalcanal, or the White Cliffs of Dover." Yet Dewey would soon try to turn Pearl Harbor from a national rallying cry into a political embarrassment for the President, about which his silence would seem an admission of guilt.

Walter Trohan, McCormick's veteran sleuth in Washington, had kept passing on to the publisher both rumor and reality about Roosevelt's poor chances of survival into a fourth term. On August 6 under Trohan's byline, the *Tribune* had broken the story "Heart

Specialist Is with Roosevelt," identifying Lieutenant. Commander.
Bruenn as a "New York City" rather than a Navy physician. (Later,
after whispers about Lahey, the indefatigable Trohan would mis-
place Bruenn in Boston.) Almost every Dewey speech included
lines that a vote for FDR would make Harry Truman, an untalented
tool of party bosses, president. Trohan even reported to Dewey, via
an intermediary, a rumor that the President's press secretary, Steve
Early, was so worried about his own professional future that he was
making discreet inquiries about a post-election job.

Long before that, Trohan and his colleagues had concocted
front-page stories to infuriate the White House and delight the
cranky McCormick. In mid-1941 the War Department under
General George C. Marshall had summoned a promising young
major on the promotion list, Albert C. Wedemeyer, to coordinate
the contingency planning of a "Hitler first" strategy of engaging
Germany in Europe before the Nazis could redeploy forces from
newly invaded Russia, which seemed barely hanging on, and
wring defeatist concessions from isolated Britain and an unprepared United States. Three days before Pearl Harbor, on December 4, 1941, the super-secret Wedemeyer document made the
Tribune's front page. Leaked to isolationist senator Burton K.
Wheeler of Montana by an Army colonel he would never identify,
it was offered via the *Tribune's* Chesley Manly to Colonel Mc-
Cormick. The banner headline "F.D.R.'S WAR PLANS" and the
revelation of projections for a ten-million-man army to retrieve
Europe confirmed to the conspiracy-minded that Roosevelt was
planning war while talking peace.

That Britain could not survive without direct American involvement had long been obvious. Since the 1920s the United States had
regularly created and revised contingency strategies for a range of
theoretical enemies, including a "Rainbow" series reflecting threats
from Japan. On assignment, Wedemeyer had studied at the German
war college in Berlin under a Hitler favorite, General Alfred Jodl, and
was friendly with outspoken isolationist hero Charles Lindbergh,

whom he had met and traveled with in Germany. Wedemeyer was an admirer of pre-war German military expertise, as was his father-in-law, Major General Stanley Embick, a former deputy chief of staff. When the "Victory Plan" was funneled by Senator Wheeler to the *Tribune* and its sister newspaper, the *Washington Times-Herald,* which charged the President with having created "a blueprint for total war," suspicion fell on Wedemeyer.

Investigating, the FBI found in his office safe a copy of the plan with passages underlined in red that had appeared in the hostile newspaper account. His underlining, Wedemeyer claimed, had been to compare his text with the press version. No one was ever charged with supplying the document to Wheeler, who had been a vocal opponent of American mobilization, acidly likening the Lend-Lease Act of March 1941, which helped rearm Britain, to New Deal farm subsidy legislation in that it would "plow under every fourth American boy." Marshall believed utterly in the loyalty of his staff and had Wedemeyer, whose personal views then were isolationist and who became increasingly conservative in politics, carry on. He would rise to four-star high command during the war, but Marshall would never assign Wedemeyer to any position confronting Germany.

The issues raised by the leak faded quickly with the raids on Pearl Harbor on December 7 and attacks on the Philippines a few hours later. New charges soon arose from the usual anti-FDR camp that Roosevelt had abetted the strikes to goad the Japanese into war by hostile economic provocations and by limitations on American preparedness in the Pacific. For the Republican opposition in Congress, an influential portion of it outspokenly isolationist until war came, Pearl Harbor was always yesterday. As presidential electioneering heated up in 1944, yet another congressional inquiry into the catastrophe was convened—"largely political," Secretary of War Henry Stimson, once Republican secretary of state under Hoover, thought, in "trying to embarrass the President." Major General Leonard Gerow, on Marshall's staff at the time of Pearl Harbor, was even recalled from his command in France to testify.

Colonel McCormick encouraged scoops likely to embarrass Roosevelt. His reporting teams, recognizing their own self-interest, fed his obsession. Attacks on the President appeared almost daily. Trohan, later *Tribune* bureau chief in Washington, thought later that the onslaught resulted from the President's miscalculation. McCormick had been a colonel in France in 1918 and ever after loved to be identified by his military rank. All that FDR had to do, Trohan mused, was to make the publisher a temporary wartime major general, as some influential industrialists had been named, and send him on bland inspection missions. But FDR had put McCormick in the White House's nethermost outcast category with Henry Ford and Charles Lindbergh, and co-opting the publisher was unthinkable.

The result in mid-1942 had been an alarming Battle of Midway headline story in the *Tribune*, the *Washington Times-Herald,* and New York *Daily News*, all anti-Roosevelt papers cut from the same McCormick family cloth: "NAVY HAD WORD OF JAP PLAN TO STRIKE AT SEA."

The story credited foreknowledge of enemy movements, obviously from code-breaking, to "reliable sources in . . . naval intelligence." The Navy knew also, it went on, that a Japanese thrust toward another "American base" (Dutch Harbor in the Aleutians went unidentified) was only a feint. Commander Arthur McCollum, who directed the Far East section of Naval Intelligence in Washington, discovered the front-page stories on June 7 as he came to work. The battles off Midway Island in the central Pacific, which badly miscarried for the Japanese, had unfolded on June 4 and continued into June 6. Comparing his intelligence advance from Admiral Nimitz in Pearl Harbor to the specifics of the press scoop, McCollum was amazed at the accuracy of the story, as was Navy chief Admiral Ernest J. King.

Assuming that the enemy now knew that its admiralty code had been tapped into, King initiated legal proceedings against the *Tribune*.

While McCormick, who had arrogantly published secret government documents before, kept the matter on his front pages as a
"Get the *Tribune* Offensive," the Navy discovered that the *Tribune's*
chief nautical correspondent, Stanley Johnston, had been on the aircraft carrier *Lexington* and then was evacuated to a transport when
the carrier sank in the Coral Sea battle in early May. While on the
Barnett, in an inadvertent security breach, he learned of enemy signals that had been decoded and picked up aboard. On debarking he
filed a story which had cleared the obtuse censorship twice, in San
Diego and Washington, on narrow technical grounds—because
only Japanese warships were mentioned, code-breaking was only
implied, and no American movements were revealed. Picking up on
the story, columnist Walter Winchell guessed explicitly "that the
U.S. Navy decoded the Japs' secret messages." When, after all the
public fuss, the Japanese did not change their JN-25 code, which
they had modified on May 27, just before Midway, the Navy quietly
dropped the proceedings.

JN-25 was decrypted only after the war began, but once the 1944
campaign heated up Governor Dewey was leaked the misinforma-
tion that military code breakers knew before Pearl Harbor that a Japanese strike force was headed for Hawaii, and that government
denials were untrue. Secretary of the Navy James V. Forrestal, who
had succeeded Frank Knox earlier in the year, alerted Roosevelt in a
longhand message to evade office scrutiny, on September 14. (The
President, who did not need any further complications in his agenda,
had just arrived in Quebec to confer with Churchill.) "My Dear Mr.
President," Forrestal began, "Information has come to me that
Dewey's first"—possibly a misreading in the source for *next*—
"speech will deal with Pearl Harbor." Forrestal went on to explain
that he had learned that an unidentified Army officer with access to
the enemy codes had leaked to Dewey's campaign staff that Japanese
signals identifying Pearl Harbor as a target had been known by Roosevelt and the military chiefs before December 7, 1941. A Jerry
Costello cartoon in the *Tribune* showed the Democratic donkey

sitting anxiously on a locked trunk labeled "THE TRUTH ABOUT PEARL HARBOR."

That a Japanese code had been decrypted before the war was true;. however, it was a diplomatic code and not a military break-through. Pearl Harbor had not appeared in the prewar decrypts. While it was a surprise that distant Oahu had been targeted, and that the attack came on a sleepy Sunday morning, harbor defenses should not have been unprepared at any time. Washington blamed, and relieved, the top commanders in Hawaii, Vice Admiral Husband E. Kimmel and Major General Walter C. Short, for inattention to their responsibilities. A committee of inquiry chaired by Supreme Court Justice Owen Roberts upheld the findings.

Decrypts of the radioed messages in code and readings (in some cases) in clear, often overwhelming in volume, suggested that the Japanese were moving large forces, including troop transports and carriers, into striking positions, presumably on the Pacific rim, toward Malaya, Singapore and the Philippines. The Japanese government had already printed and disbursed to appropriate points occupation currency for Malaya, the Dutch East Indies and the Philippines. According to coded messages that were being intercepted by American military intelligence, high-level negotiations between American and Japanese diplomats in Washington, which had gone nowhere, were about to be broken off. Unknown to the code-breakers, *Kido Butai* (strike force), under radio silence, was approaching the planned area for launching its warplanes.

On the basis of what General Marshall interpreted from the signals traffic, he had radioed, on November 27, 1941, an alert to all Pacific stations, including Hawaii, that negotiations "appear to be terminated. . . . Japanese future action unpredictable but hostile action possible at any moment. . . . Prior to hostile Japanese action you are directed to undertake such reconnaissance and other measures as you deem necessary." The Navy sent similar radiograms, beginning, "This dispatch is to be considered a war warning. . . . An aggressive move by Japan is expected within the next few days." *War warning* seemed unambiguous, but little was done. Not one of the 239 messages intercepted from Tokyo and decrypted in the six months before December 7 had mentioned Pearl Harbor. War might come elsewhere. Short and Kimmel even planned to play golf at eight that Sunday morning—a date and time rendered impossible by Japanese carrier aircraft five minutes earlier.

As the new Pearl Harbor boards of inquiry were working on drafts still withheld from the press, the *Tribune*'s Walter Trohan was leaked sensitive material by Dewey-supporting members of Congress privy to the revived investigation. Some congressmen even aired in the House and Senate what they hoped would be compromising questions. Hugh Scott, a Pennsylvania Republican, asked why the fleet on the West Coast was dispatched to distant Hawaii in the first place, and why the President hadn't personally met with the Japanese prime minister as a last resort. Unaware that an enemy force was nearing Hawaii late on December 6, 1941, the President had indeed urgently cabled Emperor Hirohito, but the message was withheld in Tokyo until after the attack had taken place. While campaigning, John Bricker accused Roosevelt of covering up "the disgraceful Pearl Harbor episode." In the Senate, Styles Bridges of New Hampshire announced that Dewey was "gathering facts" to expose a presidential whitewash.

A campaign researcher for Dewey, John Burton, had been collecting compromising data from congressional, military and journalistic leaks, as had Elliott V. Bell, a key Dewey deputy with a *New York Times* background. General Marshall recalled to an interviewer thirteen years later, "How this code business leaked out I don't know, but always somebody talks. . . . Pa Watson [Roosevelt's appointments secretary, and a major general] at one time was taking the translations of the code sent to the President and putting them in his [own] waste basket*. . . . You know that a secret only holds with two people; after that it becomes public property."

Dewey himself, at Oklahoma City on September 25, slashed back at Roosevelt's "Fala" speech as "mud-slinging, ridicule and wisecracks," deflecting charges of unpreparedness and negligence at Pearl Harbor. American military weakness until 1940 allegedly stemmed from "a Roosevelt depression." He quoted General Marshall in congressional testimony in 1940 that the army was "only 25% ready," and his aviation deputy H. H. Arnold as saying that "December 7, 1941 found the Army Air Forces with plans but not planes." He quoted Harry Truman as confessing, "After Pearl Harbor we found ourselves woefully unprepared for war." Cries of

"Another Sitting Duck" ["The Truth about Pearl Harbor"] by Jerry Costello in the *Brooklyn Eagle,* October 1, 1944.

---

* Colonel Rufus S. Bratton, a cryptanalyst, had discovered that carelessness in July 1941.

"Pour it on" came from the crowd of 7,000. Yet no one there seemed to recall that Republican and isolationist Democratic votes to support a military build-up were nonexistent in the 1930s, as were Depression-era funds, and that as late as mid-1941 General Marshall had to plead with Congress to continue conscription, succeeding in the House by only one vote.

When Marshall learned that Dewey was "gathering facts" to make Pearl Harbor itself a campaign issue, "to prove that [Roosevelt] allowed the war to develop with his knowledge or with his assistance," the general deliberately bypassed the President, and dispatched Colonel Carter C. Clarke to Oklahoma on the afternoon following Dewey's speech. Dewey had another date in conservative Tulsa, where an audience of twenty thousand had assembled at the depot to cheer him, and a full house for his rousing charge about the "motley crew" of bureaucrats "who have fattened themselves on your pocketbook and mine for twelve years." He would be interrupted by applause thirty-eight times.

Clarke was Marshall's director of the War Department's cryptographic intelligence office. Attempting to keep Pearl Harbor out of electoral politics, and to keep the Japanese from altering any codes the United States had cracked, Marshall resorted, he recalled, to "a communication direct from me to Governor Dewey with a frank statement of the situation and assurances that the President and the Cabinet were unaware of my action. To guard against accidental disclosure of the information given Governor Dewey by letter, he was requested not to read the letter unless he would bind himself to secrecy [about its contents]."

What Marshall was reluctant to tell Dewey without guarantees, as the information was super-secret, was that military intelligence was still intercepting the coded radiograms to Tokyo of Ambassador Hiroshi Oshima, a general who had been Japan's eyes and ears in Berlin since the beginning of the war. Baron Oshima, although a braggart in his confidences to Tokyo, did have easy access to Hitler and his circle. Marshall worried that the conduct of both the European and Pacific wars would be severely compromised if Oshima in Germany and his sources in Japan were silenced by campaign allegations about cracking the diplomatic code that the ambassador still employed.

Japanese obtuseness about their codes was remarkable. Before Pearl Harbor, a State Department printing room employee in the pay of the German embassy enabled Hans Thomsen to cable Berlin, "As communicated to me by an absolutely reliable source, the State Department is in possession of the key of the Japanese coding system and is, therefore, able to decipher telegrams from Tokyo to Ambassador Nomura." Learning of it, Nomura reported to Tokyo, "I have discovered that the United States is reading some of our codes though I do not know which ones." Astonishingly, the Japanese chose to believe that their most crucial ciphers were too difficult to penetrate and continued to send diplomatic traffic in their usual "Purple."

A copy of the letter about code breaking which Clarke was to fly down to Tulsa was rushed to Admiral King with an added memorandum:

> *Attached is the draft of a letter which I feel it advisable to send to Governor Dewey. It may be that you do not care to be involved in the matter and, if so, I can strike out the reference to you. In any event I would like your opinion.*
>
> *A recent speech in Congress had deadly indications and I now understand much more is to be said, possibly by Governor Dewey himself. This letter of course puts him on the spot, and I have to do it but see no other way of avoiding what might well be a [military] catastrophe for us.*
>
> *Just what he can do in the matter without [my] giving reasons I do not know, but at least he will understand what a deadly affair it really is. I had in the back of my mind the possibility, without telling him, that if he responds favorably I would secretly, here in my office,*

tell Republican floor leader [Representative Joseph] Martin the dan-*
gers of the business so that he, on the Washington side of the fence,
would understand something of Governor Dewey's attitude, without
being informed that Governor Dewey had the same facts in his pos-
session that I was giving Martin.

The whole thing is loaded with dynamite but I very much feel
that something has to be done or the fat will be in the fire to our great
loss in the Pacific, and possibly also in Europe.

G C Marshall

With King's quick approval, as the Pacific was the Navy's lake,
Marshall dispatched Clarke, in civilian garb, with the three-page
letter marked TOP SECRET. Gaining access to Dewey, Clarke
handed him the letter, which the governor immediately turned
back, refusing to make any "blind commitments." Before dismissing Clarke, Dewey demanded the colonel's word of honor that he
had indeed been sent by the chief of staff on his own. "Marshall
does not do things like that," Dewey told Clarke. "I am confident
that Franklin Roosevelt is behind the whole thing." Dewey already
knew from his sources, he said, that American military intelligence
had been decoding "certain Jap codes before Pearl Harbor and that
at least two of them are still in current use." Roosevelt, he charged,
as Clarke stood impassively, "knows about it too. He knew what
was happening before Pearl Harbor, and instead of being re-
elected he ought to be impeached."

More ignorant than Dewey realized about Japanese codes
overconfidently in use then and since, he also demanded, "Why
in hell haven't they changed them, especially after what happened
at Midway and the Coral Sea?"* He wasn't through, as a candi-

---

* Martin, a prewar isolationist, voted against rearmament until Pearl Harbor. Roosevelt despised him.

date, he insisted, with "the whole Pearl Harbor mess"—but on his return to Albany he would be willing to see Marshall himself, or the chief of staff's designee. Marshall, Dewey understood, despite his outburst, was utterly neutral politically, as were many career officers. Marshall had never voted, nor even registered to vote. The chief of staff would not have run any candidate's errands, even those of the President.

Despite his bluster, Dewey was clearly shaken, or he would have left the issue where it was, and proceeded in his prosecutorial manner to rake up what he thought he knew about pre–Pearl Harbor code breaking. He would soon encounter Clarke again. The colonel flew back to Washington, consulted Marshall, and returned to Albany with a revised letter on September 27. Its tenor was unchanged. For political purposes, Marshall charged, Dewey proposed gifting crucial military information to the enemy.

The governor had returned from his lengthy railway campaign, which appeared, from a poll of forty-eight newsmen on the train, to be going well. After Tulsa, five thousand well-wishers had greeted him, at midnight, in Springfield, Missouri, to cheer his attacks on the "long-haired braintrusters . . . who sit in ivory towers in Washington and think they know how the American people want to live." His administration would write laws "so that men will not be afraid to move in fear that you may be violating section 3, of subdivision 2, of paragraph 8, line 5 of a Washington directive."

Clarke found Dewey at the executive mansion with Elliott Bell. The governor insisted that Bell remain, and that the new letter be kept for his personal files. Clarke felt that he should ask Mar-

---

* The Japanese had modified the admiralty code, JN-25, just before Midway, and assumed they had done enough to secure it, but working feverishly, the Navy broke the new version. The "Purple" diplomatic cipher (J-19) read by the "Enigma" machine remained valid. The decrypts were known as "Magic." Traffic analysts had a more difficult task with a multiplicity of Japanese army codes, which were complicated by the Japanese language itself.

shall's permission about both matters, but hesitated, concerned about revealing, on an insecure line, the exchange with Dewey. The colonel also worried that the reception room might be bugged. Dewey assured him that it wasn't and offered to call Marshall himself—which he did. With conditions met, Dewey read the long letter aloud to Bell.

My dear Governor:

Colonel Clarke, my messenger to you of yesterday, September 26, has reported the result of his delivery of my letter dated September 25th. As I understand him, you (a) were unwilling to commit yourself to any agreement regarding "not communicating its contents to any other person" in view of the fact that you felt you already knew certain of the things probably referred to in the letter, as suggested to you by the word "cryptograph," and (b) you would not feel that such a letter as this to a presidential candidate could have been addressed to you by an officer in my position without the knowledge of the President.

As to (a) above I am quite willing to have you read what comes hereafter with the understanding that you are bound not to communicate to any other person any portions on which you do not now have or later receive factual knowledge from some other source than myself. As to (b) above you have my word that neither the Secretary of War nor the President has any intimation whatsoever that such a letter has been addressed to you. . . . I assure you that the only persons who saw or know of the existence of this letter or my letter to you dated September 25th are Admiral King, seven key officers responsible for the security of military communications, and my secretary who typed these letters. . . . I am persisting in the matter because the military hazards involved are so serious that I feel some action is necessary to protect the interests of our armed forces.

After explaining that he would have talked to the governor personally, but that might have triggered leaks and speculation in the press, Marshall went on in his message to point out explicitly that at the time of Pearl Harbor, American intelligence had intercepted only

> *Japanese diplomatic communications. Over a period of years our cryptograph people analyzed the character of the machine the Japanese were using for encoding their diplomatic messages. . . . A corresponding machine was built which deciphers these messages. Therefore we possessed a wealth of information regarding their moves in the Pacific, which in turn was furnished to the State Department . . . but which unfortunately made no reference whatever to intentions towards Hawaii until the last message before December 7th, which did not reach our hands until the following day, December 8th.*

Marshall did not divulge—and Colonel Clarke very likely did not know—that Pearl Harbor did emerge in unrelated prewar reports, none of them, to the government's later embarrassment, ever taken seriously. Ambassador Joseph Grew had informed Washington that someone at the Peruvian embassy in Tokyo had overheard talk of plans to attack Pearl Harbor. To American intelligence specialists it seemed only sake-fueled brag in an unpromising venue. In his diary, Grew had written, confidently, "I guess the boys in Hawaii are not precisely asleep." Later, the FBI had tapped a telephone conversation between the Japanese consulate in Honolulu and an inquirer in Tokyo asking about the exact docking locations of warships in Pearl Harbor, but the cross-Pacific distances between the Home Islands and Hawaii made any thinking about a strike force sailing such routes unobserved for a surprise attack seem far-fetched. Sabotage seemed more likely. That naval intelligence listening in to signals from Japanese carriers in the Home Fleet had lost contact suggested only that their destination under radio silence was Southeast Asia, long under threat. Further, a war warning to all Pacific stations was transmitted and in effect. Theoretically—but not in fact—round-the-clock sea and air reconnaissance, and radar observation, were ongoing.

What Dewey would have done with that litany of actual ineptitude, if anything, is unknown. His attention had been drawn to a broken enemy code. Marshall confided to Dewey that cracking the "Purple" diplomatic code soon assisted in wartime decrypts of other codes, which led to knowledge of enemy movements in the Coral Sea and toward Midway, and the sailing dates and directions of convoys. "Now the point of the present dilemma," Marshall's letter continued, "is that we have gone ahead with this business of deciphering their codes until we possess other [revised] codes, German as well as Japanese, but our main basis of information regarding Hitler's intentions in Europe is obtained from Baron Oshima's messages from Berlin reporting his interviews with Hitler and other officials to the Japanese Government. These are still in the code involved in the Pearl Harbor events." Exposing the crucial intercepts of Baron Oshima's communications, would create "utterly tragic consequences." The "present political debates regarding Pearl Harbor could be a gift "to the enemy, German or Jap," if they evoked "any suspicion of the vital sources of information we possess."

Elliott Bell contended that tens of thousands of people had long understood that the United States had broken the Japanese codes. Hadn't the *Chicago Tribune* carried that story after Midway?

"Well, I'll be damned if I believe the Japs are still using these two codes," Dewey insisted, backing up Bell. Besides, the governor claimed he could name "at least twelve Senators . . . that know all there is to be known about Pearl Harbor." Bell joined in, describing a Washington dinner party at which a Navy commander bragged to guests about how the deciphered codes forced the Japanese to alter warship movements—almost certainly fantasy inspired by alcohol. Cracking the naval traffic (JN-25) had actually led to the ambush, in April 1943, near Bougainville in the South Pacific, of the flight of

Admiral Isoroku Yamamoto, planner of the strike on Pearl Harbor. Clarke assured Dewey and Bell that the Japanese were still using the compromised codes and that thousands of cryptanalysts were employed around the clock, on both sides of the Atlantic, reading enemy cipher traffic. "What in hell," Dewey now demanded, visualizing the two-hemisphere war as separate entities, "do Jap codes have to do with Eisenhower?"

Clarke felt forced to elaborate on the interchanges of Baron Oshima in Berlin with Tokyo, and what they revealed of German intentions and movements as the ambassador understood them. Dewey fell silent, and stepped into an anteroom with Bell. Clarke clocked their absence as twenty-two minutes. "Well, Colonel," Dewey said when they returned, "I do not believe that there are any questions I want to ask you, nor do I care to have any [further] discussion about the contents of the letter." The codes issue had apparently become a non-starter.

Should the governor change his mind, Clarke offered, he would furnish his name, Army serial number, office address, and home and office telephone numbers. He also asked whether Dewey had anything he wished to convey to Marshall, and Clarke accepted back Marshall's original letter. The chief of staff had told Dewey over the telephone that he could make a copy for himself. Dewey described it as "protection."

"No," said Dewey. "No message." Parting, Colonel Clarke advised that he would return to Washington immediately to make his report. "Well," said the governor, "I hope we meet again under more auspicious circumstances."

Closeted with Elliott Bell, John Burton and campaign manager Herbert Brownell—and looking "like a ghost," his secretary Lillian Rosse recalled—Dewey raged that Roosevelt was a "traitor" who had willingly or accidentally cost thousands of men at Pearl Harbor their lives, and lost much of the Pacific fleet. They discussed the risks of revealing the contents of Marshall's letter and Clarke's explanations, and Brownell warned of the likely reaction from the Pentagon or the White House, or perhaps "a speech by Secretary [of State] Hull pointing out that they gave information to the enemy."

With obvious disappointment, Dewey told Burton to assemble everything about Pearl Harbor they had collected, presumably including the copy of Marshall's letter, and "put it away securely and forget it." Roosevelt had indeed tried to lead the United States into war, but through pre–Pearl Harbor provocations in the Atlantic, where the President had worked on rescuing Britain. The Nazis would not take the bait until the Japanese attacked.

The Roosevelt campaign had more public issues to deal with, especially the national disillusionment that the war in Europe would not close by year's end, as overly optimistic forecasts since D-Day had predicted. The President had not ventured such a rosy outlook himself, but officials at the reconversion-to-peacetime desks of various government agencies had been informed to plan contingencies for a German collapse by October 31. Further, Army postal officials, confident that frontline troops in Europe might be heading home before Christmas, had distributed a memorandum announcing imprudently that holiday packages already in the European mail pipeline would be returned to the United States. Even General Eisenhower had predicted a German surrender before 1944 had ended. Yet breakthroughs into Germany had failed to happen, largely due to unexpectedly bad weather for aircraft and armor and the outrunning of supply sources. The Germans had managed to cripple the Belgian port of Antwerp, counted upon to shorten munitions and fuel routes, and the disastrous defeat of a British-led airborne push into Holland at Arnhem touted by General Bernard Montgomery closed off chances to outflank the Reichswehr in the north. Newspapers on both sides of the Atlantic reported that Winston Churchill, addressing the House of Commons on September 29, had conceded that the European war would continue into 1945. Mounting public pessimism was bound to diminish the Democratic vote.

The potentially explosive Pearl Harbor matter, and code-breaking, remained under wraps, even to Roosevelt. Only several weeks into October did the President discover Marshall's intervention, on security grounds, into the campaign. Harry Hopkins had learned of the affair from the usually reticent general. "Later that day," Hopkins wrote, "I repeated this conversation to the President. The President was surprised at the action Marshall had taken but expressed no criticism of that action. He . . . felt confident that Governor Dewey would not, for political purposes, give secret and vital information to the enemy. . . . 'My opponent must be pretty desperate if he is even thinking of using material like this which would be bound to react against him.' The President wondered what officer or government official had been so faithless to his country."

After the election, Marshall sent another deputy to thank Dewey for his cooperation and to offer evidence obtained since Clarke's visits of the continuing and crucial nature of the Japanese codes. Dewey nevertheless wanted his hands-off involvement explained somehow, for the record, and after the war took arch-conservative journalist John Chamberlain, a writer for Henry Luce's *Fortune* and *Life,* for a drive from Albany along Saranac Lake, where in closed-vehicle privacy he told of Marshall's intrusion into the campaign. Chamberlain was exhorted not to identify his source. Marshall would figure it out very quickly.

Pearl Harbor did not vanish from the campaign, as opponents of Roosevelt, unaware of the tense, almost-secret meetings, found December 7, 1941, to be a continuing hot-button issue—the date and place almost a code itself. But code-breaking was no longer on the table.

Colonel McCormick's *Tribune* sleuths in Washington would continue looking for potential embarrassments to keep the White House on edge and possibly lead to an upset win over an entrenched President. As with the "Victory Plan," the alleged Pearl

Harbor codes, and the Midway exposé, there seemed always to be someone either negligent, hostile, disloyal or purchasable, offering sensitive information—or what passed for it.

Sometime in October a provocative story was passed on to McCormick by the relentless Walter Trohan that Roosevelt, anxious to have a spectacular military achievement before Election Day, was urging Lieutenant General Jimmy Doolittle to engineer another raid on Tokyo. On the drawing board before Pearl Harbor and now flying from bases in China and soon, more effectively, from the Marianas, were B-29 Superfortresses. No small-scale repeat was practical. Doolittle, a lieutenant colonel upped two grades to brigadier general and awarded a Medal of Honor after his flight of sixteen carrier-based B-25 bombers had electrified Japan on April 18, 1942, was now, with three stars, commander of the Eighth Air Force, raiding occupied Europe from England. Allegedly, while condemning another Tokyo mission as foolhardy,* he told the President, "You've made me a God-damned hero and now you'll have to listen to me." To "Pat" Maloney, McCormick's managing editor, Trohan claimed, "This comes right out of the White House." The unlikely charge could not be substantiated, and was interred in an unmarked grave. Governor Dewey would have to gain, or lose, the White House without it.

---

* The April 1942 flight, although hazardous without equal in the Pacific theater, may have helped to precipitate, as a reaction to protect the Home Islands and neutralize the American naval presence in the Pacific, the catastrophic Japanese Midway operation, which became the turning point in the war. With the occupation of Guam, Saipan and Tinian in June/July 1944, which were being prepared as air bases for Japan-bound B-29 long-range bombers, a Doolittle repeat raid was utterly unnecessary, and the imminent invasion of the Philippines would furnish a plethora of politically positive headlines.

Seven

Facing the Nation

L ate in 1943, anticipating a fourth-term campaign, Sam Rosenman had recommended to Roosevelt the Office of Public Opinion Research, directed by Hadley Cantril, a social psychologist at Princeton who had developed a lucrative sideline. Cantril had surfaced as a statistical analyst of the public mood with his book *Invasion from Mars: A Study in the Psychology of Panic* (1940), explaining the reaction to the extraordinary Orson Welles radio fantasy of Halloween night 1938.

In a memo Rosenman forwarded to the President on November 24, 1943, Cantril advised, "People are almost twice as interested in domestic affairs as international affairs." Most working-class voters—the Democratic base—sampled in his interviews felt that their post-war standard of living should not be diminished by foreign aid. Early in 1944 Cantril's associate director, Jerome Bruner, later an influential educational psychologist, published his *Mandate from the People,* in which he claimed that to "the average American,"

171

international affairs, even the war itself, "were of secondary interest to the man in the street. To him, the payoff is what happens right here at home and what is likely to happen. . . . A good job is still the bench-mark for the best of possible worlds."

At every opportunity, Roosevelt argued that Americans could only achieve the best of all possible worlds for themselves by winning the war and protecting the peace while keeping the New Deal reforms of the 1930s intact and even enhanced—as the new GI Bill promised. Republicans had to counter incumbency, with its built-in bully pulpit; suggest that the war was just short of being won, and now a non-issue; and warn that protecting the good life should be in the hands of prudent custodians who were neither radical extremists nor rash spendthrifts. They employed the Opinion Research Corporation (ORC), also located in Princeton and established by Claude Robinson and George Gallup to do survey polling. Using only five thousand respondents, Gallup in 1936 had contradicted the widely respected *Literary Digest* poll based upon two million returned questionnaires that Governor Alfred Landon of Kansas would defeat the second-term re-election bid of President Roosevelt. The ORC agreed that "home-front issues" were crucial, and recommended that Republicans should attempt to split the urban, labor and ethnic vote by alleging that Democratic professionals were dangerously incautious, irreligious and collectivist. Most big city newspapers, Republican in ownership, had long promoted such fears.

Predictably, Colonel McCormick's *Chicago Tribune* warned that "the New Deal ticket"—*Democratic* was too bland—was "supporting the Communists and building them up for the day when they plan to bring the Red Terror sweeping down America." Familiarly, the New York *Daily Mirror* labeled the President's party "the New Deal–Communist–Left Wing axis." Further pressing the Red button in every speech, John Bricker charged, "Insidious and ominous are the forces of Communism linked with irreligion that are worming their way into national life. . . . First the New Deal took over the Democratic Party and destroyed its very foundation. Now these Communist forces have taken over the New Deal and will destroy the very foundations of the Republic." *TIME* equated Bricker's brand of dogmatic oratory with old-time evangelism. "As with Billy Sunday, it was delivery rather than text which filled the big tent."

For nine weeks McCormick's *Tribune* had featured, with a cartoon, a front-page jingle,

> Back to work quicker
> with Dewey and Bricker

while it searched for an alternative verse lampooning Roosevelt. Late in September it came up with a four-color cartoon of a braying jackass holding aloft a banner,

> Back on relief
> with the Commander-in-Chief.

Swinging wildly, Dewey followed up Bricker's allegations by claiming, and repeating in nearly every appearance, that Browder was somehow "indispensable" to Roosevelt, and that FDR had pardoned Browder—although that had happened in 1942—so that the Communist leader could plan the President's campaign for a fourth term, during which he would undermine the Republic. A Communist, Dewey would charge in predominantly Catholic Boston, was anyone "who supports the fourth term so our form of government may more easily be changed." It was no help to the Democrats that Browder forecast, with his own historical spin, a dire outcome to peace if Dewey should win. The Communist chairman was speaking from the same platform in New York where on November 3, 1940, he had excoriated Roosevelt for seeking to drive the United States into an "imperialist war"—but that was before Soviet Russia had been invaded by its partner until then,

Nazi Germany. Now the President, Browder contended, was on the side of the forthcoming crimson Utopia. "This is why American Communists, even as our great Communist forbears in 1860 and 1864 supported Abraham Lincoln," he explained, "will in 1944 support Franklin Delano Roosevelt, . . . one of the three great architects of the new world a-coming."

The President knew that he had to appeal to what has since been termed the "swing vote." "Roosevelt said to me at this time," Robert Sherwood recalled, "that, if there were fifty million people who would actually vote on election day, you could figure roughly that some twenty million of them were determined to vote Democratic and another twenty million were determined to vote Republican (give or take a few million either way) regardless of the issues or the candidates." The recipe for winning was to persuade the remaining millions of "uncommitted independents, . . . and it was to these that the strongest appeals must be made. I believe that it was Roosevelt's hope that this . . . twenty percent of the population which actually held the balance of power, would increase in strength and in political consciousness and he certainly directed his own influence toward that end."

In Bricker's home state, the Cleveland *Plain Dealer*, which had supported Roosevelt "with some misgivings" in 1936 and turned to Willkie in 1940, came out early for Dewey, contending that "the only possible outcome" of Roosevelt's policies is "state socialism, followed inevitably by some form of fascism." Ironically the *Plain Dealer*'s editor was Paul Bellamy, son of Edward Bellamy, the author in 1888 of the iconic futuristic novel of utopian socialism, *Looking Backward*.

Roosevelt continued to play front-porch politics by publicly minding the White House shop, literally his platform for running the war. Unfortunately, the war in western Europe appeared to be slowing down well short of crossing the Rhine. The Democratic campaign workhorse crisscrossing the states was the tireless Harry

Truman. Traditionally the vice-presidential candidates wielded the blunt weapons. In Truman's case, his flat and rural Missourian twang, however potent his message, was no sledgehammer. "The trouble with me," he confessed to reporters covering the Senate, "is that I'm not photogenic and I'm a hell of a public speaker." He was offered whatever travel funds he needed by the Democratic National Committee. He also offered to raise money on his own. His old friend Tom Evans of the Missouri drugstore chain became campaign treasurer, and funds received were deposited in John Snyder's bank in St. Louis.

The campaign staff was small. Hugh Fulton, formerly a Truman senatorial committee aide, was campaign manager and speechwriter, and Matt Connelly, who had handled press relations, was the arrangements man. Others came in and out as needed—Ed McKim, George Allen and Paul Porter among them. The opposition targeted Truman as one of "the four horsemen of the Pendergast machine," elected "to the Senate with stolen ballots" and dedicated to "misgovernment." The other three horsemen were unidentified. Long an FDR critic, scandalmongering columnist Westbrook Pegler brought up Bess's job on the public payroll and charged that "some petty white graft" padded Truman's small senatorial salary. Clare Luce called her "Payroll Bess," and Truman, when he would refer at all to the glamor girl of the GOP ever after, would spell her name "LOOSE."

The *Chicago Tribune* kept warning that "a vote for Roosevelt is very likely to be a vote for Truman for President"—and one night on a campaign train the candidate awoke from a nightmare that Roosevelt had died, and he, Harry S. Truman, was now President. Among Republican slanders—anti-Semitism was more than an undercurrent in American life—some party hacks hinted he was Jewish. (He had a grandfather named Solomon Young, allegedly the source of his middle initial, which actually stood for nothing.) "I am not Jewish," said Truman, "but if I were I would not be ashamed of it."

An analyst of campaign expenditures joked a year later that "A visitor from Mars, dropping among us last fall, might well have thought that Sidney Hillman was a candidate," rather than Roosevelt or Truman, as Hillman-bashing often exceeded attacks on the actual nominees. Late in the campaign, in a speech to Ohio AFL members, considered somewhat to the right of the CIO, Senator Taft warned that "if Roosevelt wins, Sidney Hillman will undoubtedly sit at his right hand."

Much of the thunder from the Right came from attempts to link Hillman and his CIO Political Action Committee (CIO-PAC) to Communism; other Republican criticism came from recognition of the failure of recently passed legislation to prohibit labor unions from contributing to campaigns for federal offices. In the summer of 1943, massive anti-labor feeling engendered by industrial unrest carried the Smith-Connally "Anti-Strike" Act fashioned by Republicans and Southern Democrats over President Roosevelt's veto. The political contributions restriction was not germane to the alleged purpose of the bill, which purported to be emergency legislation to prevent wartime strikes. The measure made it illegal for "any labor organization to make a contribution in connection with any election at which presidential or vice presidential electors or Senators or Representatives [in] . . . Congress are to be voted for, or for any candidate, political committee, or person to accept or receive any contribution prohibited by this section."

The clumsily drawn provisions were easily evaded by canny labor lawyers who created committees of "political action" parallel to the unions and with separate financing. "A Buck for Roosevelt" became a PAC slogan. Such funding hardly came within individual contribution limits of $5,000—the beneficiaries of which were largely Republican candidates. Even those restrictions were fudged by gifts from individual family members, making it possible for oil billionaire J. Howard Pew and family to provide $108,996, Lammot Du Pont and kinfolk to give $39,000, Harold K. Vanderbilt $31,000 and the McCormick-Patterson newspaper family $31,000.

(On the Democratic side there were fewer big donors outside of the Warner brothers of Hollywood, who furnished $33,500; the Marshall Fields, who gave $22,000; and the shipbuilding family of Andrew J. Higgins, which contributed $20,680.) Through the campaign, the CIO-PAC would raise $1,024,814, and the International Ladies' Garment Workers Union Campaign Committee for Roosevelt-Truman would raise $183,043. These receipts were easily surpassed by the $1,659,451 taken in by the United Republican Finance Committee of Metropolitan New York and the $1,252,700 raised by the Republican Finance Committee of Pennsylvania—which was separate from the Allegheny County Finance Committee, focused on Pittsburgh—which raised $510,943. Some small supporting groups furnished more publicity than pennies. The Chicago-based Girls Who Save Their Nickels to Elect a Republican Club reported receipts of $44.74, suggesting that at least one zealous young Deweyite gave less than a nickel.

One organization set a fruit-fly record for brevity of life. Founding a national committee "to deliver the nation's farm vote to Dewey," South Carolina's anti–New Deal "Cotton Ed" Smith explained, "We have taken a nose dive into hell. I have great hopes that a miracle will gird up its loins and try another deal." With that acuity behind it, the committee vanished the next day. Smith himself was defeated in his state's primary, despite the popular appeal of his racism.

Although the total expenditure of organizations supporting Republicans exceeded the Democratic total by $5,750,000 (at a time, for contemporary comparison, when most newspapers cost five cents or less and *The New York Times* ten cents), the Democrats spent more on radio time than did the Dewey campaign— $925,000. Roosevelt even devised a One Thousand Club for wealthy Democrats, which largely financed his nationwide broadcasts. Republicans paid radio bills of $841,000. The 1944 campaigns, which spawned a large number of ostensibly independent entities like the Southern Anti–New Deal Association and Farmers

for Roosevelt, were the most expensive in history, but nothing like
the escalating costs once television came to maturity two presidencies later.

Radio furnished the administration with other problems than
air-time costs in 1944. The American Federation of Musicians
(AFM) was dominated by its union president, a one-time Chicago
trumpeter, James Caesar Petrillo. To increase musicians' income—
he claimed that 60 percent of union members were out of work, replaced by recordings—Petrillo demanded higher play fees from
radio and the employment of superfluous, non-performing musicians in live orchestras. When record companies refused and bands
and orchestras rejected compulsory hiring, concert halls were pick-
eted and "mechanical reproduction of any kind" prohibited.
Petrillo exempted the armed services from the ban on new recordings by permitting a noncommercial "V-Disc," but otherwise a
complete stoppage occurred from August 1942 until Decca
backed down in September 1943. Still, Columbia and Victor would
not relent, and Roosevelt felt that he could not intervene in a union
dispute that had no adverse impact upon the war. "It's largely a
question of the law," he told a press conference on October 13.
"People who write a story that I am acting as a dictator, at the next
moment they say I should act on this . . . without seeing whether
under the law I can act or not."

While Petrillo issued demands from his Waldorf-Astoria suite,
many union musicians not in uniform remained unemployed, and
vocalists could only record with a chorus (or a harmonica) as accompaniment. (The ban helped usher out the Big Band era, its in-
strumentalists already depleted by the draft.) With energy seeping
from live radio, and feeling that morale, and possibly votes, were at
risk, the President finally appealed to Petrillo on October 4 that it
would be "your country's gain" if the AFM complied with a War
Labor Board request ignored since June 15 and began making new
recordings. But the board could not order compliance unless a
union action "unduly impeded the war effort." A post-ban Bugs

Bunny film, *Hurdy-Gurdy Hare*, would close with Bugs Bunny hiring a non-union monkey to turn a street organ, and quipping, "I sure hope Petrillo doesn't hear about this." To have a labor union resist Roosevelt was embarrassing, but the major recording companies holding out would not retreat and give the President a psychological victory before the election.

Radio's big audience in early October was for the baseball subway series, with the underdog St. Louis Browns winning two of the first three games before the Cardinals took the final three games. Even as baseball made the front pages and the radio, Governor Dewey went on the air to propose slashing postwar taxation (as would in any case be inevitable). New York senator Robert Wagner, in a re-election bid, asserted that Dewey "is not a big enough man to lead us . . . in the critical times ahead." Democrats were constantly alluding to Dewey's height and relative inexperience to chip away at attacks on Roosevelt's age and frailty, and on a decrepit New Deal. Speaking also in New York, Secretary of the Interior Ickes, a feisty seventy, joked, "I don't have to pretend to a maturity that is not mine. . . . It is a great pleasure for me to be permitted to emerge from the home for the aged to which your effervescent Governor so graciously assigned me. . . . I believe that Governor Dewey is still in the formative stage. I would no longer say as I did in 1940, that Governor Dewey has tossed his diaper into the ring. I would have to admit that he has reached the jumper stage. He is undoubtedly growing up."

A day after Dewey's radio address on postwar spending, FDR, in his second political speech broadcast nationally, rejected, in effect, Communist support, never mentioning Browder any more than he would ever refer to Dewey by name. "I have never sought and do not welcome the support," he declared, "of any person or group committed to communism, or fascism, or any other foreign ideology which would undermine the American system of government or the American system of free competitive enterprise and private property." His remarks would not put an end to Republican innuendo about the New Deal and the far left, nor would his sweeping denunciations of "fear propaganda" from the far right "lunatic fringe." Dewey clung to Earl Browder as representing the real Roosevelt, and told an audience in Charleston, West Virginia, that the New Deal was the beginning of a Communist "corporate state," and Roosevelt retaliated by pinning the nutcakes on the Right to the Grand Old Party. After FDR compared, on radio, William Dudley Pelley's extremist Silver Shirts organization with Mussolini's Black Shirts and Hitler's Brown Shirts, Pelley's defense attorneys entered motions for a mistrial in prejudicing their client's case in a second trial for sedition. The gaunt, irreconcilable Pelley had run his splinter anti-Semitic and isolationist "Christian Party" against Roosevelt in 1936, managing to get on the ballot in only one state. Later a sympathizer fed Pelley details about Pearl Harbor losses which were banned from the press. When Pelley released them in April 1942 to allegations of treason, he went to prison, to be paroled only in 1950.

In the 1944 trial, where thirty extremists were tried en masse for sedition, FDR's Department of Justice may have miscalculated. Engaging the lunatic fringe publicly only elevated its visibility. Among the defendants was the suave Nazi propagandist George Sylvester Viereck. Another was the isolationist and bigot Gerald L. K. Smith, a Louisiana minister and self-proclaimed successor to Huey Long, who had formed the America First Party from the debris of the America First Committee, which had expired after Pearl Harbor. Also in the dock were Elizabeth Dilling, whose The Red Network accused just about every liberal-minded organization from the National Council of Churches to the Society of Friends of being toadies for Moscow; and Gerald Winrod, who attacked Catholics, Jews, Blacks and labor unions as being unpatriotic.

Smith, also a Silver Shirt, got a boost from John Bricker, who declared to the appalled Dewey that he would welcome Smith's support, as that of any other American. "That's how elections are won," he explained to a reporter. Smith reciprocated the favor by nominating Bricker as vice-presidential candidate for the America First Party, which Bricker in embarrassment would rush to disavow. (It would have increased Bricker's totals by 1,781 votes in Michigan and Texas.) Three weeks after the election, however, the presiding judge, Edward C. Eicher, died, and the unwieldy and languishing "Great Sedition Trial" ended in a mistrial. Smith would go on to spew his hate on radio for thirty more years.

The white-maned, hatless Bricker would cross the Midwest several times by rail, even pausing at the tracks in tiny Lamar, Truman's birthplace. He would also speak in the Northeast and the West, giving more than two hundred speeches. To Indiana editors at French Lick, a resort complex south of Bloomington, he declared in a national broadcast that a fourth term made the central issue of the campaign "Shall the United States continue to be a Republic?" Were Americans "unable to govern themselves"? "It is time," he declared, "to elect a President who will clear everything, not with Sidney, but with the American people." The message was the same as Dewey's but the style was his opposite. *TIME,* covering the "sawdust trail" through Missouri, Kansas, Oklahoma and Texas, wrote about "The blue and honest Bricker eye, the hearty Bricker handshake, and most of all the deep Bricker platform voice, full of enthusiasm, platitudes and love of his fellow man. . . . He was a man the people at whistle-stops could understand. . . . By the time he reached Oklahoma he was happily exhibiting two ten-gallon hats, a lariat, and a pair of spurs, gifts from the grateful citizenry en route. When a critic out front challenged his pronunciation, he said, 'Listen, I came off a farm in Ohio.'"

As Bricker's campaign special clacked through conservative Utah he wrote to his teenage son, Jack, "I have been going very hard—making several speeches every day. This is the first night that I have not had a dinner meeting with a speech afterwards." John Zook, Bricker's chief speech writer, advised an assistant to build in warnings about the inadequacies of Harry Truman, which implied Roosevelt's fragility. "It's about time we give Mr. Truman the once over. We can't say out loud but he is REALLY the candidate for president—not vice-president—on the Democratic ticket."

With Fred Canfil at the wheel, Truman drove south via Gulfport, Mississippi, in early October, boarding a campaign train to whistle-stop to California and Washington. From New Orleans he broadcast over fifty-four local stations upriver on the Columbia network at 7:30 on the evening of October 12. He stressed what listeners wanted to hear—flood control assistance—an issue above politics along the Gulf. The train, with a Pullman for Truman bringing up the rear named for African explorer Henry Morton Stanley, left at eleven o'clock to chug westward overnight. Truman dreaded, he wrote to Bess, having to encounter "all those crackpots"—the crowds of the merely curious that were the inevitable burden of political candidates.

On the road separately from Truman, Secretary Ickes on October 10 used the western venue of Salt Lake City to accentuate the positive and remind voters of the great public works and conservation projects that the Roosevelt administration had achieved, both to improve the national infrastructure and to create useful jobs. It was a record, said Ickes, that had "not been written in forgettable words but in unforgettable facts, such as great dams and reservoirs, roads and bridges, power lines and aqueducts, restored range and protected forests." Still, he could not resist reminding the electorate of Dewey's inexperience allegedly compensated for by attacks on Democrats. In Newark, New Jersey, in a radio broadcast on October 16 before the Independent Committee for Roosevelt, Ickes gibed that he was "glad that Governor Dewey is going to follow me on the air tonight. I understand that he proposes to talk about 'Honesty in Government.' That will be a double adventure into the unknown by Mr. Dewey. He knows little if anything about the Government and, judging by his campaign speeches, he is totally unfamiliar with honesty."

Some of Truman's own sallies West were whistle-stops—a term only in use since the 1920s, although employed as far back as Lincoln. Politicians arranged to have trains flagged down, whistling to an unscheduled halt at communities too small for an address publicized in advance. The candidate would then appear on the rear platform to hail or to address a handful of voters. Most towns en route were not stopping places, Tom Evans recalled to Merle Miller, "and Senator Truman gave me the job of standing outside, on the back of the platform, and waving at the people as we went through. Of course I'm much taller . . . , but I do have gray hair, and I wear glasses, and I can wave. And we went through so fast that people never knew the difference."

One early-morning whistle-stop was Uvalde, Texas, on the route from San Antonio to El Paso. "Old Jack Garner," FDR's vice president for his first two terms, Truman remembered, "came down to see me, and we talked a little about this and that; he'd been out in the cornfields that day, . . . and he said, 'Harry, do you think there's any chance you'd find the time to strike a blow for liberty? Somewhere in the world it must be twelve o'clock.'"

"Cactus Jack," a hard drinker whatever the day or hour, as long as it was allegedly past noon, craved "a slight libation" (of sour mash bourbon) and was sure that Truman traveled with a supply of Southern comforts. He invited Garner aboard, "and we both had one" before the campaign train moved out.

It was not always easy to keep the campaign train on schedule because Truman had arranged a pay-as-you-go method of financing. Evans was ostensibly chairman of the finance committee for the campaign, but Truman wouldn't accept a donor's money until he was certain that it would not generate adverse publicity. Not all dollars were the same comfortable shade of green. The train would loop westward around the states, then north to Seattle and expensively eastward toward New England. Eddie Jacobson, Truman's buddy in the 129th Field Artillery, then partner in the Kansas City haberdashery business in the early 1920s that went sour, "was really a whiz at raising money," Evans said. "I don't know how he did it, but he'd pick up the phone and call somebody, and while we never got great amounts, we always got enough money to get the train moving again. . . . We'd be in some town, and we wouldn't have enough money to pay to get the train to the next town. But with Eddie—we managed to have enough to make the full journey."

Crowds in California were large and enthusiastic. Truman was so exhausted after press conferences and receptions in San Francisco and Berkeley that he went to bed at 7:00 p.m. in order to be ready to speak from the Pullman platform at Klamath Falls, Oregon, at 7:30 the next morning. At Eugene, Oregon, a thousand people gathered at the station, and he claimed to Bess that he shook hands with all of them. Calvin Coolidge had once advised a political aspirant, "They'll expect you to make a lot of speeches, but don't talk any more than you can help. Just be sure to get around . . . and shake hands with everybody. I could never figure out why, but the American people seem to enjoy shaking hands more than doing anything else." Truman and Bricker both shook tens of thousands of hands.

For Truman, Portland, Oregon, meant a clean shirt, a radio appearance, a dinner and handshakes with six hundred, "and the state chairman stood on one side and pawed me over while he introduced me." "He was in bed at midnight and off for Vancouver, Washington, at 8:15 a.m. Then came Olympia, Tacoma and Seattle—where listeners to his radio address cheered so lengthily "that my radio time ran out." The next morning he was up at five. Truman's audiences ranged from ten thousand in Seattle ("where Dewey spoke to five thousand") to three lady schoolteachers in Avery, Idaho, a whistle-stop. He spoke to them earnestly, as if they were the entire population of the state. In Butte, Montana, Representative Mike Mansfield had him to lunch before the *Henry M. Stanley* set off for Minneapolis and St. Paul.

Campaigning by rail is now as obsolete as the rusting trackage. The television screen has replaced the hustings, and even alleged "town meetings" are often staged with carefully selected audiences. "You get a real feeling of this country and the people in it," Truman mused nearly two decades after his presidency, "when you're on a train, speaking from the back of a train, and the further you get away from that, the worse off you are, the worse off the country is, and the easier it gets for the stuffed shirts and the counterfeits and the fellas from Madison Avenue to put it over on the people."

As Dewey offered another speech excoriating Earl Browder, presumably the shadow opposition candidate for the White House, Bricker, little covered by the daily press, pounded a similar drumbeat during 15-hour days. While Truman rumbled by rail to big cities and further whistle-stops, news came, on October 7, that Wendell Willkie had died of a coronary thrombosis at fifty-two. After taking middle-of-the-road positions on losing in his party's primaries, he had denounced both party platforms, but Republicans had worried that Willkie might come out for Roosevelt, against whom he had run strongly in 1940. Some even thought, before Truman's choice, that Roosevelt might tap Willkie for the ticket, but he had backed away from all feelers, and the President first denied the approaches and then conceded at a news conference (on August 15), "Well, yes—privately." (Earlier he had even thought of appointing Willkie as czar of industrial production, but FDR had dropped the idea as politically risky.) Posthumously praising the political maverick's "tremendous courage," Roosevelt noted that it was in character for Willkie "more than once to stand alone and to challenge the wisdom taken by powerful interests within his own party."

Dewey had tried, without success, to secure Willkie's endorsement, eventually during a frosty telephone call from Albany to Manhattan securing Willkie's agreement to consult the Republican nominee's dour foreign policy adviser, Wall Street lawyer John Foster Dulles. But Dulles was unlikely to charm Willkie. Late in September Drew Pearson's syndicated *Washington Merry-Go-Round* had been tipped to radio commentator Walter Winchell, who urged his listeners to watch for it. Pearson had described the dealings of Dulles's law firm, Sullivan & Cromwell, with clients like General Franco in Spain, Pierre Laval in occupied France, and prewar German agents. As Willkie knew, several major newspapers, including the *New York Mirror* and the *Washington Post*, omitted the column. To newspaper friends in Albany, Willkie confided, "I don't trust the little bastards. . . . The whole purpose of the thing is to take some pictures. They just want to show me off like some prize bull." He died on October 8, a few weeks after meeting privately with Herbert Brownell at Henry Luce's suite in the Waldorf Towers. Allegedly he had told London newspaper baron Lord Beaverbrook, then in New York, that he—Willkie—intended to come out for Roosevelt before the election. Luce and Brownell wanted to derail that possibility. Over drinks and dinner—and more drinks—Willkie grumbled and growled about Dewey and declared, "I want you to know . . . that your man is going to be defeated and I am going to run for President in 1948 and will be elected." According to Luce, "Finally, around midnight, Willkie got up and lumbered off."

After issuing a statement of perfunctory tribute, Dewey attended the funeral on October 9 at the crowded Fifth Avenue Presbyterian Church, while an estimated sixty thousand onlookers gathered outside. Willkie's dream of the White House was over. Almost certainly it could not have been, if at all, as a Republican.

Willkie's close friend Russell W. Davenport, a former editor of Luce's business-oriented *Fortune*, would publish, in most major state newspapers, on October 30, "An Open Letter to Fellow Republicans," paid for by a New York Independent Republican Committee, calling for Willkie supporters, for whom his death was "a national tragedy," to vote for FDR. "If like me, you are an enrolled Republican," he confessed, "you will find surely find it distasteful to vote on the Democratic Party line—the party of Tammany and [Ed] Flynn." He recommended voting on the internationalist Liberal Party line—"Row F on the voting machines symbol—the Liberty Bell."

Willkie's front-page demise contributed further to rumors about Roosevelt's fragile health, especially from talkative physicians at the Mayo Clinic and Columbia Presbyterian Hospital who had connections at Bethesda, from which Howard Bruenn had vanished. With medical conferences high in rail priority, leading physicians were among the most frequent travelers during the war-restricted travel limits. Learning of what might be dangerous talk that had gone on since early summer, Assistant Secretary of State Breckenridge Long, perhaps the most far-right politically in a sub-Cabinet post, but an FDR loyalist, contacted the President's press secretary, Steve Early, who called the office of FBI director J. Edgar Hoover. His agents quietly interviewed physicians at Bethesda, who denied any statements attributed to them but conceded that discussions about FDR's likely heart disease had occurred there and elsewhere. Attempting in mid-October to put a stop to the talk, Bob Hannegan publicly condemned "the whispering drive," and Ross McIntire lied, "in view of rumors in political circles and elsewhere, the President's health is perfectly OK. There are absolutely no organic difficulties at all."

At a press conference on October 17, a reporter ventured, gingerly, to much laughter, "Mr. President, [did] you read the ominous reports about your health, printed by some of the more rugged correspondents?"

Laughing himself at the curious choice of adjective, Roosevelt said, "Look—don't—don't get me commenting on the word *rugged*, because I might say things I would be sorry for. On some of them, I know more about their health that they know about mine."

Seeking bloc and ethnic votes that could massively shift voters, both parties went after the substantial Polish constituency, largely in the Middle West. The Red Army had pushed into prewar Poland, divided greedily in September 1939 between Hitler and Stalin. Russia intended to keep its gains, setting up a puppet regime of Communist exiles and stonewalling the hapless government-in-exile in London.

While Dewey called for a restoration, Roosevelt, recognizing the realities, declared that Poland "must be reconstituted as a great nation," fudging the delicate issue of boundaries and government. Because the Soviets were poised to smother all of central Europe, FDR and Churchill, settling secretly with Stalin, had accepted the pre-1914 frontier in the east, compensating Poland with German territory to the west certain to be overrun. Roosevelt had often quoted to intimates what he claimed was an old Balkan proverb: "It is permitted to you in time of grave danger to walk with the devil until you have crossed the bridge."

Pravda derided Dewey's views on the nation's future as supporting "the pretensions of Polish imperialists"—possibly a propaganda plus for the Republicans. Yet the facts on the ground were what counted. The Red Army was the most powerful land military force ever constituted and was already in control of much of what had been Poland. During the campaign, vague words from FDR about Poland were political caution. On his instructions, Ambassador Harriman in Moscow had told Vyascheslav Molotov, Stalin's Foreign minister, that "the Polish-Soviet question must not become an issue in the . . . presidential campaign." Roosevelt hoped that "whatever the Soviet Government publicly stated would be on a constructive side. . . . It was time to keep the barking dogs quiet."

Another ethnic bloc was addressed a few days later. Roosevelt spoke from the White House by telephone to a vast Columbus Day dinner for 9,500 attendees at the Commodore Hotel in New York, sponsored by the Italian-American Labor Council, promising that the United States would stand by Italy, now liberated from "fascist gangsters." The Council's Four Freedom's award was accepted for the President by Attorney General Francis Biddle.

After a weekend in Albany, Governor Dewey set out to deliver an attack on Roosevelt in Kiel Auditorium, St. Louis. (Missouri remained a swing state despite native son Harry Truman.) Taking aim at Truman's Pendergast origins without naming names, Dewey declared once more that the Roosevelt government "has been taken over by the combination of corrupt big city bosses, Communists and fellow-travelers." The New Deal's domestic failures, Dewey would claim at every opportunity, were as nothing compared to its chaotic foreign policy: "Can an Administration which is so disunited and unsuccessful at home be any better abroad?" A White House statement would accuse Dewey of "distortion and dishonesty." Truman, at the Shrine Auditorium in Los Angeles, addressing an overflow crowd and citing Dewey's lack of war experience of any kind, wondered what it would have meant to the nation to have had a "war President like the Republican candidate. . . . Can you imagine the effect on the war?"

Always the prosecutor, yet predictably buttoned-up, Dewey could not master the politician's art of being likeable, and he found it uncomfortable before audiences to appear folksy. "Smile,

"Five seconds for [a] smile, six minutes and 23 seconds for [a] speech and three seconds laughter for each joke—a cinch, Governor" by Eric Godal in *PM*, September 13, 1944.

Governor," a press photographer shouted during a reception in Michigan. "I thought I was," said Dewey. A cartoon in the unfriendly *PM* showed a handler with Dewey on the rear platform of his campaign train rattling through cow country, advising, "Five seconds for smile, six minutes and 23 seconds for speech, and three seconds laughter for each joke—a cinch, Governor." Herbert Brownell recalled, ruefully, a rodeo on a Nebraska ranch staged to draw crowds to a Dewey appearance, where the candidate stepped off his special train "wearing a black homburg hat—no sombrero or ten-galloner for him." (Donning any hat was unusual for Dewey.) "He announced that instead of going directly to the grandstand, he had to go to the hotel to put the finishing touches on his speech. Eventually he arrived at the rodeo (still clutching the homburg) while it was still in full swing, earning a big boo rather than the acclaim we had hoped for." Bricker, his running mate, was the party populist, a press photo showing him at a whistle-stop leaning down from the rear platform to shake hands with a boy seated on a pony in cowboy regalia. Dewey despised such campaigning.

Wherever Bricker traveled, he appealed to the laboring class undecided vote by accusing the CIO of trying to "buy" a fourth term for the President "with money extracted from the honest and patriotic workers of this country." Liberal journalist John Gunther described Bricker as "intellectually . . . like interstellar space—a vast vacuum occasionally crossed by homeless, wandering clichés." Except for die-hard newspapers on the Right, Bricker seldom received front-page coverage. In the eight columns of *The New York Times* front page during the thirty-one days of October, a report about Bricker appeared once.

At a *New York Herald-Tribune* forum on October 18 at which the President declined to appear, Dewey denounced Roosevelt's "secret" and "one-man diplomacy," and his failure to project a postwar vision for Germany. "Dewey has been hollering about 'secret diplomacy,'" E. B. White wrote to *The New Yorker* editor Harold Ross.

"But secrecy is the stuff any diplomacy is made of. Hitler is the only honest writer on this subject." Germany's post-Hitler future was a more delicate matter. The President had, hurriedly and mistakenly and to his cost, bought Treasury Secretary Henry Morgenthau's proposal that defeated Germany be divided, its industrial infra-structure (and war-making potential) destroyed and its people turned to agriculture. Morgenthau's idea for postwar Germany looked good at first glance but would have been an economic catas-trophe for liberated Europe. Germany would have to be, as it had been, the economic engine driving the Continent.

Roosevelt had offered the idea, which would have appealed to Stalin, to Churchill. Although shocked by the Carthaginian pro-posal, Churchill agreed to it, to the consternation of his circle. He may have been thinking about how postwar Britain would be able to fulfill its Lend-Lease obligations, and needed to offer FDR a carrot. After Quebec, Roosevelt had to withdraw the proposal while pretending it never really happened. He was experienced at denying inconvenient facts.

When the President's own people were horrified at the grim prospect of non-Soviet Europe with its industrial fulcrum gone, and the scheme was leaked to the press, Roosevelt resorted to damage control. He called in Secretary of War Stimson and contended that Morgenthau, intruding into foreign policy, had "pulled a boner." Then the President called in ailing Secretary of State Cordell Hull, who was preparing to retire, and assured him that it was premature to determine the future of "a country we do not yet occupy."

By Friday, October 20, all the candidates were either on the political trail or preparing to do so. Late to the firing line, Roo-sevelt had considered his travels to Hawaii, Alaska and Quebec, his dinner appearance in Washington, and his radio talks suffi-cient to inform the nation that he was actively presidential, but Rosenman warned FDR that he had to show himself "before a large public gathering" or the health issue would become a cam-paign impediment. Accordingly, the President told a Cabinet meeting, "There has been this constant rumor that I'll not live if I am elected. You all know that's not so but apparently Papa has to tell them." New York City was put on the agenda.

Nationwide, however, Americans were focused on the Philippines, where Army and Marine forces had just landed on the central island of Leyte, bypassing big, sprawling Mindanao to the south. In Hawaii, Roosevelt had given MacArthur the go-ahead, which he understood had to take effect before election day. For the general, retaking the Philippines was a win-win situation. He was not going to be president in 1945, having been rebuffed embarrassingly in the primaries, but making good his public vow to return to the Philippines, however abetted by Roosevelt, might put him on top in the next campaign for the White House. Further, the achievement would tarnish Tom Dewey, whom he disliked.

The governor had regularly criticized the President's alleged failure to back up MacArthur, who had behind him not only a huge army and air force but Nimitz's navy. The most formidable battle fleet ever gathered in one place—larger than the entire British Navy—had been decimating Japanese air and sea power around the Philippines. Roosevelt's proxy victory 8,000 miles away would also be MacArthur's. "You have," the President radioed to MacArthur, "the nation's gratitude and the nation's prayers as you and your men fight your way back to Bataan." To Admirals Nimitz and Halsey—"Bull" Halsey was commanding in Philippine waters—Roosevelt, touching all bases, sent messages praising "the magnificent sweep" of the fleet over the Japanese and the "fine cooperation" with MacArthur.

New York Police Commissioner Lewis J. Valentine cancelled all leaves for Saturday, October 21, and recalled all officers from vacation to provide massive security for the President, who was to arrive at the Brooklyn Army Base Terminal in Bay Ridge at 7:30 that morning from Pennsylvania Station, and then tour Brooklyn, Queens, the Bronx and Manhattan. Democratic National Chairman

Hannegan denied that the 51-mile itinerary was arranged to demonstrate the President's ability to handle four more years in office. "After the people have seen him," Hannegan explained, "they can make up their own minds as to his vigor and health. The people will have a chance to see him as do the correspondents twice a week." Privately Hannegan was very worried.

With unstable braces a problem, Roosevelt advised organizers of the dinner meeting at the Waldorf to place microphones at the head table. He would speak seated. Drafting lines for his foreign policy talk, to be pieced together by him with additions and corrections, were an army of top writers—Harry Hopkins, Robert Sherwood, Sam Rosenman, Archibald MacLeish, Adolf A. Berle, Russell Davenport, Dorothy Thompson, Raymond Gram Swing, Ben Cohen and Chip Bohlen. The assembled version went through ten drafts. Accenting the positive, Sherwood questioned references to past isolationism. As soon as this war is over, Roosevelt warned, isolationism "may well be stronger than ever."

The President saw little but arrogance in the inflexible Dewey, yet polling data inched them closer. Despite the numbers, Roosevelt may have been buoyed that morning by Walter Lippmann's influential "Today & Tomorrow" column in the staunchly Republican *New York Herald-Tribune*. A reluctant convert to FDR's "patrician populism" (in 1931 he had dismissed Roosevelt as "a kind of amiable boy scout"), Lippmann had been won over by the President's rapid restoration of public confidence. Roosevelt's failing health after three terms impelled him to prefer a Republican restoration, but he had no confidence in Dewey, and remained on the fence. On an afternoon shortly before Roosevelt's appearance in New York, Helen Reid, co-owner with her husband of the newspaper, came into Lippmann's office and said, "Walter, I don't know exactly how you feel, but I do hope you will take a stand in this election." Increasingly unhappy with Dewey's political flabbiness, especially with his unrealistic bid for the ethnic Polish vote by promoting the impossible cause of the exile Poles to regain power in Warsaw, now overwhelmed by the Russians, Lippmann told Mrs. Reid, "Well, if I do, it will probably be against you." Unhappily, she said, "That will be quite all right, just so long as you take a stand."

In the *Tribune*'s October 21 issue, the morning of FDR's motorcade, Lippmann wrote that he was left by the Republican ticket with no choice but to support Roosevelt. "I cannot feel that Governor Dewey can be trusted with responsibility in foreign affairs. He has so much to learn, and there would be no time to learn it, that the risk and cost of a change during this momentous year seems to me too great." Lippmann would go even farther in his concluding column on the campaign.

Street crowds in New York seemed no problem despite the increasingly bad weather. Ten thousand police were on duty around New York when Roosevelt began his tour, in the back seat of an open green Packard convertible so that he would be easily visible, from the Brooklyn Army Base into which his campaign train had backed. Chill, drenching rain was already falling from darkened skies—the edge of an Atlantic hurricane. The temperature had dropped to 40°F. Admiral McIntire advised the President to cancel the motorcade. Pointing to the maps in the morning papers, and the scheduled times he was expected at various points in the city, FDR declined. He was assisted into his familiar blue Navy cape and tucked into a fur lap blanket. He tugged on his gray fedora and adjusted his glasses. Huddled in rain gear, Mrs. Roosevelt sat with him. Mike Reilly was alongside on the right. He had already arranged for changes of clothing for his chief at stops on the route.

As the motorcade formed, with rubber-jacketed motorcycle police leading and Secret Service men in raincoats riding the running boards of the President's car, an open truck preceded the Packard, with newsreel cameramen in rain slickers filming the events as best they could. Roosevelt understood that he was not only going to be visible, within hours, to rain-soaked millions in person, but, within days, to many more millions across the nation on movie screens.

After a cursory inspection of the Army base, FDR greeted seventy thousand cheering sailors and workmen at the Navy Yard, raising and lowering his soggy hat and wiping the rain from his glasses as he went by. Roosevelt's Packard turned toward Flatbush and Ebbets Field, home of the Dodgers. Soaked but eager crowds lined the sidewalks, shouting encouragement; women blew kisses. At the ball park the motorcade splashed in from the left field entrance while enthusiasts in the grandstands waved their umbrellas. At second base, the Packard was driven up a wooden ramp to an open platform. Reilly bent down to lock the President's braces into a standing position and lift him smoothly out of the car and assist him to the lectern. There, already hatless, while rocking slightly in the wind and rain, Roosevelt eased himself out of his Navy cape, raised a hand in greeting, and as his thinning hair and gray suit were being drenched, his words echoed from loudspeakers in the stands. "I have never been to Ebbets Field before," he said, "but I have rooted for the Dodgers. And I hope to come back here some day and see them play." He claimed that he was there in part to push the candidacy of Senator Robert Wagner, a labor icon, for re-election. "We were together in the [State] Legislature . . . thirty some years ago. . . . We have been close friends ever since." He closed not with any self-promotion—his very presence was that— but with the praise that Wagner "deserves well of mankind." As the drenched President was assisted to his car, spectators rose in a standing ovation.

At Mike Reilly's order, the President's motorcade veered to an unscheduled stop at a Coast Guard station. Inside, Roosevelt was assisted into a small infirmary where a change of clothes was waiting. While he was stripped, toweled, rubbed down, given a shot of whiskey and re-outfitted, an aide shook the rain from his Navy cape and FDR's signature fedora. Then, with police motorcycles leading the way, blinking through the downpour with flashing red lights, the caravan proceeded through crowded Queens streets and over the Triborough Bridge, completed with New Deal funds, into the Bronx, to the Naval Training Station at Hunter College. In the Navy armory, well-drilled WAVES in dress blue were lined up for inspection. Out again into the streets, the President lifted his sopping hat left and right to cheering but soaked crowds, the rain pasting down his sparse hair.

Mike Reilly recorded only one security scare. "Going through the Bronx . . . I looked up and saw somebody throw something from a window. It was a bull's eye, and as it came to the car I knocked it down. It turned out to be a well-wrapped ham sandwich." Inching south through Harlem, the motorcade proceeded south through Broadway and Seventh Avenue toward Times Square, and into 34th Street, where at Fifth Avenue the tower of the Empire State Building was clouded in mist. Below, the denizens of the loyal Garment Workers Union, the power base of David Dubinsky and Sidney Hillman, crowded the sidewalks in the tens of thousands, cheering while holding soggy newspapers over their heads. Close to the Arch at Washington Square, progress ceased at East Eleventh Street in Greenwich Village, at what FDR referred to as "Mrs. Roosevelt's apartment." He had never seen it. Reilly's Secret Service men surrounded the car on all sides while the President was lifted out and assisted under the building's canopy to the rented ground-floor flat that was Eleanor's private space. In a bedroom his sopping clothes were again peeled off; he was given a hot bath, rubdown and a glass of bourbon, and was dressed in dry clothes. A wheelchair waited. He was helped into it and propelled himself into the sitting room, where, with the First Lady chatting happily from a wing chair, he asked for another drink. He had defied, triumphantly, 51 miles of rain and wind, and was wreathed in smiles.

Police Commissioner Valentine estimated that FDR had been seen by three million New Yorkers. Via newspapers and newsreels, nearly a hundred million more would marvel at his guts and stamina. *The New York Times* would front-page that "the two facts of Mr. Roosevelt's ride through the rain and his standing [to speak] at

A shower of paper from factories and office buildings in the Manhattan Garment District greets the presidential campaign cavalcade in the rain, October 21, 1944. *FDR Library*

Ebbets Field are counted on to put at rest the rumors that the President was in bad health and unable to stand."

After resting, and reviewing his speech to the Foreign Policy Association, the President was assisted into a dinner jacket and black tie, mixed another drink for himself, and left in a closed car up Park Avenue for the Waldorf-Astoria, arriving in the ballroom at 8:10. Below the hotel, in a tunnel for the New York Central tracks, his Presidential Special waited. The two thousand mostly wealthy diners—two-thirds of them Republicans, including Secretary of War Henry Stimson—were tucking into their appetizers when Roosevelt entered and was helped to the dais. No attendees were unaware of FDR's vigorous campaigning day. All rose and applauded.

Roosevelt toyed at his dinner, checking the time. The address was to be broadcast. His theme was the establishment of a workable world security mechanism before the end of hostilities, to guarantee the peace. Because Governor Dewey had straddled the issue, concerned that he might lose the isolationist vote, the President went after the Republican Right for having no interest in the rest of the world after 1918, despite wars and revolutions. In the 1930s, many American schools, he noted, had even left a large blank on maps in refusal to recognize the existence of calumniated Soviet Russia. He was for realism. One lived in the present. (When his speechwriting advisers gingerly cut that several times from drafts of his address, he brushed off their misgivings with "All right, boys, leave it out of the speech if you want. I'll ad-lib it"— and he did.)

"These days," he continued, "I hear voices in the air attacking me for my failure to prepare this nation for war, and to warn the American people of approaching tragedy." Both Dewey and Bricker had issued the charge, but it had been put most viciously by Congresswoman Clare Boothe Luce, who had claimed in Chicago that Roosevelt was "the only American President who ever lied us into a war because he did not have the courage to lead us into it. . . . The shame of Pearl Harbor was Mr. Roosevelt's shame." The President now spelled out "the record." Republicans in Congress had been against preparedness, Selective Service, the repeal of the arms embargo, Lend-Lease, and, only a few months before Pearl Harbor, against extension of the draft—"voting against keeping of our army together." If the Republicans were now to win the presidency and control of Congress—effectively, he soft-pedaled, they had that control through Southern Democrats—"inveterate isolationists would occupy positions of commanding influence and power." They already had on their side "the McCormick-Patterson-Gannett-and-Hearst press."

Peace, FDR concluded to enthusiastic approval, could only succeed "where there is a will to enforce it." He understood that

Americans would not soon "attain a Utopia. Indeed, in our own land, the work to be done is never finished. We have yet to realize the full and equal enjoyment of our freedom. . . . That task, my friends, calls for the judgment of a seasoned and a mature people. This, I think, the American people have become. . . . We now are, and we shall continue to be, strong brothers in the family of mankind—the family of the children of God."

To sustained applause, cheers and the stomping of feet, Roosevelt was assisted to an elevator conveying him and his party to the sub-basement and the waiting train, poised only a few blocks north of Grand Central Station. Press Secretary Bill Hassett followed with Grace Tully. Soon Hassett predicted in his diary that the election "is in the bag. . . . My own fears and misgivings about the President's health under the terrific load he is carrying are dissipated, vanished like the morning dew."

As he wrote, the presidential train moved slowly northward along the Hudson toward Hyde Park. Reporting for the International News Service, Robert Nixon, thinking of FDR's New York City vigor, reflected, "There were terrific contrasts. You thought at times that the man was failing, but then he would spring back just like a grasshopper."

Eight

The Service Vote

Roosevelt repeatedly retold a story about a soldier weeping as he was to be relocated from a much fought over Pacific island—prematurely, he insisted—because he was being relieved before he had killed a Jap. A sympathetic colonel suggested that if he would go out into the bush and shout "To hell with the Emperor" an enraged Jap would jump out of his foxhole and the GI could shoot him. Not long afterward the colonel found the soldier still crying. "What happened?" the colonel asked. "Didn't my solution work?"

"I did what you said," the GI confessed, "but the Jap jumped up hollering, 'Rozvelt a son-a-beetz.' I couldn't shoot him: I'm a Republican, too."

Men of voting age—and they were mostly men—in uniform hardly knew another president than FDR. He had been the dominant personality in America since 1932. They were not *for* him as much as they were *against* the nation's enemies, and he was commander-in-chief. GI war aims had little to do with partisan politics. They wanted to win the two-ocean war—and go home. Some contemporaries, they realized, had dodged the draft somehow, or shirked war work, but servicemen knew that they lived precariously in an unequal and dangerous world. Many whom they admired had donned uniforms—baseball's Ted Williams and Joe DiMaggio, boxing's Joe Louis, the movies' Clark Gable, Jimmy Stewart and Tyrone Power.

The comics' Joe Palooka had even entered the peacetime draft before Pearl Harbor, and Ham Fisher, his creator, had Roosevelt's permission to draw the President in as an occasional character. Young Terry, of *Terry and the Pirates,* was in the Army Air Forces in China. Dick Tracy was in naval intelligence but still managed to confront his usual cast of bizarre adversaries. Snuffy Smith was in the Army and Barney Google in the Navy. Despite Popeye's droll past as a sailor, he was clearly too absurd to be written into the Navy. Clark Kent—Superman—also had to be exempted, as he would have overwhelmed the war. Before Pearl Harbor he had been briefly pitted against the Axis, but was withdrawn in a rewrite. His creators solved the problem when he reported to his draft board in his everyday character as a newspaper reporter. There (presumably without his concealed monogrammed tights) he easily passed the pre-induction physical—but for the eye examination. Because of his X-ray vision, he read off the wrong chart—the one hung in the last booth down the corridor. Superman was judged 4-F. Even Tillie the Toiler had signed up successfully for military service and was a WAC.

Only one strip openly took political sides, although no one in it was eligible for a service ballot. "Little Orphan Annie" was seemingly too young for a uniform, but her anti-FDR creator, Harold Gray, had her criticize rationing, labor unions, Communism and government wartime strictures in general, and create a children's "Junior Commandos" in which she wore a "JC" armband thought fascistic by the Left and christened herself its colonel. Her guardian, Daddy Warbucks, an idealized representative of Big Business, led scrap drives and was a superpatriot critic of the New Deal, despairing of the way the country was going, and finally dying, but postwar protests from the Right would resuscitate him.

Not being regular readers of the *Congressional Record*, or of partisan newspaper editorials, soldiers and sailors were seldom angry at anyone but Hitler and Hirohito. A service joke going the rounds in the Pacific areas as November and December neared suggested the President's likely Christmas present for Emperor Hirohito, who prided himself on expertise as a marine biologist: a deep-sea diving suit so that he could inspect his Navy. The gallows humor was unlikely to gain votes for Governor Dewey.

About 11.3 million Americans were in uniform, perhaps nine million of them of voting age. (An additional seven million citizens had migrated from their home districts to work in war industries elsewhere, many of them not registered to vote in their new locations.*) Not since 1864 had soldiers in wartime, far from home, participated in a presidential election. Then, as in 1944, the party in opposition realized that the commander-in-chief would be the preponderant favorite unless the war was going badly. Even having a popular general compete against an incumbent president did not change service attitudes. George McClellan lost resoundingly to Abraham Lincoln.

In 1944, FDR was running against a youngish governor who had no uniformed experience beyond the Boy Scouts. Before the campaign had reached absentee ballot stage, Marquis Childs reported in *Washington Calling* most correspondents back briefly from overseas believed that GI Joe was predictably for the President. "The correspondent of a conservative newspaper, who is anti-Roosevelt in his own leanings, returned from a tour of the

---

* Such civilian problems were rarely reported, but a front-page photo in the *Concord (NH) Daily Monitor* on November 1, 1944, showed "war worker" William F. Wall receiving an absentee ballot from the City Clerk, Arthur E. Roby. MIT chemist Edward Herman, on atom bomb research in Los Alamos, New Mexico, could not obtain an absentee ballot as secrecy restricted him to a post office box number.

major theaters of war saying he had yet to meet an enlisted man who was not for the president's re-election." A cartoon by Stan MacGovern made the point by showing the GOP elephant looking over a puny Dewey in striped baseball uniform, awed at oversized bats labeled "Reconversion," "Foreign Affairs," "The War," "The Peace," "Tax Program" and "Post-War Problems," and appealing, "Are they all this size?" "Afraid so" is the caption.

For the Republican and Southern Democratic opposition the anti-Roosevelt strategy was limited, barring a military catastrophe, to restricting the soldier vote without appearing to deny absentee voting. Although the poll tax was only one or two dollars a year, it had kept poor whites and most Blacks from the ballot. A senator raged to Allen Drury of the United Press, "Roosevelt says we're letting the soldiers down. Why, goddamn him. The rest of us have boys who go into the army and navy as privates and ordinary seamen and dig latrines and swab decks, and his go in as lieutenant colonels and majors and lieutenants and spend their time getting medals in Hollywood. Letting the soldiers down. That son of a bitch." The President's four sons all served overseas in combat zones. But before Pearl Harbor, igniting controversy, eldest son Jimmy had been commissioned as a Marine Corps officer so that he could accompany his father as naval aide on a trip to South America. Elliott had received a prewar Army Air Forces commission and went on to hazardous wartime duty, as did James, but both sons had already involved themselves in sleazy financial dealings, tarnishing the prewar Roosevelt image. In 1944 John and Franklin Jr. were naval officers often at sea.

A cartoon by Dorman Smith in the *Milwaukee Journal* showed a tightly wrapped ballot labeled "Soldier," under the watchful eye of a drill sergeant labeled "Congress," trying to leap voting barriers of "State Laws," "Politics," "Constitutionalism" and "More Politics" in order to be eligible. Correspondent Ernie Pyle reported from Italy that most soldiers wanted to vote, but if the red tape proved frustrating, they would "say nuts to it." Other GIs had little interest in the issues. To some the prevailing and nonpolitical mood was "Home Alive in '45." Many in the Pacific, expecting a very long war to push the Japanese back to the Home' Islands, reluctantly transformed the rhyme into "Golden Gate in '48."

Predicting the worst possible outcome, poet William Rose Benét wrote, with deep sarcasm and little poetry,

> Fight, Senators, to quash the soldiers' vote.
> Fight, Orators—take the young men by the throat.
> Fight for States Rights, cry havoc, shoot the breeze.
> *Seven states do not provide for absentees.*
> Strike for your Righteous Technicalities.
> *Three more do not permit voting from overseas.*
> Forward Mississippi, forward Tennessee,
> Forward Arkansas; forward States of the Free.
> "State Jurisdiction" shout; keep up your crying.
> Far off your own young men are only dying. . . .

Denouncing the poll tax and anti-Negro restrictions implied in the congressional bill, Senate Majority Leader Alben Barkley of border state Kentucky declared, recognizing the electoral consequences, "If all the soldiers and sailors scattered all over the world . . . should at this hour announce that they would vote against the party now in power, if the opportunity were given to them, I would nevertheless feel it my duty to vote to give them that opportunity."

Enough Republicans had joined with Southern Democrats on "states' rights" grounds to defeat attempts for a uniform federal absentee ballot to enable the millions in uniform abroad to vote. Yet never before had so much of the voting population been so uprooted from their legal places of residence. Worrying the Right, a Gallup Poll of servicemen released on December 4, 1943—perhaps of little sampling validity, given the worldwide scattering of the eligible military—predicted that if President Roosevelt ran again, he would secure 61 percent of their ballots.

In January 1944, a month later, the Algiers edition of the Army's *Stars and Stripes* found in a survey that 100 percent of readers who responded to a question about the November election felt strongly that they had an absolute right to vote. Yet most Southern states, Democratic by party affiliation but covertly or openly anti-FDR, had election regulations that restricted eligibility, and Republican-leaning states also had no interest in enabling another Roosevelt term.

Promoting a uniform federal presidential ballot, Senator Scott Lucas pointed out, "We have one hundred two counties in Illinois. We have one hundred two different kinds of tickets in Illinois." Voting across forty-eight states with ballots sent worldwide would swamp the services. Senator Taft challenged "the assertion of the army and navy"—which he had invented—"that they cannot carry by air two hundred fifty tons of ballots." In 1944, in the 3,050 counties in the forty-eight states, many with gubernatorial elections, plus cities electing mayors and other officials, ballots for localities would run into the many thousands. The practical impossibility was exactly what many in Congress wanted. To retain a poll tax, a literacy test and other, largely racist, restrictions on voting registration, Democrats in Dixie states threatened to filibuster Congress into 1945. Many Republican legislators also found it in their party's interest to create absentee voting obstacles, even when, like Governor Dewey, they claimed to be "against" obstacles to voting. The New York ballot, Dewey contended, rejecting the federal alternative, was more appropriate, as it included local offices.* It was also useful opposition politics if the anticipated Roosevelt majority in the armed forces found it difficult to vote.

---

* Dewey would boast in a speech delivered in Charleston, West Virginia, on October 7, 1944, that 77 percent "of the eligible soldiers and sailors" from New York "have had their ballots mailed to them already." There would be, he predicted, "an even larger percentage of soldier votes than we will have of civilians." The question lay in how the definition of *eligible* was managed.

"That's okay, Joe—at least we can make bets." Bill Mauldin's cartoon on threatened Congressional restrictions on service voting, in *Stars and Stripes*, U.S. Army, June 1944.

There was always some complicating state issue for reluctant politicians to claim. Even when service exemptions were approved, the canny technicalities of individual state procedures threatened to make many applications useless. When Republican senator Edward H. Moore of Oklahoma spoke in favor of retaining states' rights stand-pat voting, Scott Lucas responded in a confusion of pronouns, "Someday, somewhere, if these boys have the opportunity to vote, some one-armed veteran from Italy or from some [Pacific] island battle will be running against the senator in Oklahoma and will remind him of the time he was denied the right to vote when he was over there saving his country. He will throw his empty sleeve into his face in that campaign." (Moore would evade that possibility by not running for re-election.)

The emasculated bill that reached the White House looked more viable than it actually was. In order for servicemen to obtain federal ballots they had to apply for state ballots before September 1, 1944. If the document had not arrived by October 1, 1944, they became eligible for federal ballots. It was not an accident of the law that little time existed to request a ballot, receive it and return it. Even to use the opportunity, the state in which service personnel were eligible to vote had to have authorized the federal ballot by July 15, 1944.

When the legislation arrived for the President's signature in May, he telegraphed all forty-eight governors to ask whether they intended to authorize the federal alternative. Like Dewey, seventeen claimed that their state mechanisms were adequate and that they would ignore the deadline. Eighteen agreed to accept a federal ballot. Three states permitted no absentee voting. Other governors responded so vaguely that their compliance remained in doubt. Faced with a bill that was too mean-spirited, he felt, to sign, yet with some leeway language for voting, Roosevelt would let it become law without his signature, condemning it as "wholly inadequate."

Representative John Rankin of Mississippi, an anti-Roosevelt Democrat and racist crank, hailed the ballot limitations as "the greatest victory for states' rights and constitutional government that has been won in this Capitol for 50 years." Republicans and Southern Democrats, who jointly controlled the House of Representatives when their interests coincided, gave Rankin a standing ovation. When Walter Winchell's syndicated newspaper column referred to "the House of Reprehensibles," Rankin scorned Winchell on the House floor as "that little kike."

Once the Eastland-Rankin state ballot legislation passed the House by 328–69 and went to the compliant Senate, Louisiana senator Allen J. Eastland, who name was on it, asked, seriously, "Is it necessary that all the language in the bill make sense?" Soldiers in the visitors' gallery laughed and applauded, but Eastland steadfastly voted for the bill as it was. A Bill Mauldin cartoon in *Stars and Stripes* showed his grungy GIs Willie and Joe looking over a stateside newspaper from their trench. The headline read *States'*

Rights Soldier Vote. "That's okay, Joe," says Willie resignedly, "at least we can take bets."

After *Yank*, the Army weekly, published an article about road-blocks to absentee voting, Army Lieutenant Lawrence Cane, in England, was stirred to request a state ballot. Further, he wrote to his wife, Grace, "I've also taken care of all New Yorkers in my company. I know damn well that Southern states will probably prevent voting by soldiers—so they can keep on preventing Ne-groes from voting. . . . The Republicans seem to be dusting off some moldy-looking prospects to put on sale for election this year. . . . All I can see is FDR. He gets my vote this year if it takes 6,000 miles of red tape to get it in." Cane was a rare activist among those in uniform. Most were quiet about their politics, and the traditional secret ballot remained secret—but for the unsup-ported charge by Senator Elbert Thomas of Oklahoma to a local women's club that absentee state ballots were on such thin paper that it was possible to determine without opening them how sol-diers voted.

In the end all forty-eight states furnished some means of armed forces voting, and the fought-over federal ballot permitted by twenty states was rarely employed. With a total of 3,094,042 service ballots received in the thirty states with 70 percent of the voting population, results in the other eighteen states not reporting sepa-rately very likely increased the number of soldier ballots cast to at least 4,400,000—most of them through the state-by-state machin-ery intended to eliminate voting by those of voting age restricted from the franchise at home through poll taxes and literacy tests. How many more personnel in uniform voted proved impossible to count, as some states mixed absentee and local ballots. In Missis-sippi, by law, a service ballot was to be returned unopened to a local citizen who dropped it into a ballot box along with his own vote. In Maine, town clerks mailed and received ballots which were sent to a central office with other absentee votes. In some states it was illegal for election officials to separate portions of the official canvass. In others it was required. The result was an enormous participatory success in the difficult circumstances, suggesting a real determination by those in uniform to make an electoral difference.

By War Department direction, Army Special Services officers began a campaign of information, visits and unit inspections to ensure that each individual who could be reached in existing conditions was aware of his voting rights, qualifications, and access to a ballot. To prod servicemen (and women) to request a ballot expeditiously and to vote quickly on receipt, the Department issued estimates for overseas, given the uncertainties of space and transport problems, of the time it would take for completed ballots to reach home destinations for tabulating:

> Alaskan area: nearest, 14 days; farthest, 17 days
> Pacific area: nearest, 18 days; farthest, 30 days
> Caribbean area, including Panama Canal Zone: nearest, 12 days; farthest, 16 days
> South Atlantic area: nearest, 14 days; farthest, 16 days
> Middle East area, including Persian Gulf: nearest, 18 days; farthest, 22 days
> Far East area: nearest, 18–21 days; farthest, 22–26 days
> Mediterranean area, including Europe: nearest, 18–21 days; farthest 22–28 days
> North Atlantic area: nearest, 14 days; farthest, 24 days

Even in states where absentee ballots could be counted until December 18, when the Electoral College met in Washington to formalize the outcome, it was assumed by local governments that the service vote would reflect the civilian vote. Yet it became obviously rather quickly that there were grounds for Republican fears that this would not be the case. The Commander-in-Chief was on the ballot. After military successes East and West, it was difficult, especially for participants, to criticize the conduct of the war.

Sealed absentee ballots were countersigned by designated election officers to vouch for their validity. Jerry Geiger, an air corps second lieutenant from Okemos, Michigan, signed ballots at the Springfield, Illinois, air depot, where he discovered (without asking) that most men were casting their first vote, and knowing no other president in their brief lives, had opted for Roosevelt. To encourage balloting, war cameramen overseas were permitted to photograph service personnel as they voted, although their choices of candidates were never quoted, hinted at or shown. In rather quiet England, five soldiers were photographed, ballots in hand, queued beside a curtained area labeled "voting booth." In New Guinea an officer was shown supervising the voting of his troops in home elections while seven GIs looked on, awaiting their own ballots. An Associated Press wirephoto pictured six seamen "at an advanced base somewhere in the Pacific," each holding a ballot, lined up in front of a small temporary structure under a placard advising VOTE HERE. On the wall was a sample ballot. In Australia, Navy lieutenant Ralph W. Condee mailed his absentee Illinois ballot, marked for FDR—his family was rigidly Democratic. Chicago Yeoman 1/c Russell McCauley Jr., in the Seventh Fleet on a ship hauling gasoline in Tacloban Harbor, Leyte, after 4½ years of duty, and a Republican at home, did not vote because "I felt that FDR was our best hope of ending the war," while Robert Hickman, an ensign, "opposed to a 4th term," voted for Dewey.

Most servicemen voted "to get the goddamn thing over with and go home." To get home required the end of the war. The war was the reason they were far from home. Ideological appeals in campaign leaflets or alternative rhetoric would have meant nothing, and they gave it little credence when it turned up in newspapers or magazines or mail. Many were too preoccupied with staying alive to be concerned about obtaining a ballot. Voting never occurred to Captain Murray Kaye of New Jersey, who had landed in North Africa, then Sicily, then (in Operation Neptune, as part of a special engineering brigade group) Omaha Beach in Normandy on D-Day.

TIME published a photo of Private Richard Long of New York, cartridge belt slung round him and rifle on his shoulder, explaining a long sheet labeled WAR GENERAL BALLOT to two local women in Wiltz, Luxembourg. Another, on the cover of *Newsweek*, showed a helmeted lieutenant sitting at a table in front of an open barn in Consthum, Luxembourg, with a "Service Voting" sheet on the outside wall and another on the barn door; two GIs with ballots, one with a rifle on his shoulder, explaining the details to a young woman; and two children sifting through the straw on the ground for possible war souvenirs.

In Nancy, France, Sergeant Sam Kramer of Ithaca, New York, in the Fourth Armored Division of Patton's Third Army, voted for FDR as "the better man," recalling that "90% of our company" voted for Roosevelt after a GI from Rome, Georgia, explained how to apply for, and fill out, a ballot. Vince Suppan, a forward artillery observer in France, although a registered Democrat, chose Dewey, and voted Republican in every election thereafter without changing his registration. He was, he explained, a "conservative Democrat." In Italy, helmeted Corporal Tito Farcellese was shown in a press photo "near the front line," ballot in hand, authenticating his identity to Captain William H. Atkinson.

A Press Association photo from China, staged to demonstrate racial camaraderie, showed four GIs with absentee ballots, the two whites flanking an Asian and a Black. In Atlanta, Georgia, Army cadet nurse Rachel N. Williams was photographed with a ballot and described as possibly the youngest service voter in the nation. Georgia law newly permitted anyone properly registered to vote if eighteen before the polls closed. No other state allowed voting at her age. At Temple University in Philadelphia, Apprentice Seaman Jack Hargleroad, in medical school in midshipman's uniform courtesy of the Navy, weighed his concerns about Roosevelt's "ego" with "changing horses in midstream," then voted for Roosevelt.

Direct political appeals could not be made to service personnel, but they could be targeted indirectly. Roosevelt had labeled as "fantastic" the charge that his administration intended to keep men in the military after the war to avoid vast unemployment. But it kept being repeated, Dewey observing that the President's own Director of Selective Service, Lewis Hershey, "appointed by Mr. Roosevelt and still in office," had said as much. The War Department's plan for "speedy discharges" had fixed no dates or deadlines, and Hershey had put his foot in his mouth. Addressing Democratic Party workers, the President noted, obviously for transmission to service eyes and ears, that the George-Murray Reconversion Act specifically prohibited keeping men in military service "for the purpose of preventing unemployment." For soldiers to get home, however, the war had to be won.

While Nazi Germany looked on warily, Tokyo radio took sides. Air Forces sergeant E. F. Carr of Massachusetts, who had already been awarded the Distinguished Flying Cross, wrote home from the Pacific, "Tokyo Radio is really hot for Dewey. They think he is a great guy and they want us to think so. Dewey may be O.K. But if Tokyo doesn't want Roosevelt, they must have a good reason, and I think the reason is that they're losing the war." A serviceman otherwise unidentified, in a letter to the editor of the *Boston Globe*, claimed to represent contrary service opinion. "Mr. Roosevelt is an old man. Mr. Dewey is a young man with lots of energy. That is why we prefer Mr. Dewey for President." Another with opposite views, Pfc. Rodolph H. Turcotte, writing from a military hospital, observed, "When I vote for Mr. Roosevelt, it will be the first time that I voted for a Democrat." He put the choice in medical terms. Offering Mr. Dewey as President "is like proposing that a company aid man, a private or a corporal, be made chief surgeon of an Army hospital." At Valley Forge Army Hospital, infantry sergeant Bob Brandt of the 16th Regiment, First Division, having seen action in the Mediterranean and again in France, and later overseas in the diplomatic service, voted for Roosevelt. At Camp Kilmer, New Jersey, Sergeant Herbert Reiman of the Bronx, in the 335th Regiment, 84th Division, about to board a troopship, voted for FDR. The 84th would soon be in Belgium, in the "Bulge." About to ship out to Italy, Pfc. Andy Coletti of the 10th Mountain Division, a bugler and radioman from the Bronx, re-thought his intended vote for Roosevelt after "bright college kids" in his unit reminded him that the President had promised before the last election that American boys would not be sent to fight on foreign soil. Coletti marked his absentee ballot for Dewey.

Staff Sergeant Guy Taylor of Mayville, New York, a radioman with the 131st Infantry, 33rd Division in a headquarters unit in Versailles ("SHAEF rhymes with safe," he recalled*), voted for Roosevelt "because there wasn't anyone better." Some younger voters had inherited the political loyalties of their parents, marking their ballots automatically as if at home. Others later remembered their service loyalties. Seamen aboard ships in the Pacific recalled voting for FDR "because he is a Navy man." (Roosevelt had been assistant secretary of the Navy throughout the earlier world war.) But not Jack Murphy, later a captain. His father had worked for Wendell Willkie in 1940 and had been promised a White House job if Willkie had won. Willkie was not on the ballot this time, but father and son voted Republican anyway. In San Diego, Al Schroeder, M.D., a new medical officer at the naval base en route to the Seventh Fleet in Leyte Gulf in the Philippines, and still "struggling to adapt to the Navy," voted for Roosevelt. On a landing craft in the Pacific, Lieutenant Roland S. Larsen, recalling "lots of support for FDR" in his area, cast a ballot for Roosevelt as "our hope for the future." On the destroyer USS *Bailey* in the Pacific, Gyrocompass Yeoman Warren I. Colehour "didn't want to change presidents" and voted for Roosevelt. Aboard the carrier *Yorktown* in the central

---

* Supreme Headquarters Allied Expeditionary Force, General Eisenhower's command.

Pacific, Lieutenant Leon Frankel, a Navy flier who survived to earn a Navy Cross for sinking the destroyer *Yahagi* off Okinawa the next April, voted for the President as "the best qualified candidate." On the island of Espiritu Santo in the New Hebrides, east of Australia, Lieutenant Wesley Pearl of the 23rd Chemical Company returned his absentee ballot to Washington, marked for Roosevelt. Like Pearl, few recalled much discussion about politics or candidates. They voted for getting home.

In England, Staff Sergeant Irving P. Rothberg of the 14th Troop Carrier Squadron in Barkston, near Grantham, marked his ballot for Roosevelt. Pfc. Ray Nagell, with the 321st Regiment of the 101st Airborne in Belgium, voted for "our candidate"—FDR. "Our" seemed accurate. Where tallies were possible, the President, it would turn out, garnered more than 70 percent of the uniformed vote. Yet FDR was not every GI's candidate. First Lieutenant J. Norman Johnson of the 82nd Airborne, waiting in Soissons to move into Belgium, followed family loyalties and voted for Dewey. Returning home after two years overseas, a serviceman from Newport, Rhode Island, registered his outrage, in a letter to the editor, about Roosevelt's obvious appeal for the Catholic vote through praise of failed 1928 presidential candidate Al Smith. Former governor Smith, Roosevelt's predecessor in Albany, had taken "a walk" from the Democrats in 1936 and never returned. In effect it was a vote for Dewey.

A Coast Guard "Yeoman" writing from "Somewhere in California" to *The Nation* reported that he had no difficulty obtaining an absentee ballot—it took only three weeks.

> When the ballot arrived, I zipped open the envelope, whipped out my pen, and cast my vote. . . . My next step was to get an officer to sign my ballot. At the exact time I desired the presence of an officer, a short ensign walked by. I told him what I wanted, and handed him my pen. He was neither reluctant nor angry with me because I wished to exercise my right to vote. As a matter of fact,

the ensign and I had quite a long political discussion. He told me
he was voting for Landon, and I assured him he couldn't win. We
parted the best of friends.

Governor Alfred Landon of Kansas had won only the electoral
votes of Maine and Vermont in 1936.

On the eve of Election Day an editorial writer in *The Christian
Century* worried, "Will this be the last civilian election?" When war
veterans returned, "Will they vote as ex-soldiers? If so, we may just
have had our last 'civilian' election for a long time." And he named
a litany of political figures, famous and less so, who were serving in
the armed forces and would come home to furnish a "crop of candidates" exploiting their military records, authentic or inflated, or
who would have their war visibility exploited by political parties.
Such candidates would indeed emerge, but the voting public tem-
porarily in service would put away its uniforms and vote as it
always had—for personalities, and issues, and the familial legacies
of party loyalty.

The chances of a state's electoral votes turning on service ballots loomed only if current contests proved close. In states like
Connecticut, the military vote was tallied on election night as part
of the general vote, with no separate identifications. The town of
Sheridan, overwhelmingly Republican, where 258 residents cast
ballots, recorded only 19 GI votes, a rather low percentage. Eleven
states would count some or all their absentee soldier ballots after
election day. Pennsylvania, with 35 electoral votes, would not begin
its count until November 22. California, with 25 electoral votes,
would tally them on November 24, and Nebraska's deadline for its
6 votes was December 1, as was Rhode Island's 4 votes. Washington's tally date for its 8 votes was December 5, as were the 8 votes of
Florida. If service ballots were crucial, the final outcome would be
in doubt for days, or weeks.

Nine

The Closing Weeks

U pbeat after New York City, and massive sea-and-air victories off the Philippines,* the President used his Sunday at Hyde Park to pose for newsreel shots with Fala, then to go for a brisk drive with Eleanor in his customized hand-operated Ford convertible through masses of colorful autumn foliage—again an opportunity for press cameramen. In the last weeks of the campaign, moviegoers nationwide would see him seemingly relaxed and fit. Churchill would cable on October 23, "I was delighted to see the proofs of your robust vigor in New York. Nevertheless I cannot believe that four hours in an open car and pouring rain with a temperature of 40 and clothes wet through conform to those limits of prudence which you would be so ready to prescribe if it were my case." The PM could not think about anything but the imminent election.

---

* FDR sprang one "flash" on reporters on October 24—that he had just received word that "in the Philippine area [an enemy fleet] has been defeated, seriously damaged, and routed."

"My journey to New York was useful," FDR replied, "and rain does not hurt an old sailor. Thank you for your advice nevertheless. I am in top form."

At Hyde Park he had more than a couple of drinks before dinner, according to Grace Tully, then wheeled himself to work at his corner desk on the ground floor. He had to deal with communications about travel to a Big Three meeting, possibly as early as November or December. To satisfy "U.J."—as he and Churchill referred to "Uncle Joe" Stalin—it would take place at a mild Black Sea port, if they could not persuade Stalin to more neutral Cyprus. "My doctors advise for the time being," Stalin cabled his gravely ailing colleague, "against long journeys." Whatever the date, it implied an expected electoral victory, for a lame-duck leader could bind the United States to nothing.

After Roosevelt's display of urban theater, Governor Dewey altered his closing strategy. Rather than deliver a nationwide address on farm policy, he switched to a more dramatic response on world affairs. (For foreign policy he regularly invoked John Foster Dulles, praised in Luce's *Life*—two presidencies too soon—as the next Secretary of State.*) Already on Dewey's schedule was a whirlwind three-day tour of Minnesota, Wisconsin and Illinois. In Chicago he spoke to an overflow audience at the convention hall where he had been nominated, after heading a parade through Chicago's Loop, where the crowds were estimated at a half million. Middle West trends appeared promising for Republicans. In return for campaign contributions of a thousand dollars—then real money—Dewey charged, the Roosevelt ticket sold "special privilege" entitling donors to influence Administration policy. The "One Thousand Club" represented "in crude, unblushing words . . . the ultimate expression of New Deal policies." (The President told reporters that

---

* Dulles had diplomatic experience dating back to the Hague Conference of 1907 and as a prominent lay Presbyterian had long been involved in international conferences of churchmen. Yet his Wall Street law firm had also handled the incorporation of the America First Committee.

he was surprised to get a membership certificate himself for his "regular contribution. . . . I didn't even know that I was eligible.")

Dewey, asked by newsmen aboard his special train en route to Cleveland for his reactions to the President's Waldorf-Astoria speech, in which Republicans were condemned for voting against prewar preparedness, declared that he would "fill in the context which Mr. Roosevelt forgot." Did he see eye-to-eye with Roosevelt on postwar international cooperation? "I practically never see eye to eye with the President," Dewey snapped. "Congress, and only Congress," Dewey had told his Minnesota listeners, as well as a national audience on radio, "has the constitutional power to determine what quota of force it will make available [to keep the peace]." Despite majorities, Roosevelt had shown "that he cannot work with a Congress of his own party." Only he—Dewey—could close "the gaps" in American foreign policy, which now included dangerous accommodations with Communism. Otherwise he predicted, "again, as in 1918, . . . a disastrous conflict between the President and the Congress. To that I will never be a party. It is too important to hang by the slender thread of one man's continuity in office."

Harry Truman was campaigning in the West, his train reaching Seattle in mid-October, then turning east into Idaho and Montana. From Butte on October 21 he wrote to Bess, exuberantly,

> Everywhere the train stops for a minute there are big crowds and back platform appearances. . . . At two Idaho towns they dismissed the schools and all the kids were at the station. I' am very popular, at least with the kids in these towns. I've made 26 speeches since leaving New Orleans and I was only supposed to make three up to this point. But we knocked 'em over in Los Angeles and San Francisco, and even *TIME* is coming out with a special edition with me on the cover Nov. 6. "Ain't that sompin." It's a satisfaction to make 'em like it.

His allusion was to the Luce publications, which were giving more than sympathetic attention to the Dewey-Bricker ticket, and *TIME* may have used a cover portrait of the rather plain, bespectacled Truman rather insidiously—to suggest in the run-up to Election Day that he was, in effect, the presumptive presidential candidate—the unattractive other end of the "slender thread."

The week before *TIME*'s Truman cover, *Life* would publish a three-page editorial by former Foreign Policy Association chairman Raymond L. Buell in its October 30 issue, dated nearly a week in advance, "Should Liberals Vote for Dewey?" Buell was on the staff of *Fortune,* sister publication of *Life* and *TIME,* the latter which would also declare on October 30 that the prospect of a fourth term was sufficient reason "to throw the rascals out." *TIME* had already filled its columns in October with rallying points for Dewey, who "had a field day with a hatful of hapless Administration quotes. . . . Republicans everywhere were heartened by the stiffness of his mustached upper lip. . . . [H]is fame as the fearless young prosecutor was secure. . . . [a] rapid success story, from small-town editor's son to governor of the biggest state. . . . A crisp, vigorous young man . . . who had perfect stage presence. . . . He was cool, precise, tough-minded. . . . He was the only candidate discussing the issues."

Roosevelt, on the other hand, even aside from "Term IV," was personally suspect. "Perhaps Franklin Roosevelt doesn't like the Communists," said Dewey, "but look how they like him." Dewey had been alternating between Communism and monarchy in characterizing a fourth-term candidacy. Although the President joked about the contradiction, "Term IV" evoked the numerical image of monarchy. FDR had long been attacked in royal terms. Cantankerous poet Robert Frost, one of the more colorful critics, scoffed at "His Rosiness."

Unintentionally, *TIME* was sandbagging Dewey. Only "Republicans"—a minority of voters—seemed "heartened" by Dewey's stiff upper lip, and the accent on "young man" and "young prosecutor" called attention to his national and international inexperience. Campaign manager Brownell worried that in newsreels, "the black mustache loomed out of proportion and made Dewey look like a villain, and many people formed their opinion of the candidate from these newsreels." *The New York Times*, nevertheless, reported on October 27 that the governor was indeed "heartened by the receptions he has received" in Chicago, Minneapolis and Milwaukee, "and his advisers express the belief that there has been a great swing to him recently." The campaign raised more money, and more of his speeches would be broadcast nationwide in the closing weeks. Reassuring, too, were the numbers of newspapers editorially supporting Dewey—60 percent of the press, compared with 22 percent for FDR. Yet the news columns were seldom so skewed. A president made news.

Roosevelt was back at the White House for a luncheon on Tuesday, October 24, with Anna as hostess, for Averell Harriman, his ambassador to Moscow, who had been working on arrangements for the next meeting with Stalin and Churchill. FDR predicted a close election but expected to still be president when he saw Stalin. To Harriman, Roosevelt appeared "very much thinner than when I had seen him in May and therefore the lines in his face made him look considerably older. He was, however, vigorous and determined in spirit." Stalin, Harriman emphasized, remained adamant about fixing postwar Polish boundaries as long demanded. With the Polish vote in key states in question, FDR said, he felt "helpless to do anything constructive" until the election was over. To Harriman, he showed "little interest in Eastern European matters except as they affect sentiment in America."

The luncheon, begun at 1:15, lasted until three, "ruining his afternoon appointments." Although a serving ambassador is nonpolitical by tradition, Harriman—very wealthy with railroad and banking interests—asked for permission to buy radio time to endorse the President's re-election. He felt unable "to pretend that I had lost all political emotions upon accepting a government position."

Buying access to a nationwide audience on NBC cost him $5,000 for fifteen minutes of air time—equivalent many decades after to something in six figures. Ten days later he cautioned listeners that although Governor Dewey may have altered his rhetoric, "his past views are well known," and he was supported by former and present isolationists. On the other hand, "Never in the history of the world has one man—Roosevelt—had the confidence of the peoples of so many nations and their leaders. . . . This confidence we can ill afford to lose at this critical and formative time."

Following the governor to Minneapolis, Harry Truman questioned Dewey's foreign affairs bona fides by urging him to reject eight "isolationist" Republican senators running for re-election "or the people must assume he is another Harding." Strongly internationalist, Senator Joe Ball of Minnesota, a maverick Republican, had been dodging an endorsement for Dewey for weeks, and had now come out for Roosevelt. "If Dewey means it," Truman charged, Dewey had to call for the defeat of Robert A. Taft of Ohio, Gerald P. Nye of North Dakota, Charles W. Tobey of New Hampshire, John A. Danaher of Connecticut, James Davis of Pennsylvania, Clyde M. Reed of Kansas, Alexander Wiley of Wisconsin and Eugene D. Millikin of Colorado.

"I hope you heard the President," Truman reminded his audience "the man the Republicans would have you think is a tired old man, when he told you in stirring, vigorous words last Saturday night about his program to win the war and to secure the peace—the peace we fought for in the last war and that Harding and the Republican reactionaries lost in the Twenties. That must not happen again."

Worried that it could happen, especially if the conservative Midwest resumed its familiar voting patterns, Mayor Kelly turned to Turner Catledge, in Chicago to report on a Democratic rally headed by another mayor, the feisty Fiorello La Guardia of New York. "What do you think," Kelly asked, en route to the Coliseum, "about Roosevelt coming out here to make a big speech in Soldier

Field?" Bertie McCormick's *Tribune* had published an editorial, "Mr. Roosevelt's Health," on October 17, declaring that it was "one of the principal issues of the campaign and cannot be evaded by false appeals to delicacy."

La Guardia, after the New York City triumph, was all for a Chicago appearance to further defuse concerns about the President. "We've just got to get him to come out," La Guardia claimed. "A tremendous crowd out here will clinch it."

"Okay, gentlemen," said Catledge. "Do I have a story, or not?" Kelly agreed to a story, "But be careful because we haven't got his consent yet. The story is that we are urging him to come out here."

After the dispatch appeared, Roosevelt sent for Catledge, who felt squeamish, remembering his previous visit to the White House in March. "But when I walked into his office, a new man was sitting there beaming at me. He was still thin and emaciated, but he had life and spirit in his face." Catledge thought, "It's the campaign that's revived him—politics is this man's life blood."

The President asked whether he was "in trouble" in Illinois and ought to "go out there," but as a reporter Catledge could not take sides. "You don't even know if I'm for you or against you." Roosevelt tilted his head and laughed. He knew how many electoral votes were at stake in the Midwest. "Why don't we make a little deal?" he offered. "You write a story that says I'll go, but you say it on your own. Don't tell Fiorello or Ed Kelly I said I was going, because I'll tell them later. But go ahead and say it's going to be done."

Largely anti-FDR, newspapers made perverse capital of the President's seemingly sudden resort to campaign travel. Earlier he had told a press conference that he would be too busy running the war to politic in the traditional manner, but the motorcade in the rain through four of New York's boroughs suggested to some editors not his resilience but his increasing concern over the closing in of the electoral percentages. Even the temperate if conservative weekly

The Christian Century warned in coming out for Governor Dewey that the President was

> laying the foundation for a fifth term campaign. One thing to be expected with confidence in 1948, if Mr. Roosevelt survives until then, and has four more years in office, is that there will be a "crisis" at that time and Mr. Roosevelt will have what can then be made to look like a corner on the experience market. . . . If there were no other issue in this campaign than the issue of the fourth term, this in itself would be decisive in convincing this paper that it must oppose Mr. Roosevelt's re-election.

With the likelihood of a substantial electorate reluctant to vote for a fourth term, the President had also been pondering whom, from the outside, to woo as a visible convert to the cause, and decided mistakenly upon Joseph P. Kennedy. Wealthy, shady and increasingly conservative, the entrepreneurial Boston Irishman, for financial and political services rendered, had held New Deal posts in the 1930s, culminating in his disastrous appointment in 1938 as ambassador to London. In England he had linked himself to defeatist and appeasement circles, becoming a political embarrassment once war with Germany began. Late in 1940, with the Blitz underway, Kennedy returned, never to have another post under the President. On a Christmas trip back home in December 1939 he had been invited to the White House to discuss Roosevelt's policy of armed neutrality with a British bias. "You and I have always seen this thing the same way," FDR fudged. Both knew that was entirely false.

Even then the two despised each other, but Kennedy retained powerful political clout in strongly Catholic New England. Remaining to observe a press conference, he returned afterwards to Roosevelt's desk. "Did you see me finish off another candidate for President this morning?" FDR asked. "That relief question in Ohio finishes Bricker and yet I never mentioned his name." The President had ridiculed the isolationist, ultra-conservative governor of Ohio for trying to balance his state budget on the backs of the unemployed seeking relief aid. Since Roosevelt had raised the issue of politics, and 1940 loomed, Kennedy felt free to ask, "What about this 3rd term? You'll have to run."

"Joe," he confided, according to Kennedy's diary, "I can't. I'm tired. I can't take it. What I need is one year's rest. . . . I just won't go on unless we are in [a] war." Pearl Harbor was two years away.

In London the next April, Lord Halifax, the Foreign Secretary, asked Kennedy if he thought that Roosevelt would run again. The ambassador "thought he might if he saw the US possibly involved, but only if the situation in the war in Europe was in a hectic state." A few days later the Germans invaded Denmark and Norway, and a month after that the *Reichswehr* began tearing through Holland, Belgium and France.

When in Boston late in October 1940, with the third-term campaign underway and nearing its close, Kennedy knew he was through as ambassador. Yet Roosevelt asked him to deliver a supportive radio address. More isolationist than ever, although willing to aid Britain just enough to "buy time" for the United States to hunker down, Kennedy wavered. He was additionally bitter over being bypassed (as obviously untrustworthy) on matters normally ambassadorial. Clare Luce urged him to refuse Roosevelt, cajoling that he would be "doing America a terrible disservice" for "you'll probably help to turn the trick for him." Reluctantly, he agreed to a pro-Roosevelt speech, which was broadcast on the evening of October 29, 1940, over 114 stations of the Columbia Broadcasting System. "A new hand [in office]," he concluded cautiously, "cannot give to these problems [of war and peace] that careful, thorough and intelligent attention which they must immediately have if our nation is to be secure."

The President telegraphed Kennedy, using an adjective with an Irish lilt, that it was "a grand speech" but offered no new job. On December 7, 1941, when organized isolationism crumbled in an afternoon, Kennedy wired the President, "In this great crisis all Americans are with you. Name the battle post. I'm yours to command." Kennedy was snubbed. Claiming, dubiously, later that in the chaos of Pearl Harbor he was never given the telegram, Roosevelt never acknowledged the message.

At 11:45 a.m. on Thursday, October 26, 1944, responding to an urgent request relayed by Grace Tully, Kennedy, bespectacled and his thinning hair now gray, was at the White House for the first time in three years. He assumed that he was being bought off, and was eager for Henry Morgenthau's uneasy seat in the Cabinet. (The "Morgenthau Plan" had damaged the Treasury secretary.) The President's real aim seems to have been to ward off a rumored broadcast supporting Dewey. On the way to 1600 Pennsylvania Avenue, Kennedy called at the British Embassy, where Lord Halifax was now ambassador. When Halifax asked whether he had come down to make a speech for the President, Kennedy said, "Positively not. I have no confidence in the outfit. I didn't think Roosevelt was well enough to carry on, and I thought we had the makings of an unholy mess." He also had much closer concerns. In August his eldest son, Joe Jr., twenty-nine and politically ambitious, had died when his explosives-packed B-24 disintegrated over the English Channel. Flying to his rear was Roosevelt's son Elliott. His photo-reconnaissance Mosquito light bomber was nearly flipped over by the blast.

Kennedy's younger son Jack, critically injured when his patrol boat *PT 109* was cut in half by a Japanese destroyer in the Solomons, had been evacuated to the States and was healing slowly at the Chelsea Naval Hospital in Boston. In September, the elder Kennedy's titled English son-in-law, husband of the former ambassador's daughter Kathleen, had been killed in action. Her father's defeatist reputation lingered in England, and the widowed Kathleen would write to Jack sarcastically on October 31 that she had "just read in the paper this morning that [Archbishop] Archie Spellman brought back [from the Vatican] a tremendously high decoration to Daddy. What was that for? His children's war record?"

Roosevelt praised the heroism of Joe and Jack. Kennedy was unmoved. "If I hadn't been warned by the stories of his illness," he told his diary, " . . . I would have been shocked beyond words. He sat behind his desk, and his face was as gray as his hair, [he] put out his hand in a very friendly manner, and asked me to sit down. . . . I was convinced that he is far from a well man. He is thin; he has an unhealthy color. His hands shake violently when he tries to take a drink of water." Kennedy recalled that some of Roosevelt's words were slurred, and that he had memory slips about names and numbers; but he retained "a great deal of his old charm." The President asked for his estranged colleague's thoughts about the election. It should be close, said Kennedy; he thought the odds he had heard of 3–1 in Roosevelt's favor were "too high for the evidence as we all saw it. . . . I told him"—this was Kennedy's later spin on the conversation—

that in my opinion the so-called 5 per cent vote that had yet to make up its mind was for the first time, not an independent vote, but was the old line Democrats—the Irish and the Italians—all of whom should be in the Democratic column but this year were off for two or three good reasons: First, they felt that Roosevelt was Jew-controlled. Second, they felt that the Communists were coming into control. Third, that this group [of ethnic voters], along with many others, felt that there were more incompetents in Roosevelt's Cabinet than you could possibly stand in this country. . . . They will write you down in history if you don't get rid of them.

The President apparently ignored the anti-Jewish slurs, if actually made—Kennedy's letters and diaries are replete with obsessive anti-Semitism—and blamed Italian antipathy in the United States, if it existed as charged, on how the British were handling Italy. He thought that any domestic Irish unhappiness related to the hostility of independent and stubbornly neutral Ireland toward Britain.

After some discussion of de Gaulle and Stalin and Churchill, Kennedy's diary entry for the meeting concluded with Roosevelt's concession that he understood the "unwillingness to commit" to the fourth-term campaign, but that the press, knowing of the visit, "would want to know what took place in here, and I am perfectly willing to tell them." Nevertheless, "since I imagine some of it might be unfair," the President said that he would report only that they discussed postwar employment plans—which indeed was how the visit had been initiated.

Kennedy went on to James Byrnes's White House office to share their mutual bitterness. Byrnes acknowledged that he would shortly make one speech for the President, "simply a gesture," and planned to resign one week after the election. (In a nationally broadcast address on October 30, Byrnes would declare that a change in the presidency "would inevitably delay the winning of the war and jeopardize the peace for which our boys are fighting and dying.") Kennedy felt reassured that Dewey still had a chance. But an index to how the Catholic vote would go was that C. G. Paulding, in an editorial in the Roman Catholic organ *Commonweal* on October 27, closed with, "Another candidate is frivolous. I shall vote for Mr. Roosevelt."

Going to Chicago on the *Henry M. Stanley,* Truman found that the unfriendly Hearst newspaper chain had claimed that he had once worn the white hood of the Ku Klux Klan. Fortunately, in 1922 he had hastily withdrawn his application, naively made when seeking votes, after learning of the Klan's motives; yet on October 27 while at the Blackstone Hotel he received a telegram from his brother Vivian that the smear had been reborn. An elderly Missourian, O. L. Chrisman, after two hours of persistent questioning by "a representative of a New York newspaper," had signed a statement that he had "seen Harry S. Truman at a Klan meeting." But Chrisman added that if Truman "ever became a member of the Klan I did not know it. . . . The newspaper man tried repeatedly to get me to say that Truman had appeared on the platform and had made speeches at Klan meetings. This was not true." Still, the *Mirror* in New York, not giving up on the smear, published a cartoon late in the campaign showing the Democratic donkey scrubbing Truman, in a washtub, to remove the stains labeled "KKK." "And who knows," says the apron-clad donkey, "you may be president some day."

The Hearst press allegation proved to have no legs and went into the burgeoning detritus of campaign rhetoric. The *Kansas City Star*, pro-Truman but anti–New Deal, editorialized, "There ought to be a time for the statute of limitations to run out on it." Exploiting the political gift, CIO president Philip Murray charged to a labor group about opposition meanness, "On November 8, when you go looking for the men who have been wearing the hoods during this campaign, you'll find a hood somewhere along the highway. Pick it up and under it you'll find a little man named Tom Dewey."

On October 27, the day following the Kennedy interview, although Roosevelt was tired and ailing, he marshaled his flagging energy to suggest otherwise. Opposition newspapers had already denounced his campaigning as departing from his vow on accepting the nomination not to electioneer in the "usual sense." FDR countered that the Dewey press was quoting only half a sentence, as he had added that he would respond to all misrepresentations made to score political points.

Roosevelt's next campaign target was Philadelphia, where oilman Joseph Pew, a long-time bankroller of Republican candidates, had just made the first political speech of his life. He predicted "the greatest Republican sweep in history, from one end of the country to the other." Roosevelt, he charged, was not campaigning for himself, but to make Senator Truman the next President. "We will not stand for this."

One week after the New York City motorcade, FDR was out of the White House and in the back seat of his open Packard. Again in

foul weather, he waved his sodden fedora in a chilling wind to wet
but exuberant crowds in Wilmington at 11 a.m. and spoke briefly
from the rear platform of the *Ferdinand Magellan*. Then came
Philadelphia and industrial Camden, across the Delaware, where
the President discovered that a ramp had been built in front of the
City Hall, where he had not been scheduled to speak. From a waiting microphone he offered reluctant greetings, and a large New
Jersey crowd cheered lustily in the rain. It was "the only time I ever
saw this kind of a surprise sprung on the Boss," Bill Hassett noted.

Not until the last hour of the 40-mile motorcade in Philadelphia
did the sun break through briefly. As in New York City, the tour
had shrewdly included military installations. The President had
arrived from Washington at the Baltimore & Ohio railway station,
with its distinctive Victorian cupola, at 24th and Chestnut Streets
on the east bank of the Schuylkill River. As his signature Navy cape
was splashed with rain he passed throngs on Broad Street, was
driven south to the Navy Yard, and to the huge Quartermaster
Depot, continuing across the long suspension bridge on the
Delaware to shipyards in Camden (and his unforeseen talk), then
back through Germantown and Chestnut Hill. On Broad Street a
policeman's mount had fallen in front of the leading Secret Service
vehicle and broken a leg. The halt to the motorcade was so brief
that Roosevelt was unaware it had happened.

The President then returned through more crowds to the B & O
station, where he changed clothes and rested until his scheduled
speechmaking event at nine in the evening. The baseball grandstands in Shibe Park at 21st Street, home of the doormat Philadelphia Athletics, were full as his Packard ascended a wooden ramp at
second base. After a battery of microphones fixed to a board was
placed across the wound-down windows, Roosevelt removed his
hat to loud cheers, and when the ovation failed to fade at his hand
signal, he began anyway, with the familiar opening he used for his
radio addresses, and going on to claim a militant Republican predecessor, his "Uncle Ted," for his side:

My Friends,

    I am glad to come back to Philadelphia. Today is the anniversary of the birth of a great fighting American—Theodore Roosevelt. This day—his birthday—is celebrated every year as Navy Day, and I think that Theodore Roosevelt would be happy and proud to know that our American fleet today is greater than all of the navies of the world put together. And when I say all the navies, I am including what was—until three days ago—the Japanese fleet.

    Since Navy Day a year ago our armed forces—Army, Navy and Air Forces—have participated in no fewer than twenty-seven different D days, twenty-seven different landings in force on enemy-held soil. Every one of these landings has been an incredibly complicated and hazardous undertaking, as you realize, requiring months of most careful planning, flawless coordination and literally split-second timing in execution. The larger operations have required hundreds of warships, thousands of smaller craft, thousands of airplanes, and hundreds of thousands of men.

Then, pausing dramatically between each word, he went on, "And—every–one–of–these–twenty-seven–D days–has–been–a–triumphant–success." The roaring cheers could be heard on radios across the land. (The enthusiasm might have been more muted had the casualties in contested landings been revealed.) Shortly, FDR added, "I wonder what became of the suggestions made a few weeks ago that I had failed, for political reasons, to send enough forces or supplies to General MacArthur?" It was obvious to listeners that "D day" planning and the apportioning of military strength among vast theaters of operations oceans apart were not hasty responses to attacks by a "prominent Republican orator" who had described the Roosevelt government as old and tired, and "the most spectacular collection of incompetent people who ever held public office." Nor, it was obvious, had the Administration made "absolutely no military preparations for the events that it now claims it foresaw." That was a "pretty serious" charge, said the President, "because the only conclusion to be drawn . . . is that we are losing this war. If so, that will be news to most of us—and it will certainly be news to the Nazis and the Japs."

The Japanese navy, he went on, had just received "the worst licking in its history," and Admiral Halsey's fleet proved American prewar preparation—construction of every battleship involved, all but one of the cruisers, and half of the aircraft carriers in the battles off Leyte had been begun or authorized before Pearl Harbor.

To furnish some idea of the magnitude and the complexity of operations, past, present and future, he offered a few numbers about "the miracle of production" intended to boggle the mind:

> The scope of the two-ocean war has meant moving supplies along . . . at the rate of almost three million tons a month, requiring 576 cargo ships to leave our ports with supplies every month. It has meant moving more than 14 million barrels of gasoline and oil a month, requiring 156 tanker sailings each month. And all those ships and all those tankers were built in American shipyards. . . . The whole story of our vast efforts in this war has been the story of the incredible achievements—the story of the job that has been done by an administration which, I am told, is old and tired and quarrelsome.

As the cheers echoed through the stadium, the President waved his soggy fedora, and his Packard descended the platform and wheeled on to his waiting train, for an appearance in Chicago the next evening, October 28.

As the *Ferdinand Magellan* proceeded overnight toward Fort Wayne, Indiana, where a platform address was scheduled, Dr. Gallup released his latest poll figures, estimating the popular vote (servicemen excluded) as 49 percent for Dewey, 51 percent for Roosevelt. Realizing that there were misgivings about FDR's health, despite the commanding episode in the New York City rain, and then Philadelphia, the President told the crowd at the station, "I am in the middle of a war, and so are you. . . . It is quite a job, but I am perfectly able to take it, and so are you." A few days earlier, a *Fortune* poll—the magazine was a Luce monthly for the moneyed—estimated Roosevelt at 53.5 percent against Dewey's 46.5. The apparent narrowing of the gap—on Gallup's part—prompted newspapers to headline, "PRESIDENCY RACE IS NECK AND NECK."

While Roosevelt was in Philadelphia, John W. Bricker campaigned in Kansas City. His speech to Missourians was at odds from the President's claims of continuing military successes and their prewar origins. For eight years before Pearl Harbor, Bricker contended, Mr. Roosevelt had ignored German and Japanese aggression, leaving the nation unready. During those years, Bricker charged, FDR was "spending billions of taxpayer dollars on non-useful make-work and boondoggling" and "neglecting the defense of the United States. Even now the President is committing the same kind of blunders in foreign relations. He is pursuing a personal course of personal, secret diplomacy." Aside from validating treaties, a power given the Senate, the President possessed constitutional authority to conduct foreign relations—but Bricker counted on the public's being unaware that serious diplomacy was seldom conducted in newspapers. Until war came increasingly close, he claimed, Roosevelt promoted disarmament and put "attacks on business" ahead of preparedness. For the faithful, Bricker was advancing a parallel history of prewar and wartime America.

As the President's train rolled through Pennsylvania and into Ohio, he read over the draft of his committee-written Chicago speech. Although he had approved the draft when he first saw it, he was now dissatisfied. Twenty-eight electoral votes in Illinois were at stake. A copy of the text had been left at the White House for Isador Lubin, a veteran Department of Labor economist, to recheck all the facts. Lubin telegraphed a raft of corrections to the Army Signal Corps car on the campaign train, and longer responses to queries were placed aboard the train at scheduled stops. One responded to a query about the source of a quotation that, in the end, was scratched from the Chicago speech: "For Judge Rosenman from Lube. The statement 'Hitch your wagon to a star' appears in an essay entitled 'American Civilization' by Ralph Waldo Emerson. Boy, am I proud of this one. Please remember that I am an economist. . . . I am neither a littérateur, poet or playwright. What in hell have you got Bob [Sherwood] there for?" During the night and following day, into October 28, a Saturday, fresh drafts of the speech were typed out until Roosevelt approved its combining persuasive statistics about postwar employment projections with his expected informality.

At six in the evening, as the train pulled into a siding in the Dearborn yards, the President folded the finished speech into his inside jacket pocket. Looking out the window and seeing the steam rising from other trains, and the steamy breath of railwaymen, he asked warily about the temperature. It had dipped to 14 degrees above zero, and a strong wind was blowing across the choppy surface of Lake Michigan. Overcoat-bundled politicians, including Mayor Edward Kelly and Frank C. Walker, the Postmaster General and a former party chairman, began boarding the train. Despite the weather, Kelly told Roosevelt, 110,000 chilled Chicagoans had already filled cavernous Soldier Field, ten minutes away, and an estimated 125,000 had jammed the parking lots around the floodlit stadium on Lake Shore Drive, where loudspeakers were being affixed for the overflow. Dating from the 1920s and christened as a war memorial, it was best known for the Jack Dempsey–Gene Tunney heavyweight bout in 1927.*

---

* Soldier Field had not yet become the gridiron for the NFL Chicago Bears.

The President had experienced foul weather in New York and Philadelphia, but Chicago produced a more extreme dimension of inclemency. He was bundled warmly into his Packard once it was lowered from the train, and a twelve-vehicle motorcade pressed through the crowds, slowing to a near stop two blocks from Soldier Field while police walked ahead to clear a path. Once inside the arena, the open Packard circled dramatically, then moved toward a spotlighted platform where a tray of attached radio and public address microphones was waiting.

Pulling out his papers, Roosevelt realized that the powerful lights were refracting from his glasses, making his words swim. Other difficulties would emerge once he began. As he read his signature "My Friends" into the cheering of the throngs, inside and out, his voice over the amplification bounced back in the dark vastness, and he understood that because of the reverberations he

FDR waving to the crowd at windy Soldiers' Field, Chicago, from the bank of microphones at his open car, October 28, 1944. *FDR Library*

would have to slow down his speech. "Standing by his car," lanky playwright Robert Sherwood wrote, "I had the impression that some remote sections of the gigantic crowd present could not have a very precise idea of just what it was that he was saying; however that did not bother him as long as his words were getting through clearly over the radio."

The whirring of the newsreel cameras added distracting sounds, and Mayor Kelly, sitting next to the President and picking up the cadenced delivery, unrealizingly began repeating each word to himself, the cameras picking up the inadvertent comedy. Jim Beary of the Secret Service noticed, and recognized what movie audiences would see. He whispered to Mike Reilly, who whispered back, "Slip the Mayor a note." Beary hastily printed, "YOU ARE MOUTHING THE WORDS OF THE PRESIDENT. IT WILL BE EMBARRASSING TO HIM." Crouching, Beary slipped the scrap of paper to Kelly, which drew more camera attention to the Mayor, but he clammed up instantly. Bareheaded and in the intense cold, Roosevelt continued, unaware.

"Anyone could see," Bill Hassett observed from ground level, "that the Boss was having an uphill job trying to appeal personally to such a throng at such a distance."

Republican politicians, the President charged, were saying, in effect, "These incompetent blunderers and bunglers in Washington have passed a lot of excellent laws about social security and labor and farm relief and soil conservation—and many others—and we promise that if elected, we will not change any of them. . . . These same quarrelsome, tired old men . . . have built the greatest war machine the world has ever known, which is fighting its way to victory, and . . . if you elect us, we promise not to change any of that either. Therefore, say these Republican orators, it is time for a change. . . . These inefficient and worn-out crackpots have really begun to lay the foundations of lasting world peace. If you elect us, we will not change any of that either." But, the President added,

Republicans also promise to do nothing that would lose the support of any isolationists. "Why, we won't lose the support of even the *Chicago Tribune.*"

He wanted to lay out a blueprint for the American future, he continued. "I shall give the Republican orators some more opportunities to say 'Me too.' . . . When our men and women return from this war," he resolved, "they shall come back . . . to a place where all persons, regardless of race, and color, or creed, or place of birth, can live in peace and honor and human dignity—free to speak, free to pray as they wish, free from want, and free from fear." He then offered a Utopian prophecy which re-emphasized his State of the Union speech of the previous January 11. Conceding then to his frailty, in a departure from his usual practice he had sent the address to Congress rather than reading it in person. Although this was a foreshadowing of his diminishing health, he read it himself on radio in a Fireside Chat that evening, calling it a "Second Bill of Rights." In Chicago he outlined it, simply, again. What it lacked in eloquence it gained in understanding. Each sentence was punctuated by such cheers, despite the chill off Lake Michigan, that he had to pause at every semicolon:

> The right of a useful and remunerative job in the industries or shops or farms or mines of the nation;
>
> The right to earn enough to provide adequate food and clothing and recreation;
>
> The right of every farmer to raise and sell his products at a return which will give him and his family a decent living;
>
> The right of every businessman, large and small, to trade in an atmosphere of freedom from unfair competition and domination by monopolies at home or abroad;
>
> The right of every family to a decent home;
>
> The right to adequate medical care and the opportunity to achieve and enjoy good health;

The right to adequate protection from the economic fears of
old age, sickness, accident and unemployment;

The right to a good education.

Roosevelt's detractors had long scoffed at his "pipe dreams,"
but he vowed in Chicago, "After this war has ended, then will come
the time when the returning servicemen can grow their own apples
on their own farms instead of having to sell apples on the street
corners. . . . We are not going to turn the clock back." Many
decades later that faith in a bright tomorrow seems elusive—
clouded by factors which Roosevelt could not foresee. Yet the
vision endures.[*]

The President left Chicago to ear-splitting cheers, en route to
Washington. Early Sunday morning, his campaign train paused at
Clarksburg, West Virginia, and then at Grafton, where at a service
stop he wheeled out to the rear platform of the *Ferdinand Magellan*
and waved to a delighted crowd. At Clarksburg, the schedule called
for a ten-minute platform talk, but the crowd was large and enthusiastic and the sunny morning pleasant after Chicago. On braces
which the throng could not see, he stood and chatted in convivial
informality to a Bible Belt audience for far longer than he anticipated. "It was a great comfort," he said, "to come on a Sunday in a
campaign year, because on Sundays my life is made much more
comfortable by not having to think about politics. Unfortunately, I
have to think about the war, because every day, including Sunday,
dispatches come to me, on this train even, to tell me of the progress
of our boys in Europe and in the Pacific and in the Philippines. I
can't get rid of that."

---

[*] The "Second Bill of Rights" litany, mapping out a still-elusive American future and
captured on film in Chicago, reappears in Michael Moore's perversely titled *Capitalism: A Love Story* (2009). Manhola Dargis in a *New York Times* review (September 23,
2009) describes the scene as "the most galvanizing words in the movie . . . , moving
beyond words. And chilling."

Instead of politics, he said, he would "preach a sermon on trees." West Virginia's surface coal-mining, its chief industry, he realized that Sabbath morning as his train clicked through the state, was denuding the beautiful hills; and he thought of the line in Joyce Kilmer's poem, "Only God can made a tree." It was a great shame, he contended, that economic necessity was stripping the luxuriant landscape. "That is something in this country we have fallen down on. We have been using natural resources that we ought to have replaced. I know we can't replace coal—it will be a long time before all the coal is gone—but trees constitute something we can replace."

He told of a town he knew in Germany when he was a boy, and his parents had taken him traveling in Europe, where the people did not have to pay taxes for two hundred years because they were supported by logging of the great forests in the Taunus Mountains at the edge of their community.* The forests, he explained, had been given to the townspeople by the ruler of the principality because decades before, they had helped turn back an invading French army. In reverse, said the President, such a gift could be made by the American people to their grandchildren and great-grandchildren by reforestation of the country as an investment in its own future. In his family, he said, his father had practiced such conservation, but Roosevelt did not add—would it have been too political to mention, on a Sunday?—that when he had registered to vote in his district along the Hudson, he listed his occupation as "tree farmer." Hyde Park raised Christmas trees.

As October drew to a close, with a week of the campaign remaining, Governor Dewey huddled with his speech writers in Albany to prepare a major radio address to be delivered in Buffalo on the night of October 31, the last Tuesday before Election Day, and a

---

* Roosevelt at ten, in 1892, went to a local German school in the spa town of Bad Nauheim in Hesse for six weeks.

shorter talk en route in Rochester. Then he planned to make an intensive rail tour of New England. He told the writers to "pour it on." Yet he had already poured it on. "We need a house cleaning in Washington," he bristled to a sympathetic audience.

> I should like to clean house on those political satellites which have fastened themselves on your pocketbooks and mine for twelve years. I should like to get rid of that crew to whom my opponent is so indispensable. We should start of course with Harold Ickes and [Secretary of Labor] Madame Perkins and then we would go through with the elegant collection of loafers contributed to the Government by the Kelly machine in Chicago, the Pendergast machine in Kansas City, and those destroyers of civil liberty on the Federal payroll from Jersey City. [The Jersey City boss was Frank Hague, mayor for eight terms and notorious for corruption and for clamping down on political critics. FDR kept his distance.] Then we would go through the Sidney Hillman crew of the PAC, and finally, or perhaps first of all, clean out those who hold their offices and whose political and philosophical affiliations are with the gentleman whom my opponent had to pardon so he could wage this campaign—Mr. Browder.

In Chicago the President had pledged sixty million jobs in a burgeoning postwar economy that would need to employ former war workers and returning troops. Sam Rosenman, drawing on estimates from his sources, had placed the highest estimate at fifty-seven million. When the President's writers asked him what figure he wanted to use, he said, "Oh, let's make it a good round number—sixty million." By 1947 that count would be exceeded.

In Buffalo, ridiculing the likelihood of such unprecedented postwar prosperity, Dewey archly described the promise of millions of new jobs as "worthless, even if it is repeated again—and again—and again." The locution was characteristically Rooseveltian, and intended by the governor to be derisive, but Dewey's audience, anticipating no humor from him, remained silent. He waited; finally some laughter arose. "Your next President," Dewey continued, "will never make you a promise that he does not hope with all his heart and soul to keep." He also announced his support for a constitutional amendment to limit presidents to two terms of office. "Four terms, or sixteen years," he said, "is the most dangerous threat to our freedom ever proposed."*

Also on October 31, while Governor Dewey took the train to Buffalo, Senator Truman rode the rails to New York City, to speak at Madison Square Garden. In a show of Democratic unity, he appeared on the same platform as Henry Wallace. It was to be a Liberal Party show, the group legally limited to New York State. Truman's backers were counting upon Wallace loyalists, at the left of the political spectrum, to demonstrate enthusiasm for the ticket if the outgoing vice president overtly furnished the incentive. The crowd was large and restless, and the platform empty at the scheduled hour. With no sign of Wallace, Truman hesitated going onstage, and fund raiser and organizer George Allen, realizing what seemed afoot, expected that if Truman went on alone he risked catcalls. Wallace would then enter late, down the center aisle, tear the roof off with cheers, and embarrass Truman in the morning headlines.

"Mr. Truman goes on when Mr. Wallace goes on," said Allen. Allegedly, Wallace had forgotten his glasses and had returned to his hotel to retrieve them, opening the likelihood of a demonstration for himself alone. Eddie McKim was with Truman in the Garden offices when Wallace finally arrived "in a very sour mood." McKim recalled to Margaret Truman that "they walked

---

* Ironically, the limitation issue came up in Congress under a Republican president, when it appeared that Calvin Coolidge might run for a second term on his own beyond the partial term he inherited from Warren Harding. A bipartisan Senate resolution in 1927 declared it to be "the sense of the Senate" that no president should serve more than two terms.

through the entrance onto the platform arm in arm and smiling at each other, but I think they were about ready to cut each other's throats." In the row behind the rostrum sat Frank Sinatra (who had named his young son Franklin); Orson Welles, who, with his singular basso profundo, introduced Wallace with incantatory passion; and Helen Keller, who quietly read a Braille advance version of the speech, imagining the "thunder of a waking conscience." As Welles left the rally, guiding Miss Keller, crowds shouted, "Wallace and Welles in '48."

The sub-headline in *The New York Times* about Wallace and Truman read, the next day,

> They Enter Garden Arm in Arm
> but Vice President Fails to
> Return Nominee's Praise

The demonstration for Wallace after Welles's introduction had gone on so long that it ate into costly radio time and he was finally cut off—"like Orson Welles . . . the other night," Roosevelt told newsmen. "I was in the middle of listening to him, and they shut down on him." Very likely FDR missed what followed. "Every minute of this," Wallace shouted into the din, "is costing somebody money." His key lines as the hall quieted were that the "people's war" had to be followed by "a people's peace" under "a truly liberal party," which was only possible through Roosevelt's re-election. Wallace had already released to the media the text of his address, which included a grudging phrase that Truman was "not a reactionary Democrat." Liberal Party publicists had distributed to newsmen typed slips that Wallace was to insert after that—a sentence reading, "The record of Truman shows that he is a genuine internationalist and a consistent supporter of liberal domestic policies." Wallace failed to use the line. "Some people tell me," he told the Garden audience, "that here and there you can find someone sulking in his tent because he doesn't like something a reactionary Democrat has done. Well, neither Truman nor Roosevelt is a reactionary Democrat. Moreover, I say to you that if any reactionary Democrat has offended you, he has probably offended me a thousand times as much. But I want to say to you that I am out working with all brands of Democrats who are in favor of Roosevelt."

Truman received warm yet less than enthusiastic cheers from the crowded house of resentful Wallace admirers, including hundreds of standees. Clearly angry at Wallace's antics, Truman inserted into his compliments for the Vice President prepared for the press—an innuendo-charged phrase that Wallace was "the greatest Secretary of Agriculture this country ever had." It drew vigorous if misunderstood applause.

Henry Wallace and Harry Truman at a rally, where both spoke, appearing friendly for the camera, at Madison Square Garden, New York, October 31, 1944. *Truman Library*

Although it might have foreshadowed something ominous about the New York electoral turnout—that Wallace ultras might stay home—Truman was unruffled. As they left the Garden he asked Eddie McKim, "Do you think that thing was planned, staged deliberately?"

"I think it was," said Eddie.

"Well," Truman judged, "that's a funny deal, but it didn't work."

Ten

The Last Stretch

Despite the harsh weather and grueling pace to which the President had committed himself, his political swings to New York, Philadelphia and Chicago had not perceptibly damaged further his precarious health. Examining him on October 29, with little more than a week to go in the campaign, Dr. Bruenn, always now a shadowy presence in FDR's entourage, noted, "During the past month [the President] has engaged in more than the usual amount of activity [and] a complete disregard of the rest regime." Bruenn's pulse and blood pressure readings were, to his surprise, positive. Roosevelt seemed to thrive on his renewed thrust into electioneering. "Patient," Bruenn added, "appears well stabilized on his digitalis regime."

Summing up what he knew from Bruenn and his own observations, Admiral McIntire wrote later that "the manner in which the President came through [the campaign] made me doubt my accuracy as a diagnostician." (At Quebec, Roosevelt had seemed frighteningly frail.) From September 20 to November 1, McIntire set out the statistical record as "Temperature—98.6—no elevations; general appearance—color good; present weight—172. Lungs clear, heart—no cardiac symptoms at any time—sounds are good in character; pulse rate ranges 68 to 74. Blood pressure of labile type; systolic ranging from 165 to 180; diastolic 88 to 100; electrocardio-gram shows no changes from that of May [5] examination." He had seldom been that thorough. It was Howard Bruenn who was thorough.

Late in the campaign, FDR's health was still an issue in the press. It was "the last-minute whispering stage," Marquis Childs wrote from Chicago on October 27. "Some people hate the Presi-dent so much that the wish is father to the thought that his health is seriously undermined." Childs took the view that one could not doubt supreme medical authority:

> Behind [Roosevelt's] public appearances is the record itself. The President's physician during his three terms of office has been Vice Admiral Ross McIntire. McIntire, who is also Surgeon Gen-eral of the Navy, presumably values his high professional reputa-tion. Would he endanger it by giving his expert opinion that his patient was in good health if he were not actually a healthy man? I think not. Quite apart from his own sense of professional honor, he would have too much to lose.

"I am going to make a trip to New England through Hartford, Bridgeport, [and] Springfield, and then come into Boston to wind up my campaign," the President had reported to Joe Kennedy. Though Kennedy assumed that he was to respond, "I'll be seeing you there," he ignored the cue. He could not own up to Roosevelt that he not only blamed the President for the two-ocean war but considered him implicated somehow in the death, in action, of his favorite and first-born son, Joe Jr. Obviously the mid-air catastro-phe was unplanned, but grief-possessed paranoia remains beyond reason. That it was a Roosevelt whose plane, behind Kennedy's, was rocked by the blast was a macabre coincidence.

Within months the European conflict that the prewar isolationist had hoped to avoid had also invalided Kennedy's second son, Jack, and widowed his daughter Kathleen. Joe Kennedy's millions and his influence—and his family's political future—now seemed worthless. When Harry Truman campaigned in Boston on the heels of Dewey's visit and looked in on Bob Hannegan, who operated from a suite at the Ritz-Carlton overseeing arrangements for a Roosevelt stopover, Truman found Kennedy there. Hannegan had not given up on the Massachusetts moneybags and at the least wanted Kennedy to keep silent. "Old man Kennedy," Truman recalled, "started throwing rocks at Roosevelt, saying he caused the war and so on. And then he said, 'Harry, what the hell are you doing campaigning for that crippled son of a bitch that killed my son Joe?'"

"I stood it just as long as I could, and I said, 'If you say another word about Roosevelt, I'm going to throw you out that window.'" As they glared at each other, Hannegan pulled Truman out of the room. "Come out here," he said. "I'm gonna get ten thousand dollars out of the old son of a bitch for the Democratic Party." Later Hannegan asserted that he did. But to Walter Trohan of the *Chicago Tribune*, covering the campaign, Kennedy again blamed Roosevelt for getting America into the war. Kennedy claimed that he would have contemplated suicide if he thought that as ambassador in London he had "any part in causing the war to be fought." Trohan kept the tirade to himself.

Joe Kennedy's version of the meeting with Truman could not have been more different. The next February he wrote belatedly in his diary,

On Sunday afternoon [October 29, 1944] at Hannegan's request, I went to Boston to meet Harry Truman. Came to see me in my [hotel] room and begged me to make a speech. They both believe that Roosevelt won't live long, particularly Hannegan. He has made this statement to me a number of times before, and they felt that Truman will be President and will kick out all these incompetents and Jews out of Washington and ask fellows like myself and others to come back and run the government. Truman assured me that is what he would do. . . . I couldn't in conscience come out for Roosevelt. . . . They both finished up by saying that knowing my experience they didn't blame me a bit.

Kennedy did not come out for Dewey, but his silence about Roosevelt implied enough. When Dewey spoke to an audience of twenty-four thousand in a jammed Boston Garden on Wednesday evening, November 1 (an estimated ten thousand others failed to get in, and listened outside), he was introduced by House minority leader and prewar isolationist Joseph Martin, who asked the crowd, "Do we want next January 20 [to be] a coronation or an inauguration?" He got a resounding "No!"—presumably for the former. But Dewey turned to his familiar charge, making a bid for the Catholic vote by again connecting Earl Browder, whom he quoted as calling all religions "bad for the masses," and Roosevelt, who allegedly had sprung the Communist leader from prison "in time to organize the fourth-term campaign." Projecting a Red scare had become the last-stretch theme of the Dewey campaign. "In America," he told Bostonians, vigorously pressing the paranoid button, "a Communist is a man"—women did not seem to matter—"who supports the fourth term so our form of government may more easily be changed." The President, he charged, had "only softly disavowed Communism." Among the dignitaries in the front rows was General Hugh Drum, now retired. He had been the senior officer in the Army in 1939 when Roosevelt had passed him over for a relatively obscure one-star general, George C. Marshall, to become chief of staff. Drum had since become, as a consolation prize, commanding general of the New York State National Guard.

Beginning at Pittsfield, the first platform stop in Massachusetts, Governor Dewey drew ovations from the faithful by promising "the biggest housecleaning Washington ever saw." The 8-mile motorcade from South Station to the Hotel Statler had been disappointing. Beginning at 4:10 p.m., it had conflicted with working hours of possible supporters. Some loyalists unable to be on the sidewalks hung out of shop and office windows, and from rooftops, to wave and cheer. Unsympathetic observers shouted the now-familiar "Where did you get the gas?" Others yelled "We want Roosevelt!" But en route to Boston through Worcester, when the slowly moving special train passed a dozen firemen fighting a rooftop blaze, they paused to doff their hats.

Traveling by rail to Baltimore the next day for a rally at the Lyric Theater at noon, where pro-FDR shouting nearly drowned Dewey out, he charged that the campaign was not between Republicans and Democrats but between "those who believe in our system of government" and "those who have kidnapped the Democratic party in order to change our system of government."

Dewey then entrained north into Pennsylvania to the coal-mining bastions of Scranton and Wilkes-Barre, chancing an 18-mile drive between the two cities, where he met with vocal hostility, although mining union czar John L. Lewis was passionately anti-Roosevelt. "I never saw 18 miles take so long to get through in my life," Dewey told his handlers.

Lewis had already labeled Sidney Hillman a stand-in for Browder and Roosevelt, and a "Russian pants worker." Supreme Court Justice Felix Frankfurter observed that the innuendo went even further. "The use that has been made of Sidney Hillman's Lithuanian birth—which is a cowardly way of saying that he is a Jew—is one of the saddest things in my life. Only one thing is sadder—the way those who themselves would not indulge in such poisoning of the American atmosphere are silently allowing others to do so." Hannegan worried each time Hillman spoke for FDR in the Lithuanian-accented English he could not soften, and thought it might be disastrous when Hillman (and Orson Welles) stood in for Roosevelt on October 18 in New York at the *Herald-Tribune* Forum.

The outspoken Hillman was not easily cowed. He declared that Dewey as president would be "a catastrophe for the country" and accused the Republicans of "Red-baiting and Jew-baiting." Yet Dewey did not take advice easily. He had asked Charles Breitel, counsel to the governor and his former law partner, to look over the text of the Boston speech. Breitel told Dewey frankly that it was no good. When Dewey asked for particulars, Breitel explained, "You've got that Hillman piece in there. You're speaking in Boston and everybody will know you're trying to get the Irish Catholic vote. It's going to look like a cheap play at a time when the Jews in this country are terribly sensitive, when they feel terribly threatened; they don't even know whether they'll survive this war . . . and to a group they believe is largely unsympathetic, if not anti-Semitic, you've got this stuff."

Dewey pointed out that he had praised another Jewish labor leader, David Dubinsky, but Breitel downplayed it as "obvious cover." The governor's political adviser Elliott Bell retorted that Breitel, a Dewey loyalist, was "carrying the torch for the typical Communist line." When, listening in from the next room, Frances Dewey popped in and offered that she had read the speech, she was asked what she thought of it. "Bricker could have written it," she said.* Still, her husband toned nothing down, portraying Hillman as "stalking the country" in the interests of Communism. It worked for true believers, but it was obvious that as the days dwindled, Dewey was becoming even more shrill in pandering to the urban electorate he saw as essential to winning the big states. *The New York Times* headlined the speech as "Dewey Predicts 'Red Menace' Rise if Roosevelt Wins. . . . Perils Religion, He Says." In the *Boston Globe* a "Soldier's Wife" wrote with undisguised sarcasm, "Oh boy, pal, that was certainly a magnificent speech of

---

* Earlier, "a Republican biggie" suggested, unsuccessfully, "You'd better mute Clare Luce. She'll cost you a lot of votes." Dewey said, "That's funny. My wife told me the same thing."

Dewey's. . . . Did he have Hillman on the ropes! And those punches
he threw at Browder!"

At a Madison Square Garden "Everybody for Roosevelt"
rally the next evening, broadcast on NBC, Secretary Ickes accused Dewey of "desperate, contemptible fanning of the flames
of religious hatred. . . . I never heard a candidate for a high office
talk so recklessly. The campaign has proved that Thomas E.
Dewey is no George Washington when it comes to telling the
truth. . . . Time after time, page after page, comment piled upon
comment, the Dewey campaign line and Nazi and Japanese
propaganda have been identical." An array of speakers followed,
including shipbuilder Andrew Higgins, whose efficient landing
craft by the thousands made a succession of D-Days possible,
and were then being constructed wholesale for the invasion of
Japan. That the war would be coming closer to the Home Islands
was unconcealed in an announcement by the War Manpower
Commission that the Navy was seeking three thousand additional physicians. The chief of the Navy's Bureau of Medicine,
Vice Admiral McIntire, asked to comment, observed, "Even this
figure will not meet actual needs."

Rumor had it that pollster George Gallup was privately a
Republican and was adjusting his figures to keep the election
percentages close—leaning toward the Dewey-Bricker ticket in
hopes of persuading undecided voters to chance a winner. Ernest
Cuneo, an OSS agent under "Wild Bill" Donovan and a former
Democratic strategist, told William Stephenson, who ran a British
lobbying and intelligence service in New York, "Dewey is calling
Gallup up so often they have to have a [special] clerk to answer
him. . . . Imagine a guy shaking so much." Stephenson cabled
Cuneo's sweeping pro-Roosevelt predictions to London as if they
were his own: "My estimates have consistently conflicted
markedly with those of Gallup and other pollsters and political
pundits . . . and now show greater divergence from largely accepted

view than previously. . . . My current analyses indicate victory for FDR in minimum repeat minimum of 32 states with 370 electoral votes and maximum of 40 with 487 electoral votes."

Stephenson may have been buoyed by pundit Walter Lippmann's final *Herald-Tribune* syndicated column before going "overseas on a newspaper assignment." Internationalist yet conservative, and the leading opinion maker in journalism, Lippmann confessed that he had hoped that Dewey would demonstrate "that he was prepared to assume quickly the tremendous responsibilities of a war president." His campaign, Lippmann deplored, "showed that he did not know what was going on and had not taken the trouble to find out." Dewey's promise of "housecleaning" Washington was actually "a threat of administrative chaos." Further, he had failed to show "a sufficient understanding of foreign affairs and of the function of a war president." Instead, "the Governor has exhibited the recklessness of a novice who does not know which guns are loaded." His strategy, Lippmann's parting column went on, "has been based on a fundamental misconception, in fact on mere wishful thinking. It is that the war is just about over and that therefore he is offering himself not as a war President but as a peace President. This has been a complete misjudgment of the real situation." All Dewey has demonstrated, Lippmann concluded in reluctantly dismissing him, is that he is "a relentless prosecuting attorney, not that he is fit and ready to be a war President."

Perhaps the most significant aspect of Lippmann's thinking was his quoting Alexander Hamilton, from the *Federalist Papers* of 1788, on term limits, as "a profoundly conservative and practical [Founding Father] view": "Without supposing the personal essentiality of the man, it is evident that a change of the Chief Magistrate at the breaking out of a war, or any similar crisis, for another of even equal merit, would at all times be detrimental to the community, inasmuch as it would substitute inexperience for experience, and would tend to unhinge and set afloat the already settled train of the administration."

Opposing, with obvious pessimism, its own star columnist's view, the *Herald-Tribune* published a "Time for a Change" editorial, and a cartoon captioned "Relax, Samson, Your Haircut Isn't Finished." Samson, labeled as "American Way of Life," is sprawled on a bed while Delilah ("New Deal"), wielding huge scissors that have left locks of Samson's hair ("Lost Liberties") on the floor, warns him, "Now just go back to sleep for another four years! I'm not quite through!"

Taking nothing for granted, on Thursday evening, November 2, with the election to come on Tuesday, Roosevelt made a fifteen-minute nationwide broadcast from the White House. By loudspeakers, it was heard at a crowded Madison Square Garden rally chaired by Harold Ickes. The radio format was explained as in lieu of appearances in Detroit and Cleveland. The President had explained his curtailment of campaign travel to a news conference on Tuesday, October 31, as "this war comes first." He could not spare the time away from Washington, Roosevelt said, although he may have been hoarding his physical resources for a grand Boston finale on the weekend.*

Asked by reporters whether he had bet on the election himself, Roosevelt told the newsmen that he had—twenty-five cents—"an even money bet on a certain state."

"Doesn't that disqualify you from voting, in New York State?"

To laughter, the President explained the relevant law. "No. If it's made outside the State of New York, it's all right."

Speech writer Sam Rosenman (he had help in persuasion from political pundit Max Lerner) felt that a campaign address without a visible audience was always "an inappropriate vehicle. . . . The enthusiasm of the crowd and its reaction to the candidate's words create an atmosphere that a cold microphone in a secluded room

---

* FDR's failure to campaign in Ohio may have enabled Senator Taft to squeak in for re-election.

cannot furnish." There were more compelling explanations for Roosevelt's undramatic acceptance speech from Camp Pendleton, and his nearly disastrous address from Bremerton Naval Base months earlier, but Rosenman felt that the radio appeal piped into Madison Square Garden was "dull, stuffy, and ineffective." Still, Roosevelt warned the audience and the nation against "wicked" whisperings. "As we approach election day, more wicked charges may be made and probably will, with the hope that somebody or someone will gain momentary advantage." The audience at the Garden was primed to be enthusiastic, and radio listeners elsewhere may have sensed their vibrations.

Following FDR, party chief Hannegan pitched a direct appeal to Catholic voters. "My faith," he declared, "stands as a mighty bulwark against Communism." Roosevelt's policies for social and economic justice were "essentially the same as those which have been advocated by the spiritual leaders of my church since the days of Leo XIII." The President had made his own more subtle bid. For an "on the record" lunch at the White House he had Archbishop of New York and Military Vicar of the Armed Forces the Most Reverend Francis J. Spellman. The future cardinal was usually "off the record."

Late on November 3, after a press conference in which the President outlined his pre-election schedule, he boarded his special train in Washington for a whistle-stop journey to Boston, including platform appearances en route in Connecticut and Massachusetts. He had just weathered a press controversy over his endorsement by elderly and conservative Senator Carter Glass of Virginia, which was denied from Lynchburg by his son, Powell Glass. Soon after, Steve Early recalled reporters to his office and said that he had telephoned Senator Glass, often an FDR antagonist, at the Mayflower Hotel. "He wanted me to tell the President that he was voting for him and to give the President his love."

Although the South harbored a very different Democratic Party than had rallied in Madison Square Garden, it remained essential to Roosevelt's re-election. Maps in the press of the way various states were leaning continued to show a "Solid South" of Democratic electoral votes and little sign of the Republican presence that would emerge in the contentious Civil Rights era beginning four years later.

As the President began his last-stretch campaign trip, Dewey was closing his travels, returning to Albany on Friday with only a final trip to Madison Square Garden for a radio-covered speech on Saturday evening. Ironically, he would be remaining overnight at the poorly chosen Roosevelt Hotel—named, voters did not remember, for the President's Republican "Uncle Ted." "The return to Albany this morning," Warren Moscow of *The New York Times* reported,

> by way of a freight line of the Delaware & Hudson Railroad from Scranton, Pa., marked the end of about 30,000 miles of traveling . . . on a special train, to which the correspondents said a hasty good-bye this morning. It had taken them through coal country and cattle country, from coast to coast, from war centers to towns where the war seemed remote. Only once had it been late, the day it was wrecked at Castle Rock, Wash., and it genuinely was rated as one of the most efficiently run campaign trains of all time.

Along with Roosevelt's own staff en route to Boston were thirty newspapermen, radio commentators, press photographers and newsreel men. In the party, Bill Hassett wrote, was Mike Hennessy of the *Boston Globe,* "spry as a cricket and keen as a razor, seventy-nine, who has covered every national election campaign since 1892." Other than the President's cadre of Cabinet officials (and Admiral McIntire), correspondents and confidants, was Orson Welles. (Frank Sinatra, who had given $5,000 to the campaign, would catch up with the entourage in Boston.) Welles had been hospitalized with a throat infection. Once his fever had broken he wrote to the President, "This illness was the blackest of misfortunes for me because it stole away so many days from the campaign. I cannot think I have accomplished a great deal but I well know this is the most important work I could ever engage in."

Toward dawn on Saturday morning, in the heavy fog the campaign train encountered near Stamford, Connecticut, two auxiliary policemen guarding the trackage were struck by a New Canaan–bound train. One was killed and the other seriously injured. Lest it cast a pall over the proceedings, the President's train, unaffected, and its passengers uninformed, continued on, pausing near Bridgeport so that the first platform appearance would occur as scheduled.

Although the fog had not yet lifted, a crowd had already gathered. Roosevelt summed up to them the relentless attacks on him as the meanest in his political life. "I can't talk about my opponent the way I would like to, sometimes, because I try to think that I am a Christian. I try to think that some day I will go to Heaven, and I don't believe there is anything to be gained in saying dreadful things about other people in any campaign. After next Tuesday there are going to be a lot of sorry people in the United States."

It was a remarkable off-the-cuff statement, for hints by his political enemies that he was dying remained widespread, but Roosevelt's America was churchgoing. His disability, and security concerns, usually kept him from a pew, but his prayerful references were many, and he seemed sure in his inner faith that he had been tested in his crippling by an exacting but just God and that he had come through. As for his theology, he once told Eleanor, "It's just as well not to think about things like that too much."

At Hartford, a lunch-hour station stop in a city dominated by banks and insurance companies, he brought up, extempore, campaign charges that he was anti-business. At a time when working people paid for minimal life insurance policies with a nickel or a dime a week, company executives through three previous campaigns had charged that insurance policies would become worthless under a Roosevelt presidency. "Four years ago," he said,

I was told terrible things were being circulated all over the country. People all over the United States were being told that if I got reelected, all of the Hartford insurance companies would go broke. So, coming in here, I expected to see vast, empty buildings not being used and employing no people. . . . And yet they are still here. And the joke is that the insurance companies, not only of Hartford but of other places, are better off than they have ever been before. . . . And they are making the fantastic claim this year that your government is now engaged in some deep-dyed plot to take over the insurance business.

People, he observed, "cannot be easily fooled by that type of propaganda." Their policies and savings were safe. "That was not true in 1933 when I took office."

The opposition, he added, turning a traditional charge against the Democrats upside down, was the party of unsound money. "Time and again the Republicans in Congress voted overwhelmingly against price control, and in favor of letting prices go skyrocketing. So I make an assertion. The Democratic party in this war has been the party of sound money. The Republican party has been the party of unsound money. If the Republicans had their way, all of us—farmers, white-collar workers, factory workers, housewives—we would all have our dollars cut by inflation and a higher cost of living." The crowd cheered; the President waved his fedora; and the campaign train was soon underway for Springfield and Boston.

Refining the Boston speech kept Sam Rosenman and Robert Sherwood busy en route—"practically up to the moment we had to leave the train"—as Roosevelt chatted up reporters and local officials. Boarding the train at each pause, including Springfield, were political worthies invited for ego massage, including Representative John McCormack, House majority leader, who would introduce the President; and Maurice J. Tobin, mayor of Boston and candidate for governor. At Worcester, where no whistle-stop speech was scheduled, isolationist Senator David I. Walsh, no friend of the Administration, joined the dignitaries. Although greeted cordially for the press cameras ("I'm glad to see you, Dave," followed by "I'm glad to see you looking so well, Mr. President"), the balding, heavy-jowled Walsh told reporters that while he would vote the party line he would give no speeches and not appear at the Boston rally.*

As Dewey returned to Albany to prepare for his last major address, in New York City, the press largely ignored his running mate, John Bricker, and also Bricker's counterpart, Harry Truman, both still on the hustings. They were appendages to the ticket, covered on the inside pages of most papers, if at all. Asked at a press conference in Providence, Rhode Island, what difference there was between David Walsh and eight Republican isolationist senators whom Truman had unsuccessfully charged Dewey to "repudiate," the vice-presidential candidate said sharply, "No difference, but he is serving two more years and we have a chance to reform him."

The presidential special arrived at the Brighton Yards at 5:20. Roosevelt was to have dinner aboard the *Ferdinand Magellan*, then leave in a small motorcade for Fenway Park, home of the Boston Red Sox, at 8:30, and speak from 9:00 to 9:45. For unspecified reasons, perhaps because it would have taken place after dark, the White House Secret Service detail had ordered cancellation of a planned street parade, and on grounds of security ruled out seating in several grandstand sections. Leaving nothing to chance, the preliminary entertainment would begin at 6:30 with Kate Smith singing "God Bless America" and Frank Sinatra singing "America the Beautiful." Bobby-soxers squealed. Congressman James M. Curley would warm up the audience with an attack on the Dewey-

---

* Tobin was elected governor and became Secretary of Labor in 1947. Senator Walsh, to almost no one's disappointment, was defeated for re-election in 1946.

Bricker ticket. Bostonian tenors Phil Reagan ("When Irish Eyes Are Smiling") and Morton Downey ("It's the Same Old Shillelagh My Father Brought from Ireland") would sing. At 8:00 a gaggle of state ticket candidates would each speak briefly. Then came Orson Welles, who quoted the Catholic weekly *Commonweal* that "no labor leader ever hunted down Communists more vigorously than Sidney Hillman in his own union." The Republicans, he charged, had no program beyond negativism. "By free enterprise they want exclusive right to freedom. They are stupid enough to think that a few can enjoy prosperity at the expense of the rest."

When the crowd of forty-five thousand occupied every available seat, Boston police shut the entrances, and as in Chicago, a roaring throng that had overflowed the ballpark area gathered stubbornly before loudspeakers outside. The President's Packard was to enter via the centerfield gate and ascend a ramp to a platform set with microphones. "We were coming into the ball park in an open car under the great arc lights," Welles recalled. "There was a Secret Service man on our running board. I was sitting next to Roosevelt. I was riding with him because he didn't want to ride with a local ward heeler. . . .* When we got to the entrance the Secret Service man had forgotten whether they were to turn right or left, and I said, 'Mr. President, you've never gone wrong when you've turned left.' So he roared with laughter and we turned left."

As the auto entered the stadium, circled the field, and mounted the speaker's platform, the crowd chanted, "We want Roosevelt!" The big football scoreboard still read as it did for the final play of the Boston College–Syracuse game, "4TH DOWN—3 TO GO." At the microphones (his address was carried by the radio networks), Roosevelt waded directly into the matter of Republican appeal, via the exaggeration of Sidney Hillman's influence, to religious differences:

---

* Also in the Packard were McCormack, Hannegan and state party chairman William H. Burke Jr., perhaps the politician FDR had in mind when he invited Welles to occupy the seat.

When I talked here in Boston in 1928, I talked about racial and religious intolerance, which was then—as unfortunately it still is, to some extent—"a menace to the liberties of America."

And all the bigots in those days were gunning for Al Smith.

Religious intolerance, social intolerance, and political intolerance have no place in our American life. . . .

Today, in this war, our fine boys are fighting magnificently all over the world, and among those boys are the Murphys and the Kellys, the Smiths and the Joneses, the Carusos, the Kowalskis, the Schultzes, the Cohens, the Olsens, the Swobodas, and—right in with the rest of them—the Cabots and the Lowells. . . .

It is our duty to make sure that, big as this country is, there is no room in it for racial or religious intolerance—and that there is no room for snobbery.

Then, without identifying Dewey by name, and to howls of laughter, Roosevelt went after the contention that his party and his administration had sold its soul to the Communists:

Just the other day you people here in Boston witnessed an amazing demonstration of talking out of both sides of the mouth. Speaking here in Boston, a Republican candidate said— and pardon me if I quote him correctly—that happens to be an old habit of mine—he said that, quote, "the Communists are seizing control of the New Deal, through which they aim to control the Government of the United States." However on that very same day that very same candidate had spoken in Worcester, and he said that, with Republican victory in November, "we can end one-man government, we can forever remove the threat of monarchy, in the United States."

Now really, which is it, communism or monarchy? I do not think we could have both in this country, even if we wanted either, which we do not.

Everybody knew, Roosevelt said, that he was reluctant to run again. Alluding to opposition talk about his physical condition, he quoted Al Smith as saying to him, "It is perfectly evident that you don't have to be an acrobat to be President." It got a roar from the audience. According to Robert Sherwood, the President would confide to Harry Hopkins that he was "particularly resentful about the whispering campaign which he believes was an organized affair."

"Now that the campaign has developed," he told his Fenway Park audience, bypassing the health issue, "I have become most anxious to win—and I say that for the reason that never before in my lifetime has a campaign been filled with such misrepresentation, distortion, and falsehood. Never since 1928 have there been so many attempts to stimulate in America racial or religious intolerance." In truth, misrepresentation, distortion and falsehood were endemic in American presidential campaigns, continuing without pause well into the next century. In a view from Britain, a writer in the November *Contemporary Review* observed, "It should be borne in mind not only that the discussion of any problem in America—whether this be of a political or artistic or social or personal nature—is even at the best of times characterised not only by a truculence, but by a disregard for facts, which would scarcely be possible to imagine elsewhere."

Roosevelt charged his always-nameless opponent with making speeches conceding the necessity of retaining New Deal reforms, while the Republican vice-presidential candidate—he would not identify Bricker by name either—was carrying on violently anti–New Deal tirades. "The American people," Roosevelt continued, to audience laughter, "are quite competent to judge a political party that works both sides of a street—a party that has one candidate making campaign promises of all kinds of added government expenditures in the West, while a running mate of his demands less government expenditures in the East." (Roosevelt would write his son James, "I made a very hurried and hectic tour in the last few weeks—mostly in bad weather—but the results were worth it. The little man made me pretty mad.")

Since radio network time cost the campaign big money, the President concluded his appearance in the Red Sox venue with a baseball metaphor. Although the Republicans had threatened wholesale housecleaning of the government,

> Have you heard one word of specific criticism of any of the progressive laws that this Administration has proposed and enacted? Have you heard any talk of sweeping out any of these laws—or sweeping out any of the agencies that administer them?
>
> Oh, no; on that subject the Republican politicians are very uncharacteristically silent. This Administration has made mistakes. This I freely *assert*. And I hope my friends of the press will not change that to *admit*.
>
> But, my friends, I think it is a good batting average. Our mistakes have been honestly made during sincere efforts to help the great mass of citizens. Never have we made the inexcusable mistake—we know some who have—of substituting talk for action when farms were being foreclosed, homes were being sold at auction, and people were standing in breadlines.

To tumultuous cheers, the FDR Packard rolled down the ramp as the President held his hat held aloft, and left Fenway Park for the Brighton Yards and Hyde Park, where the President, once the last two cars in the train were detached, would remain through Election Day. And as he closed, the networks prepared for a competing closing on radio at ten o'clock by Governor Dewey from Manhattan.

Both events on the air were preceded by a report from Washington that neither candidate publicly acknowledged. A survey of fifty-six leading political journalists from across the nation collected and pooled by the Washington Bureau of *The New York Times* forecast that Roosevelt would win the election with at least

332 electoral votes, 66 more than the majority necessary, and that 116 of them would come from the "solid South." Dewey was predicted to receive no more than 199 electoral votes. The reporters polled also estimated Republican gains in the Senate, and just enough additional seats in the House to win a majority there, and to overturn Democratic committee chairmanships. The survey assumed that the service vote would parallel the civilian vote, creating no surprises.

The final Gallup Poll showed the President leading in states with 206 electoral votes, and Governor Dewey with 255, close to enough to win, but with 70 votes "on the line." It was the best Republican news to date, based on an alleged "quickening pace" in Dewey's direction. In his diary, Bill Hassett observed, wryly, "Dr. Gallup is carrying water on both shoulders and a bucket on his head besides." *Newsweek*'s last issue before Election Day, representing estimates by "118 political writers" nationwide, cautiously forecast FDR ahead in 27 states, with 249 electoral votes, and Dewey leading in 20 with 247—too close to call—with Pennsylvania's 35 electoral votes a tossup. With a possible 300,000 service ballots, forecast to go two-thirds for Roosevelt, a Republican "trend" in the state seemed crucial to win. Both party chairmen characteristically foresaw sweeping victories, Herbert Brownell refusing to concede a single loss of a state outside the South. Predictably, Robert Hannegan forecast a landslide greater than the third-term victory in 1940.

The most curious prediction came in a letter to the editor in the *Syracuse Post-Standard.* "Bertrande" wrote that his friend John Dalrymple predicted that the President would be "re-elected by the smallest plurality given him in his four campaigns." Dalrymple also claimed that a new, as yet unforeseen, circumstance will cause both Japan and Germany to come to their knees, literally, within six months." John Dalrymple, the writer confided, "was in a position to know." He had died, aged twenty-six, in 1910. His insights had come as a "spiritualist tip." (Apparently Dalrymple's shade had counted the electoral votes in advance, and presumably learned about the atomic bomb although he hurried its deployment.) Dewey's staff clipped the letter for the campaign files.

In Madison Square Garden, and on network radio, Dewey claimed that the President's "own confused incompetence" had already prolonged the war. Further, Roosevelt's awkwardly withdrawn endorsement of the Morgenthau Plan (unidentified by name) to turn an occupied Germany into a docile economy devoid of industry had already "stiffened the will of the German people to resist." Threatening the "disposing of the German people" was allegedly as good as creating "ten fresh German divisions." Although General Eisenhower had predicted that the war might end "this year," Dewey reminded his audience, President Roosevelt "last Thursday . . . decided to tell us that the war had still a long way to go." (Churchill also told Parliament that he believed that war in

"Racket-Buster Dewey"—a last-minute Dewey appeal, by Jerry Costello in the *Brooklyn Eagle*, November 4, 1944.

Europe would not only continue beyond Christmas but even beyond Easter.) Breaking into the *Heimat*—as had already occurred at the frontier city of Aachen—would alone have heightened German fears as well as home-front resistance, went unmentioned in Republican rhetoric. That there was still a longer way to go in the other and parallel war in the Pacific went without notice. Choruses of anti-Roosevelt jeers followed each charge.

Dewey returned to Albany on Sunday afternoon to prepare a Monday-night pre-election address, again on all four national networks—NBC, Blue (the future ABC), CBS and Mutual—for 11:00 to 11:15 p.m., recognizing that it would be three hours earlier on the West Coast. Besides, the Democrats had booked the networks for an hour-long get-out-the-vote rally at 10:00 p.m.

The President had returned early Sunday morning to Hyde Park, where Republican officials predicted that Roosevelt's own Dutchess County would go for Dewey by 12,000 votes, twice the plurality achieved by Wendell Willkie in 1940. Predictably GOP, the county had gone for Hoover in 1932 and Landon in 1936. The local congressman whom Roosevelt loved to revile, isolationist Hamilton Fish, was no longer running from FDR's home territory, redistricting having removed Hyde Park to a neighboring jurisdiction. It was at Newburgh, Representative Fish's new headquarters, Republican officials reminded voters, that Roosevelt had remarked in 1940 that after his third term there would be another President.

Eleven

Election Day

syndicated George Lichty "Grin and Bear It" cartoon on November 6, the Monday before Election Day, featured an overweight, sour and string-tied clubman with bulging vest and cane. Lichty was having it both ways, caricaturing a comic-strip congressman rather than either presidential contender. A sign in the background read, "GALA SEN. SHORT VICTORY SUPPER . . . COME ONE COME ALL." The candidate is cautiously explaining to the *maître d'*, "and as the election results become apparent, I'll let you know whether it'll be a single or separate checks!" An authentic senator, Ohio's Robert Alphonso Taft, from the major league baseball city of Cincinnati, as an anxious Republican thought that the race hinged upon the "strong feeling of a small percentage of the people that we had better not take out a winning pitcher in the eighth inning."

Baseball and other contests surfaced on November 6 in a newspaper advertisement sponsored by the "All-American Athletes for Dewey," a largely moneyed and past-their-prime group that had

sent checks to the co-chairmen—the iconic Babe Ruth, who had
dominated the major leagues from 1916 into 1934, and the 1931
Wimbledon men's champion, Sidney B. Wood Jr., now a lawyer.
"TWELVE Years of One Man Rule Would Dry Up Any Sport—
"the double column contended, "SIXTEEN would kill It! WE'RE
VOTING FOR DEWEY." The signers in the *World-Telegram* in-
cluded Ty Cobb, Tris Speaker, Walter Johnson, Bucky Walters, Bill
Tilden, Red Grange, Jim Thorpe, Johnny ("Tarzan") Weismuller,
Gene Sarazen, Babe Didriksen, Jim Jeffries, Jesse Willard, Pop
Warner, Billy Talbert and Gertrude Ederle. If their trophies could
vote, Tom Dewey was a sure thing.

Dr. Bruenn recorded that Monday before the President set off in
an open car through the Hudson Valley district (in which he would
cast his ballot the next day) that Roosevelt's "blood pressure
levels, if anything, were lower than before." Campaigning seemed
better medicine than prescribed inactivity. Five White House advisers, Robert Sherwood recalled, had invested five dollars each
in "a pool" on the likely FDR electoral vote: "Watson–400;
Rosenman–431; Hopkins–440; Early–449; Sherwood–484."
Rosenman held the stakes. On a yellow slip tucked into his White
House desk, Roosevelt himself predicted a more conservative
total: 335 to Dewey's 196.

He drove out to the Post Road with Bill Hassett (and the accompanying Secret Service detail) soon after one o'clock. Lying in
wait, press and radio correspondents, photographers and newsreel
men, joined the procession. Eleanor did not accompany her husband. "They always stop in the same places," she told her young
acolyte Joe Lash, "and I think the one at Beacon is the very spot
where the President made his very first campaign speech when he
entered politics as a young man, running in a 'hopeless' district for
the State Senate." Probably realizing that her absence would be
talked about, Mrs. Roosevelt would catch up to the FDR party at
his last stop in Poughkeepsie.

FDR with Henry Morgenthau Jr. (center) on a final campaign tour through towns in the Hyde Park area, November 6, 1944. Office buildings in Poughkeepsie are in the background. *FDR Library*

At Wappingers Falls the President suggested to the crowd from his open Ford that if he ran often enough he might even carry Maine and Vermont, the two states—and eight electoral votes—he lost to Alfred Landon in 1936. He spoke again briefly at Beacon; then the cavalcade boarded the ferry for Newburgh, across the Hudson, where FDR spoke to workmen at the Eureka Shipyard. In the town he asked the crowd for "a little hand for the legislature" for redistricting the area out of the clutches of Representative Ham Fish. By the time they reached Kingston the mild November day had turned cold, but Roosevelt, still jolly, turned his crack about his isolationist *bête noire* around and, hardly seriously, mourned the fact that the state legislature had taken his congressman away from him.* En route back toward Poughkeepsie, the procession paused at a roadside eatery where Secretary Morgenthau, a Dutchess County neighbor riding

---

* Fish would be ousted altogether, losing his seat after twenty-four contentious years.

with the President, ordered sandwiches and much-welcomed hot coffee. Many riders, now chilled, were also in open cars.

Eleanor was waiting on Market Street at the red-brick Nelson
House, then the best hotel in the city. There, and around the corner
on Mansion Street, at the Poughkeepsie Post Office, an impressive
WPA (thus New Deal) structure, an overflow crowd waited. Off to
the northeast, Ernest M. Hopkins, presiding at Dartmouth College,
had just announced his support of Governor Dewey, declaring that
nothing was "more vital to the country's long time welfare than to
establish a limit to the number of terms a president shall serve." In
Poughkeepsie, supporting another term for Roosevelt, Dean Mil-
dred Thompson of nearby Vassar College, from the second-floor
portico of Nelson House (which had an elevator), introduced the
President, bareheaded in the biting cold, who called the occasion
the end of "another sentimental journey."

The term meant something more to audiences than it had before
1944. "Sentimental Journey" was the hit tune introduced by Doris
Day with Les Brown's band, about entraining back "to renew old
memories"—suggesting a wartime reunion with a loved one who
had been far away. Already popular from live performances on
stage and radio, it would not be recorded until November 20, post-
election, when James Caesar Petrillo reluctantly permitted the musicians union to end its ban.

The campaign caravan parted from Poughkeepsie in different
directions, Eleanor was on the train to Manhattan to rally campaign workers at Democratic headquarters in Manhattan. The
President returned to Hyde Park for drinks, dinner and preparations for a late-evening broadcast. Although his radio talk would be
brief, he had enlisted not only his regular writing staff but also his
daughter, Anna, and her husband, John Boettiger. Episcopal bishop
Angus Dun of Washington had sent Roosevelt a brief prayer. He
intended to conclude with that. The party had tied up the key
evening hour on the major networks for its campaign finale. The
President had the final fifteen minutes.

At the Executive Mansion in Albany, Governor Dewey readied a nationwide radio address to be delivered at eleven o'clock, just after Roosevelt's finale. For Dewey it had not been a sentimental journey, and he expected to hit hard. Each of the former prosecutor's radio speeches, S. K. Ratcliffe of the London *Contemporary Review*, wrote, was "an example of what may be called precision bombing." Before Dewey's broadcast came dinner with his wife, mother, sons and close associates, who then turned on a radio to listen, at 9:30, to a re-broadcast on the Mutual Network of the governor's speech at Madison Square Garden the previous Saturday night. Dewey retired to his study. The Dewey children—Thomas E. Jr., twelve, and John Martin, eight—were not permitted to remain up for either broadcast. Their bed-time was 8:30, and they had school as usual the next day.

The Democratic National Committee had enlisted CBS writer-producer Norman Corwin, at thirty-four the master of docudrama. "He has earned," the *New York Post* had just written, "the daring reputation of being the first to credit radio audiences with intelligence." In his wind-up Corwin utilized ordinary people from all walks of life, including war workers and servicemen telephoning from the fronts, explaining why they were voting for Roosevelt. Preceded by musical accompaniment came brief recorded plugs for FDR by movie stars and other celebrities. To keep listeners from turning their dials Corwin interspersed songs (obviously live, given James Caesar Petrillo's embargo) like "Gotta Get Out and Vote," "Don't Look Now, Mr. Dewey, but Your Record Is Showing" and, referring satirically to past Republican misgovernment, "The Dear Old Days."

At the close, at 10:45, the President was introduced by an eighteen-year-old girl from Georgia who would be casting her first vote for him. Although Sherwood and Rosenman were at Hyde Park to assist with the speechwriting, most of the brief talk, Rosenman recalled, was the work of daughter Anna. FDR began not with his familiar "My Friends," in Fireside Chat form, but with the more formal "Ladies and Gentlemen." American fighting men, he said, will be wondering what message the election will send to them "for their future lives." With "the political battle finished," he called on citizens to lay aside "partisan politics" and "face the future as a militant and united people." He invoked the Almighty on special occasion in ambiguous rather than sectarian terms, as he had done in a broadcast on D-Day. Adapting Bishop Dun's words were not any intimation of mortality or special religiosity. "Enable us," he closed, "to guard for the least among us the freedom we covet for ourselves; make us ill-content with the inequalities of opportunity which still prevail among us. Preserve our union against all the divisions of race and class which threaten it."

He did not stay up to listen to Dewey's broadcast to his "Fellow Americans," which followed. Dewey's "tactical error," *Commonweal* would report, "was to base the greater part of his appeal to people who would have voted for him anyway." If elected he would keep the managers of the armed forces, General Marshall and Admiral King. Yet he criticized, indirectly, the conduct of the war in Europe, saying, "Plainly, things have not been going as well in Washington as General Eisenhower expected and had a right to expect." With a Republican victory, however, "Their hands will be strengthened by the end of civilian confusion in Washington," while at home, too, new leadership was needed after "twelve unhappy years of turmoil and dissension." The argument against a change in the presidency during a great ordeal, he declared, going as far as he felt he could in referring to Roosevelt's health, "comes down the bald plea for the re-election—so long as he lives—of whoever happens to be President." And Dewey closed by invoking "divine guidance" and "faith in Almighty God."

At 9:20 on Election Day morning, Governor and Mrs. Dewey, with his principal secretary, Paul E. Lockwood, left Albany for New York City, arriving just after noon. They were escorted to a polling place at 148 E. 48th Street, as all three were registered to vote at the nearby Hotel Roosevelt, where Dewey kept a suite. Members of his campaign staff would gather there for what they expected, if the returns showed a close contest, to be a long vigil. Had Dewey voted from his home in Pawling, which was largely abandoned for the governor's official residence, it would have been the only time in American history that two presidential candidates cast their ballots in the same county.

In an open car the President and Mrs. Roosevelt drove toward the Hyde Park Town Hall to vote, with grandson Johnny Boettiger and Fala. Their first stop was the Hyde Park Elementary School, where the principal, Miss Davey, marshaled the children at the entrance to sing songs deliberately unrelated to the campaign. At the polling place the President signed the register, giving his occupation as "tree grower" and received ballot 251.

Newsreel photographers had hung an electric cable along the green-curtained booth, which kept the privacy curtain from completely closing and the voting machine from operating. FDR's familiar voice was soon heard, complaining loudly, "The damned thing won't work!" (To deflect Sunday sermonizers, he denied to the press the next day that he had uttered "damned." Although *TIME* published the alleged blasphemy, and clergymen predictably began protesting, the President, adept at evasion, had the White House switchboard quote him as saying, "In view of the falsity of the story, I do not think it is necessary to pay any more attention to it.")

Once the cable was detached from the booth, the curtain and the voting machine worked, and as the President emerged, cameramen took his photo. After Eleanor voted, cameras flashed again; then the Roosevelts returned home to find AP and UP teletype printers being installed, as well as a direct telephone line to Democratic state headquarters at the Biltmore Hotel in Manhattan. That afternoon—already evening in London—the President cabled Winston Churchill, "I have no reason for changing my opinion that it will be a Roosevelt landslide. The voting is very heavy in industrial centers. We are not likely to know definitely before 10:00 our time which will still make it pretty late even for you." The PM stayed up.

Harry Hopkins cabled his own bulletin to Churchill, and another to Lord Beaverbrook. Although Hopkins described himself as "the world's worst political forecaster," he predicted a sweep: "This will not be merely an election; it will be a census for Roosevelt"—a matter, he meant, of mere counting. To Beaverbrook, Hopkins added that if he were proved wrong, "I will underwrite the British National Debt and subscribe to the *Chicago Tribune*."

While Governor Dewey settled in at his hotel suite with his wife and staff (the Dewey sons were left in Albany with their grandmother), the Roosevelts, including Anna and John Boettiger and young Johnny, had an early dinner so that the dining room, with its Delano family portraits looking down, could be cleared for FDR's personal tabulation of returns. Gathered in the big library close by were Steve Early, Pa Watson, Frank Walker, Henry and Elinor Morgenthau, Sam and Dorothy Rosenman, Robert and Madeline Sherwood and Daisy Suckley. The President told Elmer Van Wagener, who supervised Hyde Park, that at eleven o'clock— "win, lose, or draw"—he would receive his Hyde Park neighbors as always on election nights. As he began surveying the early results, Averell Harriman, who had delayed his return to Moscow until he had voted, looked in, and Roosevelt told him that "Dewey's dirty tactics" had made him much more determined to win. "He expressed the hope that Dewey would no longer be an important Republican leader and that the country would be in safe[r] hands if the leadership of the Republican party went to such a man as [Leverett] Saltonstall [of Massachusetts] or [Harold] Stassen [of Minnesota], both of whom he respected greatly. I drew the inference, though he in no sense said so, that he considered the next President would probably be a Republican."

For *The New Republic*, Malcolm Cowley, its literary editor, wrote about election night in his home village, Sheridan, Connecticut, in

Harry Truman in Missouri with his family to listen to the election results on the evening of November 7, 1944. Bess Truman is seated next to the radio, with their daughter, Margaret, in the foreground. *Truman Library*

many ways a microcosm of how small communities across America, regardless of party affiliations therein, collectively tallied their votes. Sheridan's chief claim to outside recognition was that it nestled in Clare Boothe Luce's congressional district, and despite her name recognition, she was in a tough race. Larger communities, even FDR's Poughkeepsie, now had voting machines to speed the count, but Sheridan, with little more than three hundred eligible voters, had paper ballots.

Inside the Sheridan town hall, where Cowley worked through the day, having arrived at 6 a.m. to set up, no one talked politics. Like most states, Connecticut by law forbade electioneering within a prescribed distance from the polling booths—there, seventy-five feet. Inside, the atmosphere was that of an informal reception. There was a lot of laughter and local gossip. Some came in family groups. The local minister and his wife greeted the flock. Six voters were over eighty, and one was over ninety. At the back of the hall

> a table was spread . . . with pies and a big homemade layer cake; the ladies of the Opportunity Club were serving lunch to the twelve election officials. The kitchen door was open and you could smell a big pot of chowder simmering on the stove. Going in to vote was almost like paying a Sunday afternoon visit to a French village café.
>
> At eight o'clock, the two checkers, the two ballot clerks, the two box-tenders and the two booth-tenders all rose to their feet; their day was ended and they each earned $5.

As the doors were being locked, a man in the back of the hall sampling what was left of the food muttered, "But I wanted to vote." In a loud voice someone explained, "It's too late, Pop. You got here one minute too late." A poll worker took charge of the two padlocked ballot boxes, stained and greasy with age. One, which had held Remington 12-gauge shotgun shells in a former life, now held the numbered stubs of the ballots. The other, labeled "Paine's Celery Tonic," a venerable nerve remedy, contained the ballots. "That's what you Democrats are going to need tonight," another worker at the polls told Cowley, nudging him. The boxes were carried, "like a priest bearing the Host," into the Town Clerk's office through a door at the back of the hall, with a small group of observers following. There, continuing the secular ceremony,

> Eight persons took seats at a long table; on one side the Republican registrar of voters and two Republican counters; on the other side the Democratic registrar and two counters, while the town clerk sat at one end of the table and the moderator [in charge] at the head. . . . Ceremoniously he unlocked what used to be the case of shotgun shells and emptied the numbered stubs in the

middle of the table. The four counters arranged them in piles of ten, then counted the piles and the eight remaining stubs. "Two fifty-eight, right," one of them announced. The stubs were returned to their packing case. Now the Celery Compound box was unlocked and the ballots themselves were emptied on the table. They were counted like the stubs, while a dozen spectators leaned forward to see that every act was properly performed. . . . "Two fifty-eight, right," said one of the counters. "Now open the ballots," the moderator said.

The counters carefully unfolded each slip, checking to see whether it was properly marked, then placed them in three piles— Republican, Democratic or split ticket. Doubtfully marked ballots were handed to the moderator, who rejected only one, to no protests. Then the tabulating began, the Democratic counters taking the larger Republican pile, the Republicans the smaller Democratic pile. The two piles were then exchanged for a recheck,

which did not alter the results: 154 straight Republican and 55 straight Democratic votes. The 48 split ballots came next. They too were sorted into three piles according to the vote for President: Dewey, Roosevelt and other. This time Roosevelt got 31 votes and Dewey 14, the figures being added to their previous straight-party figures. There were two for [the Socialist Party's] Norman Thomas and one write-in vote for Henry A. Wallace. "Two fifty-eight, right," said the town clerk, after including in his count the ballot voided by the moderator. . . .

The split ballots were sorted into three piles once again, this time according to the vote for Governor . . . and the process of sorting the split ballots continued for each of the fourteen national, state and local offices at issue in Sheridan. Standing near the table, I could see how some of the ballots were marked and, whatever the result, they seemed to suggest a good deal of soul-searching.

Several Republicans had voted for Roosevelt and Truman, but for nobody else on the Democratic ticket. A very few Democrats had voted for Dewey. Some Republicans had voted against Representative Clare Boothe Luce and [isolationist] Senator [John A.] Danaher; in fact these two, with Dewey himself, ran a dozen votes behind the rest of the ticket.

By ten o'clock, Cowley felt that he could predict the results of the state and national elections. As they finished the hall radio was blaring the early national returns, but he felt that the local tally was more revealing, "because here I knew what the votes meant." If the President could poll more than a third of the votes in Sheridan, which was safely Republican in past contests, "he could probably sweep the country." But he guessed wrong about Mrs. Luce, having "not allowed for the big vote she was getting from her neighbors in Greenwich."

At 10:30 the Sheridan polling officials signed their reports. They put the ballots and stubs back in their boxes and locked them away in a closet. "It was a good job on both sides," one official said. "Nobody can say it wasn't right." Presumably someone called in the results to a central office: The results could not wait for the hand-delivery of the documents. After nearly seventeen hours, the town clerk turned off the lights. Wearily the worthies of Sheridan, Connecticut, dispersed to their home radios.

In the nation's capital, residents without absentee ballots observed the election by not voting and not staying home. The District of Columbia, constitutionally disenfranchised since its establishment as a non-state, enabled voting via the post office. Residents who had taken the precaution of maintaining a different legal residence mailed their ballots home. Newspaper editorials grumbled as usual, but there were more complaints in the streets about the rise in special delivery postal rates from ten to thirteen cents. Campaign parties were ubiquitous, private and public. (In the states with legal voting, liquor-dispensing establishments were shut down for the day.) The largest gathering was a Republican shindig at the Statler, where more than a thousand revelers crowded in. The Democrats held open house at the less posh Burlington Hotel. The area's leading hostess, diamond-swathed Evalyn Walsh McLean, a professed Republican, permitted socially respectable Democrats into "Friendship," her palatial home, where a band drowned out the increasingly depressing news blared on radios. Among those not at her party, and unable to vote, were six Washingtonians named George Washington. A reporter covering the election from Boston wrote on Hotel Touraine stationery that "they won't allow Democrats into the Ritz-Carlton or the Copley-Plaza"—apparently reserved for Republican victory celebrations.

Elsewhere across the time zones, an FDR victory beckoned from the early tallying. From the Hyde Park terrace at eleven o'clock, with Eleanor and Anna at his side, Roosevelt told neighboring well-wishers, including two busloads of Vassar girls who had joined them, that the returns were still indecisive but that he was confident. He would have been happy to have come back to Hyde Park for good, he said, but the war still had a long way to go. The big spruce tree to his left swayed with boys who had clambered up for a better view. Mrs. Roosevelt and Anna waved; then all three returned to their tabulations in the dining room.

At 11:40 the traditional torchlight parade of villagers reached the mansion, and the President, eschewing his leg braces, wheeled onto the porch to greet his neighbors. It was too early to make a statement, he said, "but it looks like I'll be coming up here from Washington again for another four years." When he was wheeled back in, Eleanor invited the dozens of reporters and photographers shivering outside to warm themselves into the library, where the fireplace was going strong, and to share her coffee and cheese-and-crackers. In the dining room the tickers churned out increasingly promising returns.

Ebulliently, Hopkins cabled Churchill, up in the wee hours as usual, "It's in the bag." It was already clear that the only questions were the size of the majority and when Governor Dewey would formally concede. At Nelson House in Poughkeepsie, the local Democratic campaign staff was celebrating as if the race were over. Even isolationist Representative Hamilton Fish, after twenty-four years, had gone under. At 3:16 radio networks announced Dewey's 3:12 concession of defeat, but the governor had as yet sent no message to the President.* Updated by the BBC, Churchill would cable FDR, "I always said that a great people could be trusted to stand by the pilot who weathered the storm. It is an indescribable relief to me that our comradeship will continue and will help to bring the world out of misery."

At 3:28 Roosevelt ceased waiting and dictated a telegram to Dewey, "I thank you for your statement, which I heard over the air a few minutes ago." The belated concession assumed Roosevelt's re-election and accepted "the will of the people." The Republican Party, Dewey added, in a post-campaign barb, "emerges from the election revitalized and a great force for the good of the country and for the preservation of free government in America." As Bill Hassett was on the telephone and trying to talk to Mrs. Roosevelt at the same time, FDR was in the corridor being propelled to an elevator on his way upstairs to bed. Turning to Hassett, he said, "I still think he is a son of a bitch." It was 4 a.m.

Sam Rosenman had won the White House pool. He had forecast 431 electoral votes for the Boss, who collected 432 to Dewey's 99. Roosevelt won 36 of the 48 states, with a provisional 25.6 million popular votes to Dewey's 22 million. *The New York Times* headlined, the morning after, "RECORD POPULAR VOTE IS CLOSE," but realistically it was not—merely more close than FDR's previous tallies.

---

* A concession message would arrive three days later.

The New York Times front page with the election results, November 8, 1944, showing the re-elected President with his successful running mate, Harry S. Truman.

The Times also noted that some—very likely, many—of the armed forces ballots had been marked "as long as two months ago," but little hinged on the soldier vote. Waiting for the late-tabulated service ballots in some states would not have boosted the Republican ticket, as where that vote could already be counted separately, it was obvious that it was running strongly for the President, and tilted some states, like New Jersey, more decisively into the Democratic column. In Phoenix, Arizona, the daily *Republic* published a Reg Manning editorial cartoon showing a diminutive and disconsolate Dewey perched atop a large GOP elephant headed back to a signposted Albany, trailing FDR votes behind him. Nearly four million ballots separated the candidates. Anywhere the civilian count seemed close, GI ballots expanded the difference.

And They Said He'd Lost His Batting Eye!

"And They Said He'd Lost His Batting Eye!" H. M. Talburt in the *New York World-Telegram*, November 9, 1944.

A Talburt cartoon in the *New York World-Telegram* depicted FDR, cigarette holder still clenched, on a baseball diamond prone and sliding, arm outstretched, easily into home plate (labeled "4th term"), clutching 1st, 2nd and 3rd bases in the other hand, while the Republican elephant lay dazed on the pitcher's mound. A *New Yorker* cartoon would show a businesslike wife at her desk asking her surprised husband, "What shall I do with your Roosevelt button? Do you want me to put it away again?" Fears about the President's health, and about his little-known successor-in-waiting, added to concerns about further eroding the two-term tradition, had an impact in civilian voting booths that was not nearly enough. The FDR campaign buttons could now be put away.

FDR, Harry Truman and Henry Wallace at Union Station, Washington, DC, November 10, 1944. The President was returning to the White House after spending Election Day and after at Hyde Park. *FDR Library*

FDR at the microphone at Union Station, Washington, DC, on arrival from Hyde Park following the election, November 10, 1944. Harry Truman and Henry Wallace are to his left. *Truman Library*

Epilogue

As a cold wind snapped at bunting on the White House portico, Roosevelt and Truman were inaugurated at noon on January 20, 1945. Snow had fallen two days earlier. Crowded indoors, two thousand guests would be served chicken salad. (Chicken was not rationed.) Chief Petty Officer Arthur Prettyman and Colonel James Roosevelt helped the President put on his braces so that he could stand to take the oath. He wore a dark business suit as he was helped to his wheelchair and escorted by elevator to the first floor corridor. Hatless and coatless, he emerged onto the portico leaning on James's arm and was seated next to the lectern. A chilled throng of thousands stood behind the iron fence on Constitution Avenue. In the gloom beyond, loomed the Washington Monument. With the outgoing vice president, Henry Wallace, holding a Bible for Harry Truman, the new vice president was sworn in by Chief Justice Harlan Stone. The Marine Band played "Hail to the Chief," and Bishop Dun offered a prayer for the President and the nation. Jimmy Roosevelt and a waiting Secret Service agent lifted FDR from his chair and guided him up the single step to the lectern. Holding the Roosevelt family Bible open, as the President wished, to *Corinthians 1:13,* "And now abideth faith, hope, charity; these three, but the greatest of these is charity," the Chief Justice administered the oath of office.

Suppressing winces of discomfort, reminiscent of Bremerton, the President remained standing on his painful braces for a brief fourth inaugural address. He spoke of the "supreme test" the country was going through. "I know it is America's purpose that we shall not fail. We have learned that we cannot live alone, at peace, that our own well-being is dependent on the well-being of other nations far away. We have learned that we must live as men and not as ostriches, nor as dogs in the manger. We have learned to be citizens of the world, members of the human community." Once inside again, he settled—almost collapsed—into his trusty old wheelchair, and prepared for the receptions to follow.

In the weeks remaining to the President, he made his final impact upon the postwar world he would never see. He had led his nation out of catastrophic depression and into social and economic mobility, edging toward what has long been described as "the American dream." Drawn into the most terrible war in history, he knew that the unwieldy alliance forged by circumstance was now on the verge of victory.

The grim reality loomed that the colossal Red Army could overwhelm most of Europe. Conceding that, Roosevelt and Churchill, however reluctantly, had compromised with Stalin at Yalta, on the Black Sea dividing the shattered continent, redrawing frontiers and recognizing inevitable spheres of influence. The troubled deadlock would last until the unsustainable Communist empire began imploding forty-five years later. To make unnecessary an invasion of the Home Islands of Japan, certain to be suicidally defended and awesome in casualties, Stalin's agreement had been secured, at a further ransom, to go to war against Japan once Germany had collapsed. Also, seeking an elusive postwar amity, Roosevelt had invited an United Nations assemblage to convene late in April. He expected to be in San Francisco to address the opening session.

After his long, exhausting flight to Yalta, the President, early in March, reported to Congress on the conference, beginning with an apology for sitting down to speak, as his twenty pounds of braces were no longer bearable. He then traveled to his beloved Warm Springs in Georgia for warmth and rest. There, early on the afternoon of April 12, 1945, with Lucy Mercer Rutherfurd unreported at his side while her friend Elizabeth Shoumatoff painted his portrait, he suddenly lost consciousness and died of a cerebral hemorrhage. Franklin Delano Roosevelt's fourth term had lasted eighty-three days.

Hitler, dead by his own hand, would outlive FDR by eighteen days, Nazi Germany by twenty-six. Imperial Japan would be blasted into surrender four months after the President's fourth term had been abruptly abbreviated. Harry Truman, surprising almost everyone but himself, would prove a formidable successor in the White House.

A constitutional amendment now limits a president to ten years less one day. There will never be another fourth-term election. The Rooseveltian legacy may be that we will never have further crises of such magnitude as to require one.

Acknowledgments

Credits for illustrations have been posted with the illustrations themselves. I appreciate the good offices of those who have assisted in the searches and procurement of these images.

I am also grateful, for information and assistance, to Robert Benson, Diane Bond, Stephen Budiansky, Robert Clark, Robert C. Doyle, William H. Duncan, Dennis Giangreco, Julie Grahame, Charles E. Greene, Robert Guinsler, Murray Kaye, Elizabeth Kerr, Sam Kramer, Mark Learman, Kay Li, Lannie Liggera, Judy Litoff, Matthew Lutts, Russell McCauley, Mark Mompoint, Don Patton, AnnaLee Pauls, Michel Pharand, Jack Pickering, Bob Pigeon, Ben Primer, Mark Renovitch, Richard Sommers, Sandra Stelts, Richard Swain, Gary A. Taylor, Pauline Testerman, Gregory J. H. Unwin, Mark Bennett Weintraub, Rodelle Weintraub, Richard Winslow, Paul Zimmer and James Zobel.

Sources

General

Key sources beyond those detailed below are the Franklin D. Roosevelt Presidential Library in Hyde Park, New York; the Harry S. Truman Presidential Library in Independence, Missouri; and the Thomas E. Dewey papers in the Rush Rhees Library at the University of Rochester, New York. Dewey's efficient staff compiled nine very substantial scrapbooks of related campaign documents without prejudice. Many sources are identified in the text and are not repeated below.

1: Bungled Beginnings

Roosevelt's medical episode aboard his train near Camp Pendleton is described by James Roosevelt, with Sidney Shalett, in *Affectionately,*

F.D.R. A Son's Story of a Lonely Man (New York: Harcourt Brace, 1959). FDR's letter to Eleanor, July 21, 1844, on his "collywobbles," is in Elliott Roosevelt, ed., *F.D.R. his personal letters,* vol. 2 (New York: Duell, Sloan and Pearce, 1948). Roosevelt's medical condition is detailed professionally by his cardiac specialist, Howard G. Bruenn, M.D., in "Clinical Notes on the Illness and Death of President Franklin D. Roosevelt," *Annals of Internal Medicine* 72 (1970). It is slightly abridged, also excluding electrocardiogram readings, as Appendix B in Robert H. Ferrell's *The Dying President: Franklin D. Roosevelt 1944–1945* (Columbia: University of Missouri Press, 1998). FDR's alleged "mild case of bronchitis" is reported in *TIME*, April 10, 1944. Navy Surgeon General Ross T. McIntire's self-serving account as the President's personal doctor, among other things misleading *TIME* as well as FDR, is *White House Physician* (New York: Putnam, 1946).

Daisy Suckley's cousinly relationship to the President throughout the period, through her letters and diary notes, appears in Geoffrey C. Ward, ed., *Closest Companion: the unknown Story of the intimate friendship between Franklin Roosevelt and Margaret Suckley* (Boston: Houghton Mifflin, 1995). Her thirty-nine handwritten letters are in the FDR Library. The covert revival of FDR's relationship with Lucy Rutherfurd and its encouragement by Anna Roosevelt Boettiger is described in Joseph E. Persico's *Franklin and Lucy: President Roosevelt, Mrs. Rutherfurd and the Other Remarkable Women in His Life* (New York: Random House, 2008), stretched out by "the other remarkable women."

FDR's press conference texts here and throughout are drawn from *Complete Presidential Press Conferences of Franklin D. Roosevelt,* vols. 23, 24, 25 (New York: Da Capo Press, 1972). Grace Tully's personal secretarial archive of FDR's papers was purchased and utilized by Conrad Black in his *Franklin Delano Roosevelt: Champion of Freedom* (New York: Public Affairs Press, 2003). The collection is now in the FDR Presidential Library at Hyde Park and posted on the library's website. Her reminiscences and letter extracts are in *F.D.R., My Boss* (New York: Scribner, 1949).

Walter Millis's reference to Aristides and FDR is in "A President Must Be Elected," *Virginia Quarterly Review* 20 (Winter 1944). Douglas Chandler, a turncoat as "Paul Revere," is quoted by James MacGregor Burns in *Roosevelt: The Soldier of Freedom* (New York: Harcourt Brace Jovanovich, 1970). Bernard DeVoto cites Walter Lippmann in his "The Easy Chair," *Harper's Magazine,* June 1944. Harold Ickes on the political "shambles" if FDR did not run again, in a letter to Stacey Mosser, is quoted by T. H. Watkins in *Righteous Pilgrim: The Life and Times of Harold L. Ickes* (New York: Henry Holt, 1990). A useful survey of the fourth-term dilemma by Michael J. Korzi is "Theorizing Presidential Tenure: The Difficult Case of FDR's Fourth Term," *Congress and the Presidency* 35 (Autumn 2008). FDR's retrieval of his old campaign hat was confirmed by Michelle M. Frauenberger, Museum Collections Manager, FDR Library, in a letter, November 3, 2009, to Lannie Liggera. William Rigdon's role in South Carolina as FDR's traveling secretary is reported by him (with James Derieux) in *White House Sailor* (New York: Doubleday, 1962). He would later travel to Hawaii and Alaska with the President.

Background material about Washington in 1944–1945 throughout is from the daily and weekly press as cited; from David Brinkley's *Washington Goes to War* (New York: Knopf, 1988); and from Doris Kearns Goodwin, *No Ordinary Time* (New York: Simon and Schuster, 1994). Turner Catledge's shock at FDR's physical deterioration is described in his *My Life and the Times* (New York: Harper and Row, 1979).

2: The Missouri Compromise

A description of the *Ferdinand Magellan* and its history to 1944 is in Rigdon, above, and also in Brinkley, above. FDR's food tastes for traveling are reported by Rigdon. A personal recollection of traveling Jim Crow–style from Washington southward then is that of Maurice G. Eldbridge in a letter to the editor in *The New York Times,* October 9, 2010.

Truman's letters to his wife are in Robert H. Ferrell, ed., *Dear Bess: The Letters from Harry to Bess Truman, 1910–1959* (New York: Norton, 1982). Ferrell summarizes his take on the process that evolved into Truman's nomination in *Choosing Truman: The Democratic Convention of 1944* (Columbia: University of Missouri Press, 1994). Ferrell quotes political boss Ed Flynn as allegedly being told by FDR, "Inject Truman into the picture." (It seems unlikely.) Henry Wallace's appearance at the convention is self-described, and perhaps less than accurate, in John Morton Blum, ed., *The Price of Vision: The Diary of Henry A. Wallace, 1942–1946* (Boston: Houghton Mifflin, 1973). The cartoon "The Political Education of a Vice-Presidential Candidate," by "Ding" (Jay Norwood), appeared in the *Des Moines Register.* Walter J. Trohan's recollection of Jim Farley's "Before you take it . . ." advice to Truman is drawn from Trohan's oral history interview with Jerry N. Hess, October 7, 1970, Truman Presidential Library. Margaret Truman's quoting a friend of Senator Truman as being told that the traditional role of the vice president is to merely wait for a funeral to attend in behalf of the president, and her recollection of the convention and its aftermath, are both in her *Harry S. Truman* (New York: Morrow, 1973).

Of the many variations on the FDR endorsement memo to Hannegan, Truman is named ahead of Wallace according to Bruce Allen Murphy in *Wild Bill: The Legend and Life of William O. Douglas* (New York: Random House, 2003). Grace Tully recalled the opposite sequence of names in Tully, above; however, her book is prefaced with a foreword by William O. Douglas, another aspirant believed to be on FDR's list. James Byrnes's bitter comment on being discarded as candidate about FDR's lack of backbone was recalled by a journalist and friend, Walter J. Brown, in his *James F.*

Byrnes of South Carolina: A Remembrance (Macon, GA: Mercer University Press, 1992). For Krock and the notorious "Clear it with Sidney" allegation, see Arthur Krock, *Memoirs: Sixty Years on the Firing Line* (New York: Funk and Wagnalls, 1968); and Turner Catledge, above. Truman's concern about the consequences of Mrs. Luce's "Payroll Bess" charge (and Bess was indeed on Truman's Senate payroll) is fully detailed with salary figures in Ferrell's *Choosing Truman,* above.

FDR's May 6, 1944, press conference at Hobcaw, South Carolina, is printed verbatim in *The Complete Presidential Press Conferences,* above. Dr. Harry Etter's post-Hobcaw diagnosis of FDR is reported in Evans, above. Dr. Frank Lahey's dubious medical allegations as related by a third party appeared in Jack Anderson and Joseph Spear, "Evidence Indicates FDR Knew of Cancer," *Washington Post,* July 2, 1987. Lahey's actual memo (to himself) of July 10, 1944, on his blunt assessment to Ross McIntire of FDR's cardiac prognosis after a visit to the White House was locked away and surfaced after Lahey's death in 2007 in Harry Goldsmith's self-published *A Conspiracy of Silence: The Health and Death of Franklin D. Roosevelt* (2007). The posthumous history of the personal memo, the original which is in the Lahey Clinic, Boston, is recorded in *The Boston Globe,* April 12, 2011, the anniversary of Roosevelt's death at Warm Springs, Georgia; and by David Steinberg in *The Boston Globe Magazine,* May 20, 2011. Lahey's cover-up letter to McIntire, September 12, 1944, FDR Library and also available online, is reproduced in the lurid conspiracy-theory book about FDR's alleged melanoma and abdominal cancer by Steven Lomazow and Eric Fettman, *FDR's Deadly Secret* (New York: Public Affairs Press, 2010).

FDR's impulsive wish to be buried at sea if his death occurred on a voyage is recalled by Tully, above. Roald Dahl on Frank Waldrop is from Jennifer Conant, *The Irregulars: Roald Dahl and the British Spy Ring in Wartime Washington* (New York: Simon and Schuster, 2008).

3: Fighting the Fourth Term

Ogilvy's pollster recommendations for Dewey's speeches are reported in *The Irregulars*, above. Jaeckle's rejected recommendation that Dewey visit European war sites is in Herbert Brownell with John P. Burke, *Advising Ike: The Memoirs of Attorney General Herbert Brownell* (Lawrence: University Press of Kansas, 1993). The Hokinson cartoon deploring advice given Dewey appeared in *The New Yorker*, June 3, 1944. Oswald Garrison Villard reports the canard about Dewey needing to sit on telephone books to increase his height in "Dewey Grows in Stature," *The Boston Globe*, November 4, 1944. The "stre-e-etch" cartoon on the same subject appeared in *PM* and was reproduced in *The New Republic* on July 10, 1944.

Governor Bricker's paradox offered in his speeches that Republicans were the liberal party and New Dealers reactionary appeared in *The New York Times*, February 11, 1944. That Drew Pearson got hold of a McCormick cable denouncing the Army's *Stars and Stripes* as a "Communist New Deal paper" appears in Richard Norton Smith, *The Colonel: The Life and Legend of Robert R. McCormick* (Boston: Houghton Mifflin, 1997). McCormick's allegation, reported in an Associated Press dispatch, February 15, 1944, that there were 410,000 Communists in New York, is reprinted by Herman Schnurer and George R. Geiger in "Political Dictionary, 1943–44," *Antioch Review* 4, March 1944.

Isaiah Berlin is quoted from H. G. Nicholas, ed., *Washington Dispatches 1941–1945: Weekly political reports from the British Embassy* (Chicago: University of Chicago Press, 1981). Cissy Patterson's intemperate remarks about FDR's war service are quoted in *TIME*, July 24, 1944. Roosevelt's wartime inspection trips to France, Britain and Italy in 1918 as assistant secretary of the Navy are detailed by Black, above, and in other biographies and published letters. FDR's Depression-era comment describing veterans as not a sacrosanct caste, a remark pandering to the unemployed and reversed in wartime by his pitch for the GI Bill, is quoted by Stephen R. Ortiz, *Beyond the Bonus March and G.I. Bill* (New York: NYU Press, 2008).

Rose Kimball's letter to FDR about her buying war bonds and sewing food-sack dresses, and an irate letter hoping that he fails re-election, from someone with an illegible surname, are in Lawrence W. Levine and Cornelia R. Levine, *The People and the President: America's Conversation with FDR* (Boston: Beacon Press, 2002).

4: Commander-in-Chief

Dorothy Thompson's radio riposte about FDR's health is quoted by Marian K. Sanders, *Dorothy Thompson: A Legend in Her Own Time* (Boston: Houghton Mifflin, 1973). For FDR and de Gaulle, see William Hassett, *Off the Record with FDR 1942–1945* (New Brunswick, NJ: Rutgers University Press, 1958); S. Weintraub, *15 Stars* (New York: Free Press, 2007); Jonathan Feiby, *The General* (New York: Simon and Schuster, 2010); and "De Gaulle Arrives, Meets President," *The New York Times,* July 7, 1944. FDR refers to "the temperamental Lady de Gaulle" in a letter to Cordell Hull, Casablanca, January 18, 1943. De Gaulle's "Cyrano" nose is alleged by Hassett, above. His equating himself with Joan of Arc, and then Clemenceau, is from a letter to John Roosevelt in James Roosevelt, above.

FDR's Hawaii voyage and conferences, and his Alaska voyage and return, are chronicled in Weintraub, *15 Stars*, above. Samuel I. Rosenman describes the Hawaii segment in his *Working with Roosevelt* (New York: Harper, 1952). Howard Bruenn, M.D., deals with FDR's medical condition in Hawaiian and Alaskan waters in his "Clinical Notes," above. William Rigdon covers both journeys in *White House Sailor* (New York: Harper, 1962), and also the news received aboard of the death of Missy LeHand. Missy's death in Massachusetts is described in Goodwin, above, and James Roosevelt, above. Walter Trohan's untruthful trashing of

FDR's financial maintenance of LeHand appears in his *Political Animals* (New York: Doubleday, 1975). Admiral William F. Halsey's recollection of FDR's competent handling of a destroyer in treacherous waters as civilian assistant secretary of the Navy is in his *Admiral Halsey's Story*, with Julian Bryan III (New York: Whittlesey House, 1947).

FDR's letters to Hull, Mackenzie King and others in this chapter are from Elliott Roosevelt, above. Events in both Alaska and Hawaii, and weather cancellations in Alaska, are also described by Mike Reilly with William J. Slocum in *Reilly of the White House* (New York: Simon and Schuster, 1947).

The Port Chicago explosion and mutiny is described by Gerald Astor in *The Right to Fight: A History of African Americans in the Military* (New York: Da Capo Press, 2001); and Robert L. Allen in *The Port Chicago Mutiny* (Berkeley, CA: Heyday Books, 2006). *The Crisis* for November 1944, "A Record of the Darker Races," excoriates the Navy trial board that all fifty sailors after a hasty hearing of forty-five minutes were convicted.

5: "Roosevelt's dog and Dewey's goat"

Truman's post-convention White House meeting with FDR is described in all HST biographies, and the press, but never better than he did himself in a letter to Mrs. Truman, August 18, 1944, in *Dear Bess,* above. Truman's style and adaptation to circumstances are described colorfully by John Snyder in an oral history for the Truman Presidential Library, December 8, 1967.

Dewey's uncharacteristic but effective "half a horse" quip is quoted by Scott Hart in *Washington at War: 1941–1945* (Englewood, NJ: Prentice-Hall, 1970). Dewey's cold audience manner is best described by Richard Norton Smith in *Thomas E. Dewey and His Times* (New York: Simon and Schuster, 1982). Herbert Brownell's recollections of the "flat" and "disappointing" Dewey campaign, including the cautious decision not to go after FDR's health, and risking a backlash, is in his "Working with Dewey" chapter in Brownell, above. Samuel Grafton's "mobilization of discontent" column appeared in the *New York Post* on September 15, 1944. John O'Donnell's "Capitol Stuff" description of what would happen if a candidate died was published on September 21, 1944, precipitated by the rail accident to Dewey's campaign train—and talk about FDR's health.

FDR's press conferences are in *Complete Presidential Press Conferences,* above. The impact of the film *Wilson* on the early weeks of the campaign is described in the newsmagazines and in Clayton R. Kopper and Gregory D. Black, *Hollywood Goes to War* (New York: Free Press, 1987). Felix Frankfurter on the "cowardly" use by Republicans of Hillman's Lithuanian birth as covert anti-Semitism is in Leonard Baker, *Brandeis and Frankfurter* (New York: Harper, 1984). The second Quebec Conference is described by William F. Leahy in *I Was There* (New York: Whittlesey House, 1950); Conrad Black, above; Martin Gilbert in *Winston Churchill, Road to Victory 1941–1945* (Boston: Houghton Mifflin, 1986); Lord Moran in *Churchill: Taken from the Diaries of Lord Moran* (Boston: Houghton Mifflin, 1986); and Jon Meacham, *Franklin and Winston* (New York: Random House, 2003). The illogical FDR-Churchill security suspicions about Niels Bohr at Quebec are described by Robert Dallek, *Franklin D. Roosevelt and American Foreign Policy 1932–1945* (New York: Oxford University Press, 1995).

"TRB" (Richard Strout) of *The New Republic* wrote on "The Roosevelt Years" in *TRB:Views and Perspectives on the Presidency* (New York: Macmillan, 1979). Clare Boothe Luce's curious "bet" that her cocker spaniel could "lick" Fala was reported in the staff-written "Washington Background" column of the *Philadelphia Inquirer,* September 28, 1944. Her prediction about her post-election "head" on the block was in an editorial hostile to her in *The Crisis,* November 1944. FDR's preparation for his "Fala speech" is best described by Sam Rosenman, above. The press covered the speech substantially and delightedly. Watkins's

Righteous Pilgrim covers Ickes's campaign speeches as if he were pursuing a personal vendetta with Dewey. Ickes loved the political fray.

6: Misremembering Pearl Harbor

The Dewey campaign's gamble to exploit Pearl Harbor as a campaign issue is described by Norton Smith, *Dewey*, above, and Norton Smith, *McCormick*, above; Brownell, above; Weintraub, *15 Stars*, above; Joseph Persico, *Roosevelt's Secret War: FDR and World War II Espionage* (New York: Random House, 2001), who reports Forrestal's memo to FDR on Dewey's plans to use Pearl Harbor; and Tape 14 in Forrest C. Pogue, ed., *George C. Marshall: Interviews and Reminiscences* (Lexington, VA: George C. Marshall Research Foundation, 1991). Background about which codes were broken before Pearl Harbor and which were not is best reviewed in Ladislas Farago, *The Broken Seal: "Operation Magic" and the Secret Road to Pearl Harbor* (New York: Random House, 1967); and Stephen Budiansky, *Battle of Wits: The Complete Story of Codebreaking in World War II* (New York: Free Press, 2000).

7: Facing the Nation

For Cantril, see Rosenman, above. For McCormick and for Dewey, see Norton Smith, above. Dewey's campaigning is also from Brownell, above, and the newsmagazines, especially *TIME*, "The Dewey Demerits," October 2, 1944. E. B. White to Harold Ross on Dewey is from Dorothy Lobrano Guth, ed., *Letters of E. B. White* (New York: HarperCollins, 2006). Bricker's French Lick attack on Truman is from Richard O. Davies, *Defender of the Old Guard: John Bricker and American Politics* (Columbus: Ohio State University Press, 1993); and his season of campaigning is reported in "Bricker's Sawdust Trail," *TIME*, November 6, 1944. The photo of Bricker leaning down from a rail car platform to shake a boy's hand is in the Ohio Historical Society collection. John Gunther's derogatory jabs at Bricker are from *Inside U.S.A.* (New York: Harper, 1957).

Robert Sherwood is quoted from his *Roosevelt and Hopkins* (New York: Harper, 1948, 1950). Truman's campaigning is from *Dear Bess*, above; Margaret Truman's *Harry S. Truman,* above; John Snyder's oral history, above; and John McCullough's *Truman*, above. FDR on the Musicians' Union strike is from his October 13, 1944, press conference. Details on the strike are from the daily press and from *Downbeat*, "All Recording Stops Today," August 1, 1944.

Henry Luce's intervention on the Dewey side is from Robert E. Herzstein, *Henry R. Luce* (New York: Macmillan, 1994.) Willkie is from Norton Smith's *Dewey,* above; from Herzstein, above; and from FDR's press conference of August 25, 1944. Russell W. Davenport's "Open Letter" about Willkie's death and seeking support for FDR was published in the *Rochester Times-Union* and other papers in New York state on October 30, 1944.

The details of campaign funding are examined by Louise Overacker, "American Government and Politics: Presidential Campaign Funds, 1944," *American Political Science Review* 39 (October 1945).

Walter Lippmann is from Ronald Steel, Walter Lippmann and the American Century (New York: Vintage, 1980),and his Herald Tribune syndicated columns. For Margaret Suckley, see Closest Companion, above. FDR's instructions to Harriman (and Molotov) on the Polish question are from John Lewis Gaddis, *George F. Kennan: An American Life* (New York: Penguin Press, 2011). FDR's dramatic in-the-rain campaigning in New York City is reported voluminously in the daily press and the newsweeklies, and by Rosenman and Sherwood, above. TIME refers to FDR as "the Champ." His actual state of health (he parried the question in an October 17, 1945, news conference) and rumors about it from doctors at Bethesda are described by Ferrell in The Dying President, above.

8: The Service Vote

The joke about the Republican GI and the Japanese POW that FDR told on himself is retold by Jonathan Daniels, FDR's last press secretary, in Jack Goodman, ed., *While You Were Gone* (New York: Simon and Schuster, 1946). Bill Mauldin's Willie and Joe cartoon in *Stars and Stripes* is reproduced in Mauldin, *Up Front* (New York: Henry Holt, 1945). Dorman H. Smith's cartoon on service hurdles to voting (made literal) appeared in the *Milwaukee Journal*. William Rose Benet's "The Phoenix Nest" on the service vote is from *Saturday Review*, December 18, 1943. Army censorship of some publications (but not others) reaching servicemen that might contain political content was attacked in *The New Republic*, July 24, 1944. FDR and Dewey were both given columns, pro and con, "Executive Interest in [the] Soldier Vote," *Congressional Digest*, June–July 1944.

"Control of Absentee Soldier Voting," reviews and articles on the controversy, is in *Congressional Digest* 33, January 1944. The tirade of an unidentified senator against FDR because the President's sons were all in officers' uniforms (yet all with hazardous overseas duty) is reported by Allen Drury of United Press and quoted in Brinkley, *Washington Goes to War*, above. Even less reliable is the objection by Senator Elbert Thomas of Oklahoma, reported in the *Portsmouth (NH) Herald*, October 31, 1944, that paper service ballots were "so thin" that it was possible to determine how soldiers voted.

How and where servicemen voted is gleaned from press reports and later live interviews. Rodolph Turcotte's letter appeared in the *Boston Globe*, November 6, 1944; on November 4, 1944, the *Globe* had also shown William H. Atkinson voting in Italy. A "Yeoman" who voted published a letter to the editor in *The Nation*, July 15, 1944. Sailors "somewhere in the Pacific" were pictured lining up to vote in the *Portsmouth (NH) Herald*. Richard Long is pictured voting in Luxembourg in *TIME*, October 23, 1944. Soldiers voting in China were pictured on the cover of *Senior Scholastic*, October

16, 1944. *The Illustrated London News*, November 4, 1944, showed servicemen voting at an unidentified polling booth in England. *Newsweek*, November 13, 1944, showed a GI at a polling station in a barn somewhere in Europe.

Lawrence Cane is quoted in David E. Cane, Judy Litoff and David C. Smith, eds., *Fighting Fascism in Europe: The World War II Letters of an American Veteran of the Spanish Civil War* (New York: Fordham University Press, 2003). Don Patton interviewed Ray Nagell, Leon Frankel, Warren I. Colethour, Al Schroeder and Ronald S. Larsen. Rodelle Weintraub interviewed Walter J. Hipple, Edward Herman, Jerry Geisager and Vince Suppan. Wes Pearl, Irving R. Rothberg, Herbert Reiman, Robert Hickman and Bob Brandt e-mailed SW; Russell McCauley, Jack Pickering, Sam Kramer and Guy A. Taylor responded by letter.

9: The Closing Weeks

Churchill's lauding FDR's "robust vigour" demonstrated in New York City, in a message of October 23, is quoted by Jon Meacham, above. Robert Frost's nasty references in his correspondence to Roosevelt as "his Rosiness" are quoted by John Gross in "Sunset Sails," *TLS*, January 15, 2010. The President's forays into Philadelphia and Chicago were widely reported in the daily and weekly press. Hassett, above, describes the logistics for the Philadelphia campaigning. More detail about Chicago appears in Rosenman, above (who describes Lubin's fact-checking by telegraph as the campaign train proceeded); Sherwood, above; and Hassett, above. Manhola Dargis, in a review of Michael Moore's documentary *Capitalism: A Love Story*, "Greed Is Good? Maybe, But He Begs to Differ," *The New York Times*, September 29, 2009, recalls FDR's "galvanizing words" at Chicago about "a second bill of rights." Averell Harriman's radio address, which he paid for, supporting FDR despite his status as a diplomat, is described in Harriman, writing with Elie Abel, in *Special Envoy to Churchill and Stalin*

1941–1946 (New York: Random House, 1975). Radio time was expensive, and speakers could be cut off. FDR notes in his October 20, 1944, press conference that he was listening to Orson Welles "and they shut down on him." Opening his October 25 news conference he offered his "flash" about the Philippine Sea naval victory.

Truman's relentless campaigning, widely covered, included his cool reception at Madison Square Garden among frustrated Wallace supporters and his being trashed in the press as a former Klansman. Truman comments on the Klan "damn lies" and his Boston speech in Merle Miller, *Plain Speaking: An Oral Biography of Harry S. Truman* (New York: Berkley/Putnam, 1974). *TIME* (normally a Dewey-Bricker organ) was already preparing a positive cover story on Truman, which would appear dated November 6. HST's letters offer his enthusiastic details, from Los Angeles and Seattle eastward, in Monte M. Poen, *Letters Home by Harry Truman* (New York: Putnam's, 1984). Dewey's campaigning is recorded in Norton Smith, who notes that neither Truman nor FDR used Dewey's name "in public." Norton Smith recalls Alice Roosevelt's deadly wisecrack that Dewey looked like "the groom on the wedding cake."

The malicious KKK washtub cartoon about Truman appeared in the *New York Daily Mirror* on November 4, 1944. Truman's Boston address at Mechanics' Hall, October 27, 1944, is among his papers at the Truman Library. His confrontation with Joseph Kennedy is recorded from the Kennedy side in Amanda Smith, ed., *The Letters of Joseph P. Kennedy* (New York: Viking, 2001).

10: The Last Stretch

FDR's Boston pilgrimage is reported by Leahy, and by Hassett, both above; Roosevelt's reference to "cold roast Boston" is from Grace Tully, above. The appearances of a still-ill Orson Welles and Frank Sinatra are from Barbara Leaming, *Orson Welles* (New York:

Viking, 1985), from Black and Hassett, both above, and from press accounts.

Dewey's final campaign stops, including Boston, are reported largely from Associated Press dispatches, *The New York Times*, and *The Boston Globe*. Charles Breitel's urging Dewey to eliminate the indirect anti-Jewish references to Hillman when in Boston are from Norton Smith, above. Ickes on Dewey's "reckless" talk, and FDR's thanks to Ickes, are from *Righteous Pilgrim*, above. "The little man made me mad" is from FDR's letter to his son James, November 13, 1944, in *Letters*, James Roosevelt, ed., above. British agent Stephenson reported to London before the election on his electoral vote estimates, based upon polling figures, in Jennifer Conant, above.

The "Spiritualist Tip" letter to the editor appeared in the *Syracuse Post-Standard* on November 2, 1944. The "Coronation Day!" crown cartoon appeared in the *New York Journal-American* on November 4, 1944.

11: Election Day

Senator Taft's baseball metaphor on the campaign is from his letter to David Ingalls, December 26, 1944, in Clarence E. Wunderlin Jr. et al., eds., *The Papers of Robert A. Taft, vol. 2, 1939–1944* (Kent, OH: Kent State University Press, 1997). The "All-American Athletes for Dewey" advertisement appeared in the *New York World-Telegram* on November 6, 1944, and presumably other newspapers as well.

The Democratic Party's "startling manoeuvre" on radio election eve (this opinion from a British journal) is described by S. K. Ratcliffe, "President Roosevelt's Fourth Victory," *Contemporary Review*, December 1944, and by the program's producer, Norman Corwin, in *While You Were Gone*, above. Orson Welles's four-network election-evening speech for FDR is in Leaming, above. Malcolm Cowley's

"Election Night in Sheridan" appeared in *The New Republic,* November 22, 1944. The scene at Hyde Park is from Rosenman, above, from Harriman, above and from Hassett, above, who describes FDR's "sentimental journey" by open auto around his Poughkeepsie area voting district.

Dewey's final radio address that evening is from *The New York Times,* November 6, 1944. The governor's "tactical error" of basing his appeal on people who "would have voted for him anyway" is analyzed in the *Commonweal,* November 17, 1944.

The informal electoral vote poll of White House staff, with FDR, is reported by Rosenman, Hassett and others, with FDR confiding his own estimate afterward to a press conference on November 10, 1944. The post-election cartoons are identified in the narrative.

Index

310

Index